THE QUESTION
OF
GREEK INDEPENDENCE

THE QUESTION OF GREEK INDEPENDENCE

A Study of British Policy in the Near East, 1821–1833

BY

C. W. CRAWLEY, M.A.

Fellow of Trinity Hall, Cambridge

CAMBRIDGE

AT THE UNIVERSITY PRESS

1930

CAMBRIDGE
UNIVERSITY PRESS

University Printing House, Cambridge CB2 8BS, United Kingdom

Published in the United States of America by Cambridge University Press, New York

Cambridge University Press is part of the University of Cambridge.

It furthers the University's mission by disseminating knowledge in the pursuit of education, learning and research at the highest international levels of excellence.

www.cambridge.org
Information on this title: www.cambridge.org/9781107626515

First published 1930
First paperback edition 2014

A catalogue record for this publication is available from the British Library

ISBN 978-1-107-62651-5 Paperback

CONTENTS

PREFACE

More than one hundred years have passed since the death of George Canning and the destruction, in time of peace, of the Turkish and Egyptian fleets in the Bay of Navarin. That 'untoward event' was a landmark in the creation of modern Greece from small and precarious beginnings, and the five years which elapsed before a King was found and a boundary fixed for the new State have often been treated as a mere postscript to the story of the revolt. Such a treatment has a certain justification in the history of Greece. But Navarin was a landmark also in the decline of Turkey during the nineteenth century, and may be taken as the beginning of a different chapter.

From another point of view, the years 1828 to 1833 were a turning-point in the relations of England and Russia, and cannot be ignored if we are to understand the development of a temper which ultimately led to the Crimean War, persisted through the crisis of 1878 and came to the surface at frequent intervals until circumstances brought about a short-lived alliance from 1907 to 1917. It may safely be said that Englishmen, for two or three generations, were pro-Turkish because anti-Russian, and for no other reason. The 'conversion' of British diplomats and statesmen was almost completed between the Battle of Navarin in 1827 and the Treaty of Unkiar Skelessi in 1833. In the official world, a definite change can be traced during those five or six years in the views of Stratford Canning, Aberdeen and Palmerston, and in others a hardening of views already held. The 'conversion' of the British public followed; it was attempted, with only moderate success, during the thirties, and was achieved much more completely during the fifties, of the last century. Among those who influenced opinion by books and articles, it is enough to mention the names of David Urquhart and John McNeill.

This episode in the story of British policy in the Near East has been comparatively neglected, and for an obvious reason—it falls mainly between the death of Canning and the beginning of Palmerston's career at the Foreign Office. The biographers of Canning treat it merely as the unworthy sequel to an unfinished stroke of genius: the biographers of Palmerston are plunged at once into the affairs of Belgium, and pick up the Eastern problem with Egypt already in the foreground. But Canning's legacy to his successors was a policy, brilliant indeed, but hazardous and perhaps not fully thought out to a conclusion: while Palmerston inherited a situation already developed to a point where his decision could hardly be in doubt. A connecting link may be found in Stratford Canning, who seems to have been already both the strongest influence upon our policy in the Levant and the most faithful mirror of the gradual development of opinion. This book is an attempt to fill the gap, or rather to show that the 'gap' has a structure of its own, which must be brought into relief for the sake of due proportion. The interest is focussed mainly on Greece, and I have thought it not irrelevant to relieve a mainly diplomatic narrative by a few glimpses of the turbulent stream of Greek politics and guerilla warfare. But the point of view remains in London throughout, in an attempt to understand the problem of British policy.

That policy up to the death of Canning has been set forth at length in Professor Temperley's *Foreign Policy of Canning*; but I found it impossible to make the later period intelligible without some account of the earlier years, 1821–7, based on independent study of the printed materials and a few MSS, selecting a rather different emphasis from that of the biographer and illustrating more in detail the play of forces upon the scene of action. For the period after Canning's death, I have relied upon my own researches among public records and printed sources. Two books cover some of the same ground—Mr Stanley Lane-Poole's *Life of Lord Stratford de Redcliffe* and Professor Alison Phillips' *War of Greek Independence*—but one is biography and the other centres in Greece. There are foreign studies based on French, Austrian, Prussian and Russian records, but there is no clear account of the Duke of Wellington's policy.

My thanks are due to Mr J. R. M. Butler, of Trinity College, Cambridge, for the first suggestion which led me to an interest in the Near East: to Mr F. F. Urquhart of Balliol College, Oxford, for helpful criticism: to Professor Temperley for much encouragement, and for advice which, if not always followed, has been always appreciated: to Mr P. W. Duff, of Trinity College, Cambridge, for his careful reading of the proofs: and lastly to my wife, who has lightened much of the labour of preparing this book for the press.

C. W. CRAWLEY

TRINITY HALL
October, 1930

CHAPTER I

INTRODUCTION

I

THE outbreak of the Greek revolt in 1821 found Europe politically in a frame of mind half exhausted, half expectant, and in any case unsettled. The 'moral solidarity' of the Quadruple Alliance had already been shaken by Castlereagh, who was abused at home as the ally of despotism, the accomplice of oppression. Alexander I, on the other hand, who had been hailed as the liberal and reforming Tsar, was coming to be regarded as the second pillar of the established order in Europe. After six years of troubled peace, Metternich was beginning to hope that his system was built up on solid foundations. But when Europe is at peace in herself, the East is too often ready to disturb her repose.

In the Treaties of 1815, Turkey was not mentioned and consequently not included in the implied guarantee of territory among the Powers. There was not even any specific guarantee of the treaties as a whole; Castlereagh, at first anxious for it (1815), afterwards objected to a proposal for a separate treaty of guarantee. But after the Greek revolt, he was inclined to treat Turkey as protected by the settlement of 1815, in so far as any Power was protected by it.[1] His view was consistently denied by Russia; for, by admitting it, Russia would have been renouncing a campaign of absorption, which was inevitable but probably less systematic than it appears in retrospect. In the Treaty of 1774 Russia had secured certain limited privileges for the Christians in Turkey; the Porte promised in general terms to give legal protection to the Christian worship and to churches, priests and pilgrims, without admitting any general right of interference by Russia. The treaty included more detailed stipulations of the same kind, together with some civil privileges in favour of the

[1] Webster, *Castlereagh*, pp. 51, 96, 163, 349, 378. Cf. Russian Declaration of War, 26 Apr. 1828, in *British and Foreign State Papers*, 15, 656. (This series is henceforward indicated by the reference *S.P.*)

inhabitants of the Danubian Principalities and the Islands of the Archipelago, and promised to all subjects of the Porte a limited right of emigration. These rights were reaffirmed at Jassy in 1792 and extended to Serbia at the Treaty of Bucarest in 1812. They did not apply specially to the Morea.[2] Certain points in those treaties had been in dispute ever since. The Russian Cabinet liked always to have some unsettled claims which could be pushed forward at favourable moments as an excuse for further encroachment. There was little ground for interference (except in the Principalities) under the *letter* of the treaties; the Turks, unless provoked, seldom molested the Greek Church, which was rich and powerful. But the Russians used the treaties to put forward much wider and vaguer pretensions, which they hoped that Europe would take for granted. These were practically claims to civil as well as religious protection over all the Christians, claims considered by other Powers to be incompatible with the existence of the Turkish Empire as an independent government. It seemed better even that Turkey should disappear than that it should be managed by its traditional foe.

There was, therefore, a general impression, openly expressed outside the Cabinets and privately admitted within them, that the Turkish Empire must soon collapse. Alexander filled the stage of European politics, and the power of Russia loomed in the East all the more gigantic because it was indistinct. But the weakness of Turkey and the strength of Russia were both exaggerated. Little was known as yet of the firm and ruthless character of Mahmud II: few people had the means of discovering how weak were the foundations on which the appearance of Russian power really rested. The paper strength of the Russian army was out of all proportion to the effective force which could be concentrated on the Danube; the Decabrist conspiracy of Christmas, 1825, first revealed to the world the widespread dis-

[2] For commentary, see T. E. Holland, *The European Concert and the Eastern Question* (1885); *Treaty Relations of Russia and Turkey, 1774–1753* (1877). Hertslet's *Map of Europe by Treaty* contains some of the relevant clauses in the Appendix. The Russian interpretation is set forth in Prokesch v. Osten, *Geschichte*, III, 117: future references to this work are under the initials P. O.

affection even among the highest ranks. Almost all of those implicated were under thirty years of age, and belonged to the flower of the Russian corps of officers; they inherited the traditions of the court of Catherine II and the 'contagion' picked up in Western Europe by the armies which fought Napoleon on the soil of Germany and France. Yet this revolutionary movement was national and characteristically Russian. Among those who directed Russian policy, there was a real desire for commercial supremacy in the Black Sea and for a secure commercial outlet to the Mediterranean. These objects might be achieved by treaties. But mere increase of territory was an object quite foreign to the general progress of the people. Russia was not over-crowded, and had no indefensible frontiers: many Russians themselves recognised that the Empire had outgrown itself and needed overhauling. The administration was hopelessly corrupt: Alexander began with good intentions of reform, but the system was too strong for him. Others who were less anxious for reform yet feared that the possession of Constantinople would split the Empire in two, change its centre of gravity, and take from St Petersburg and Moscow their unchallenged pre-eminence. Religious and racial sympathy for the subjects of the Porte could easily be excited on occasion, but did not yet exert a continuous or compelling pressure upon the Government, whose foreign policy was directed mainly by men of foreign extraction. The first beginnings of a Pan-Slav movement in 1823 were confined to an obscure group without influence or publicity, though the ramifications of the Greek *Hetaireia* were much wider.[3]

Belief in the irresistible power of Russia died hard, but it alternated with an equally foolish contempt. The English ambassador at St Petersburg used the language of paradox when he wrote in June 1829 that "Russia possesses fewer and less formidable means of *aggression* than any other of the Great Powers....The long continuance of the delusion was due to military display and to the high tone assumed by Russian agents in foreign Courts".[4]

[3] K. Waliszewski, *Le Règne d'Alexandre I*, 1818–1825, pp. 13, 165, 175. *Les Rapports de Lebzeltern*, Introd. p. lxxii.

[4] Heytesbury to Aberdeen, 29 June 1829, *F.O. Russia*, 180.

He was thinking no doubt especially of the blustering but wily Pozzo di Borgo in Paris and of Prince Lieven and his wife in London. Of the first, Canning said in 1824: "I know that Russia governs Continental Europe through Pozzo, now, nearly as absolutely as she heretofore governed Poland through Poniatowski".[5] Of Princess Lieven and her husband—for that is the order which more truly represents the influence of Alexander's 'two ambassadors in London'—much has been written. The princess corresponded regularly and intimately with Lord Grey on political matters: she was on terms of friendship in turn with Castlereagh and Metternich, then with Canning, Aberdeen and even Wellington. Although she feared and hated democracy in every shape, her ambitious temperament could never be content with ultra-Tory passivity: it was her business to know the men in office, and she saw when Liberalism might be turned to the account of Russia. She certainly exaggerated her own influence, and boasted of a power which she did not really possess. But she gave constant and faithful reports to Count Nesselrode at St Petersburg of the shades of political feeling in England, and she made ministers feel that Russian diplomacy was a formidable weapon.

Everywhere Russian agents served their imperial master ably, devotedly and unscrupulously, making it their one aim to increase the power and prestige of the Tsar, and constantly outstripping the instruction of their Foreign Office, which sometimes offered a mild rebuke and sometimes quietly accepted the results. While Russia was professing sympathy for her 'co-religionaries' of Greece, she was steadily absorbing the independent 'Christian' populations of Georgia and Circassia, and penetrating Persia by gradual encroachments. Moreover, these conquered peoples were treated with little ceremony: in 1830 more than 200,000 Armenians of Erzerum were inveigled across the Russian frontier with fair promises of deliverance from Turkish misrule; a few months later the remnant tried half-starving to return to their homes, but the frontier guards would not let them pass. The

[5] Canning to Wellington, 8 Oct. 1824, in Wellington's *Despatches* (N.S.), II, 316; cf. Metternich, *Mémoires*, 689.

wretched people of the Principalities, oppressed by their Greek ruling princes, dreaded the Russian armies of occupation as much as they resented the coming of a Russian officer to raise a revolt in the name of Greek liberty.[6] The Greeks of the Morea had cause to remember how Catherine II in 1770 had encouraged them to revolt, and, when the diversion had served her turn, had abandoned them to a terrible vengeance.

Other Powers feared these encroachments not only from sentiments of national rivalry but for definite material reasons. Their treaties with Turkey, which were on the whole faithfully observed, allowed them great freedom of commerce, because the Turks had no desire to compete. The proud and lazy Turk left commerce within the Empire to his Greek and Armenian *rayahs*, and to the Franks if they chose to come; until 1803 the English ambassador at Constantinople was primarily a servant of the Levant Company of Turkey Merchants, dissolved in 1825. But Russian tariffs were high, and aimed at exclusion: soon there were complaints that our considerable trade with Central Asia was threatened by the Russian advance. Moreover the fear of a Russian fleet in the Mediterranean and for the safety of the British Empire in India—or of the future line of communication with India—was beginning to be vaguely felt.[7]

Russian policy had a definite aim of expansion, which was pursued—subject to the vagaries of Alexander I—throughout the Greek revolt up to the successful climax of the Peace of Adrianople. The only hesitation was between the policy of downright conquest and that of keeping Turkey as a feeble neighbour to whom Russia could dictate at will. The latter policy promised less complication for the unity of Russia and less trouble with the other Powers; in 1829 it was from choice or necessity adopted

[6] On early Anglo-Russian rivalry in Persia, see Sykes, *History of Persia*; Webster, *Castlereagh*, p. 35; and below, chap. xv. On the Armenians, Gordon to Palmerston, 26 Feb. 1831, in *F.O. Turkey*, 198, and G. F. Martens, *Recueil, Nouveaux Suppléments*, III, 303. Reports of Col. Blutte on the Russian occupation of the Principalities, 1828–30, in *F.O.* 97/402. Cf. I. L. Evans, *The Agrarian Revolution in Rumania*, p. 192.

[7] On trade, see a letter from G. Ross, 26 Jan. 1830, in *F.O. Russia*, 189. The Russian tariff was raised in 1822 and again in 1828. On India, see chap. xv below; cf. Heytesbury to Aberdeen, 16 Jan. 1830, *ibid.* 185.

for the time, and led four years later to an actual treaty of protective alliance with the Turks at Unkiar Skelessi. Russian ambition, however natural with such neighbours as the Turks, was inevitably feared and disliked. The 'Russian menace' was not, as the Whig tradition held, a mere bogey: but Tory panic could not help British commerce. As Joseph Planta wrote in 1821: "The Turks will hold the Russians a long Tug before the latter get to Constantinople". English trade with Turkey was increasing rapidly throughout the Greek revolt, and, though partly interrupted by the Russian war in 1828–9, recovered immediately to a greater volume than before. Our export trade to the Baltic, on the other hand, remained stationary, owing partly to the high tariffs imposed by Russia and partly to the fact that much of the Mediterranean trade had been diverted to the Baltic during the Napoleonic wars, and now returned to its normal course. Yet our export trade to Russia was, until the forties, the more important, and our imports of raw materials from Russia were immeasurably greater than from Turkey. A war with Russia would, in the twenties, hurt more people in England than could a war with Turkey, especially as the former might mean the closing of the Dardanelles and the interruption of the Turkey trade as well. During the forties, the position changed, and our export trade to Turkey became the more important, continuing to increase while exports to Russia actually declined.[8]

Indifference might allow Russia to advance her plans by mere bluff, but premature and public alarm was both impotent and undignified. The middle course, which Canning attempted to follow and Palmerston found it increasingly hard to maintain, was to keep a watchful eye against undue encroachment, and to forestall it without needlessly exciting the enmity of Russia. A conflict might after all be inevitable, but Wellington's impotent irritation was even more harmful than Whig indifference. Lord Grey wrote in 1821 to Lord Holland: "The danger arising from the extension of the Russian power and influence on that side is so remote and contingent as to bear no degree of comparison

[8] J. Planta to S. Canning, 8 Aug. 1821, in Webster, *Castlereagh*, pp. 582–3. See Appendix II for comparative tables of trade with Russia and Turkey.

with the certain evil of the existence of the Turkish Empire" But twelve years later he wrote less confidently:

I certainly have not much more fear than you have of an attack upon India though this is not to be entirely put out of view. But with the influence which Russia is likely to obtain in the new Government of Greece—with that which events seem likely to give her in Turkey, the danger of her power in that quarter of the world is not remote.[9]

It is not always fair to quote isolated judgments as evidence of altered opinions, and something may be put down to Grey's increasing age and conservatism; but the change of tone after the experience of these years in Eastern affairs was common to so many Englishmen that it cannot be disregarded.

The question for the people of the Balkans was whether it was worth while to exchange Turkish for Russian misrule.[10] The Sultan's *rayahs* had little cause to envy the Poles or the Moldavians in 1830: but at least his late *rayahs* of the Greek peninsula had shaken off one yoke without succumbing to the other. How was this result achieved?

II

Since the middle of the eighteenth century, the Greeks had grown steadily in wealth and population.[11] The cultural revival

[9] Trevelyan, *Lord Grey*, p. 227, Nov. 1821; p. 355, Jan. 1833.

[10] Cf. *Coup d'Œil sur la Turquie*, by A. Mavrocordato (? 1820), printed in P. O., IV, 1–54, esp. 52–4. But it was only 'European' Greeks who fully recognised the danger. The mass of the people were devotedly attached to Russia by the ties of religion, and looked to her for salvation. Mavrocordato proposed a Greek Empire, giving Russia the southern shore of the Black Sea: he did not mind letting Serbia go to Austria. Yet the Serbs had already a far more real national existence than the Greeks.

[11] According to *New Portfolio*, II, 367, the population of the Morea was trebled between 1790 and 1820. That is probably an exaggeration. In 1823 it may have been about 400,000 (Green, *Sketches of the War in Greece*, p. 299), but cf. a statistical table (compiled from Pouqueville) in *S.P.* 11, 303. At the end of the eighteenth century the Morea exported a crop of currants worth eight million pounds annually, of which five-eighths went to England —Beaujour, *Tableau du Commerce de la Grèce* (1800), p. 132. The currant crops of the Morea in the years preceding the revolt were not equalled by those of 1840 after ten years of external peace—F. Strong, *Greece as a Kingdom* (1842), a volume of statistics.

The origins of the revolution are traced in detail in Finlay's *History*, II. The following are only a few points which seem to bear most on the troubles which followed the revolution. For the system of government in European Turkey, particularly the Morea, see Appendix VI (d).

was practically confined to the Greek communities in European cities, and to some extent the Ionian Islands. The chief centres abroad (outside Russia) were Paris, Vienna and Trieste. Lord Guilford's efforts to found a University at Corfu were discouraged by the High Commissioner, Maitland, who distrusted his Philhellenic enthusiasm and his conversion to the Orthodox Church. After Maitland's death the University was established in 1824, but ceased to flourish much after the death of its eccentric patron three years later. Conditions among the Greeks varied enormously. The islanders of the Archipelago had got possession, during the Napoleonic wars, of the carrying trade of the Levant under the protection of the Russian flag, and big fortunes had been made by the shipowners of Hydra and Spezzia, who were of Albanian origin—Konduriottes, one of the first Presidents of Greece, could hardly speak the Greek language. Syra and other islands shared in the prosperity. These islanders enjoyed something like independence, merely paying to the Capitan Pasha (the Turkish admiral and governor of the Archipelago) a yearly tribute collected by one of their own notables (called 'primates'), and in some cases sending a quota of men to the Turkish fleets. Although the municipal government was in the hands of a few of the richest men, the ships' crews always shared with the captain and the owner a fixed proportion of the profits, and decisions were taken by quarter-deck committees. There was consequently no discipline, and the Greeks, though good sailors, and good pirates, never had an organised navy during the revolt.

The peasants of the Morea were hard-working and fairly prosperous, but superstitious and fanatical. Since the unsuccessful revolt in 1770, the scourge of the brigand *klephts* had been increasing. But the *klephts* were not really a separate class; they were recruited from the same homes which they afterwards found it exciting and profitable to live by plundering. Even thirty years later Edmond About could write in an entertaining satire on the kingdom of Greece:

Ce n'est pas que les brigands épargnent leurs compatriotes et réservent leurs rigueurs pour les étrangers: mais un Grec dépouillé par ses frères se dit avec une certaine résignation que son argent ne sort pas de la famille. La population se voit piller par les brigands comme une femme du peuple se sent battre par son mari, en admirant, comme il frappe bien. Les moralistes indigènes se plaignent de tous les excès commis dans la campagne, comme un père déplore les fredaines de son fils. On le gronde tout haut, on l'aime tout bas; on serait bien fâché qu'il ressemblât au fils du voisin, qui n'a jamais fait parler de lui.[12]

Across the Isthmus, in Attica and Acarnania, life was even more unsettled. The *armatoli*, a sort of Christian police licensed by the Turks to carry arms under their own chieftains, often became mere robber bands: they were being gradually disarmed and replaced by fierce Mussulman Albanians. Lawlessness was least in the country governed with ruthless methods and a show of enlightened policy by Ali Pasha of Yanina, who had made himself practically independent of the Sultan.

The lower clergy were ignorant and not always saintly; they depended upon their occasional fees to support their families. The bishops were maintained by taxes upon laity and clergy, and were taxed in turn by their superiors; their standard of learning was low. The primates, usually small landowners invested by the Pasha with civil authority, lived at their ease, imitating Turkish dress and manners. Each district collected the tribute due to the Sultan, sometimes through its own elected representatives; the primates had a chosen agent (Vekil) at Constantinople, who with the Patriarch of the Greek Church was consulted on all the affairs of the *rayahs*. In administration and justice the hand of the Pasha fell as heavily upon Mohammedan as upon Christian subjects: indolence made him more capricious than systematically cruel. Finlay says that the Greeks enjoyed as much practical freedom as the French under Napoleon, and much more than Italians or Poles under their foreign masters. But the Christians alone were subject to the hated *haratch*, or poll-tax, and to certain galling distinctions of dress and privilege. The tax was not in most provinces collected in proportion to the existing population, but had been assessed at a lump sum at the time of the original conquest. Consequently provinces which had grown in population paid at a very low rate and others much

[12] *Le Roi des Montagnes*, c. 2.

too highly. Two-thirds of the land was owned by the Turks, whom the active-minded Greeks despised for their stolidity and ignorance. A fair proportion of the Greeks were traders who could read and write: they conducted all the Turks' business and manned their fleets. Such a relation between master and servant bred obstinate pride in the one, venality and faithlessness in the other. A sense of injustice, a growing measure of prosperity and power, combined with religious zeal to bring about this revolt of a half-Eastern people, agricultural and trading, preserving a form of municipal government, but almost untouched by Western political ideas. The French Revolution had indeed some echoes even in Greece. Napoleon had sent emissaries to the Morea, and recruited his Ionian regiments from among the *klephts* of the mainland; the Pasha of Yanina used to wear the tricolour, and the highland clans of Maina were found praying before a portrait of Napoleon beside that of the Virgin Mary.[13] But these were mere symbols, without the revolutionary spirit. The people were ready at the bidding of their priests and of the itinerant preachers to join the ranks of the *klephts* and to drive out the infidel from Greece: all had a prospect of sharing in the spoil, and the Primates hoped to replace the Pashas. They took little thought of what Greece was to be when the Turks should be gone.

The famous *Hetaireia* was founded at Odessa in 1814 and removed its headquarters two years later to Moscow. Its professed aim was with the aid of Russia to restore the Greek Empire at Constantinople, but almost all revolutions have had a similar war-cry, which the more intelligent know in their hearts to be visionary or premature. The most probable issue was a status like that of the Danubian Principalities under a native prince paying tribute to the Porte. This prospect suited the views of Russia, whose consuls and agents were often implicated in the

[13] The *Voyage de D. et N. Stephanopoli en Grèce, 1797–1798* (Paris, an VIII), is an extraordinary tale, written in the rapturous strains of the revolutionary period, of a mission from Napoleon to offer French liberty to the Mainot chiefs. The author, a Corsican herbalist, mingles together military speculations, romantic encounters with Mainot maidens, advertisements of his medical skill, and complaints of his losses in the service of Napoleon.

Hetaireia, under the double stimulus of religious sympathies and patriotic zeal. The society announced its object to be "purification of this nation and with the aid of heaven its emancipation"; each recruit vowed "irreconcilable hatred against the tyrants.... I will exert every method for their injury, and when circumstances permit, for their destruction".[14]

All this was very simple, and, when all is said, a respectable if not heroic movement. It had little in common with the Liberal movements of Europe. But several things made the case of the Greeks essentially different from that of the Serbians or the Bulgarians or any other of the subject peoples in the loose haphazard structure of the Turkish Empire, and enabled them to gain a place on the map of Europe so many years in advance of the rest.

Besides the natural activity of the people at large, and the encouragement of Russia, there were more conscious forces behind the ambitions for Greece: the Greeks of the Fanar quarter of Constantinople and the educated Greeks living abroad. The Fanariots, the 'black-coated city men' of the capital, were completely out of sympathy with the rude popular movement of the Moreot peasants. For the most part they stood aloof from the *Hetaireia*, and preferred to paralyse the Turks by becoming indispensable to them. Many of them, filling high positions in the Turkish Government, continued to do so throughout the revolution. A few, like Mavrocordato, threw in their lot with the revolt, while deploring the barbarities of its opening stages and wishing that the Greeks had been given another ten years at least to grow and to prepare.[15] The Greeks living abroad, headed by Korais in Paris, hoped to revive the ancient language and literature, and to educate their countrymen by the examples of Leonidas and the Academy. These men had far wider views for the future of their country. They hoped to create an inde-

[14] Waddington, *Visit to Greece*, Introd. pp. xviii ff.

[15] Mavrocordato to Gentz, 17 Dec. 1824, in P. O. IV, 132. But this was a letter for legitimist eyes. Th. Blancard, in *Les Mavroyéni* (Paris, 1909), has traced the fortunes of a leading Fanariot family through several generations; the picture is one of culture, ability and tortuous ambition, sudden elevation and precarious tenure of power.

pendent State after the European model, a monarchy or a republic, with a centralised constitution, an army and navy, diplomatic representatives and the rest. All these things were finally achieved under a Bavarian King. But some of the clansmen thought that they had got more than they bargained for. Most of the troubles of Greece were due less to the so-called selfishness of the Powers than to this fundamental difference between the new Greeks and the old, between the intelligence of the revolution and its instruments, almost between West and East.

The promoters were surely inspired by a great idea—nothing less than the regeneration of a whole people. For whatever measure of freedom existed in Greece, there could be no doubt at all that regeneration in this European sense was impossible with the Turks in occupation. But the only men who could perform the first task, removal of the Turks, had no views of regeneration whatever: after the revolution, Capodistrias was faced even more acutely than was Cavour with the problem of the disgruntled and clamorous veteran. The people had thrown off a brutal but easy-going rule for—they knew not what: the force of circumstances brought them a strictly paternal government. After all, it might be argued, the Morea was not likely to be anything but a land mainly of peasants and fishermen and trading-captains—was all the apparatus of Western government a boon to such a community? But it could not be expected that the West should stop to argue the merits of the case with the East; and the West not only felt its own expansive power, but was especially attracted to Greece.

III

The geographical fact that Greece juts out into the Mediterranean Sea was alone enough to prevent the revolt from being quietly snuffed out, after years of disturbance, by Turkey alone. The devastation in the Morea affected the currant trade in London and Trieste; piracy in the Archipelago threatened to paralyse the whole commerce of the Levant, which could be protected only by large squadrons in the Mediterranean. The

Turkish fleet, even before the revolt, had neither the skill nor the energy to police the seas, and the Greek leaders would do little to restore order until their claims were satisfied. English shipowners could not expect continual convoy from our own much-reduced navy. The fact that England exercised an uneasy sway over the Ionian Islands brought home still more to the Government the urgent need of finding a settlement; the 'Septinsular Republic' was nominally under the protection of England, but it could in fact only be treated as a Crown Colony under a military governor and a strong garrison.

Intervention was called for by reasons of a practical kind. But just as the Barbary pirates had never been suppressed in the interests of all Europe, owing to the mutual jealousies of the Powers and the suspicion that Russia wished for a naval base in the Mediterranean,[16] so in this case the disorder was allowed to go on for six years before anything was done. Even then the purely material arguments for intervention were on a short-sighted view just as strong for helping to suppress the revolt as for legalising it, much stronger in the eyes of Metternich and the rigid professors of 'legitimacy'. It was only the sentimental interest of Europe which supported the Greeks through the middle stages of the revolt and ensured that when intervention came at last it was not on the side of the Turks.

The 'Philhellenes' who sought adventure in Greece achieved very little in a military sense, but they raised high the hopes of the Greeks, and the name of Byron focussed the interest of Europe upon the struggle; when Byron landed, the enthusiasm of classical scholars was reinforced by the romantic admiration of readers of *Childe Harold.* Diplomatic intervention, it is true, did not become effective until enthusiasm had turned to coolness and even to disgust. The civil wars in Greece and the shady transactions in the Greek Loan[17] had done their work: in June

[16] In 1818 a proposal for concerted action was frustrated by British fears of a Russian fleet in the Mediterranean—*C.M.H.* x, 19. But cf. Webster, *Castlereagh*, pp. 463–4.

[17] Exposed by Cobbett under the title of 'The Greek Pie' in the *Weekly Register*, 28 Oct., 4 Nov., 11 Nov. 1826. The connection of Greece with the classics of course infuriated Cobbett; cf. Moore's *Ghost of Miltiades.* The

1827, just before the Treaty of London was signed, Hobhouse, the friend of Byron and a member of the Greek Committee in London, said that "everybody is disgusted with the Greeks".[18] But the interest of Europe, exhibited by the campaign of the press, by subscriptions and by innumerable pamphlets, had prevented the question from being allowed to drop. Diplomats who at first referred to Philhellenism as the "clamour of a faction" were speaking by 1823 of the "sympathy shown by the whole of Europe". The significance of this movement was quite independent of the character of the Greeks and the real conditions of Levantine politics: it lay in the European appeal of classical tradition and of Christendom oppressed, and above all in the discovery of an outlet for energies compressed by the conservative Alliance—an outlet the more welcome because relatively unconnected with the dangers of revolutionary movements at home.

Every statesman in England, and many abroad, had been brought up in classical studies, and some of them felt a warm personal concern in the fate of Greece, whatever their view of public duty. If some of the Whigs found in Greece a convenient stick to beat the Holy Alliance, others were genuine partisans. Among the Tories, Aberdeen was interested, and even Lord Eldon contributed privately £100 to the Greek Committee.[19] In the age of Sir Walter Scott, with the passing of the eighteenth century and the end of the stern struggle against Napoleon, there was renewed among Englishmen, official and unofficial, of every political creed, a strain of fine Quixotism, a temper ready

papers made endless fun of the Greek Loan, e.g. a mediocre epigram from the *New Times* in *Spirit of the Public Journals* for 1824, p. 187:

"Pray do the bonds of Hume and Co.
  Intelligibly speak,
And are the fatal words 'I owe'
  In English or pure Greek?
In Greek, and poor enough they say,
  Plainly by no Oxonian;
They're Attic promises to pay
  In dialect I-O-nian."

[18] To Eynard, 3 June 1827—Lord Broughton, *Recollections*, II, 200.
[19] *Diary of J. Q. Adams* (ed. Nevins, 1928), p. 323; 10 May 1824.

to admire adventure, a kind of generous extravagance which made our countrymen seem to foreigners a little more gloriously mad than usual.[20] It manifested itself in different forms; not merely in the avowed romantics and Philhellenes—men like Lord Guilford and Sir Richard Church—but in the zeal of the anti-slavery group, in the warm-hearted impulsiveness of Stratford Canning, in the fervour of Urquhart, a convert to the 'Spirit of the East', in Palmerston himself, the apostle of 'British common sense', and strangest of all, in those who professed themselves least moved by sentiment, such missionary disciples of Bentham as Sir John Bowring and the 'typographical' Colonel Stanhope. Bentham himself wrote in 1828 a remarkable series of letters to Mehemet Ali, calling upon this new hope of the East to secure for posterity the blessings of his enlightened rule by declaring himself independent, accepting a Benthamite constitution, and entrusting his grandson Abbas to the philosopher's own care.[21] Even Cobbett, who inveighed most against 'unpractical illusions', had no small share of them himself. One and all, these Englishmen did not care what others thought of them: they conducted their controversies with a high-handed vigour and a contempt for nice qualifications which a later age may envy but cannot imitate.

In France the enthusiasm was shared not only by Liberals, who favoured Greece out of hostility to the Holy Alliance, but by Royalists, who embarked on the wave of romantic sentiment, piloted on different courses by Chateaubriand and Victor Hugo. Charles X showed almost the ardour of a crusader, heightened by his eagerness for a diversion to support his shaky throne and by his anxiety to please Russia, on whose support he depended. In Germany, Philhellenic committees were active in practical relief, but the policy of the Government was controlled by Metternich, who succeeded in neutralising the close ties of the Prussian Court with the Tsar; only in Bavaria, under the patronage of the King, did the movement become fashionable.

[20] The Austrian consul at Prevesa wrote to Metternich that his English colleague, Consul Meyer, was not (as he thought at first) "a thorough Turk", but "a mad and true English enthusiast": 27 Nov. 1825, in *C.O. Ionian Is.* 33.

[21] *B.M., Add. MSS.* 25663.

In Russia, the Orthodox Church was a natural bond of sympathy, and Greek merchants living there spread the fame of the *Hetaireia*; but it would be idle to speak at this time of a strong public opinion outside the society of St Petersburg and Moscow. Capo d'Istria, a Corfiot by birth, used his influence with Alexander to predispose him in favour of the Greeks: like Cavour at Paris in 1856, he gave expression to the claims of his countrymen at the Congress of Vienna. But his views for Greece had little in common with those of the Western 'Liberals'; in an open letter to the Greeks he dwelt on the Church as the instrument of a revival: while teachers with a University education should be encouraged, great care must be taken not to let them stand in opposition to the Orthodox Church. Administrators would be needed: let them be trained in Russia, "a school offered us by the Christian peoples of our faith".[22] But religious sympathy did not direct the lively interest of the Russian Cabinet, which was ready enough to neglect its 'co-religionaries' if they could not be of use. When the revolt broke out sooner than the cautious friends of Greece had hoped or expected, Capo d'Istria soon lost his position at the Emperor's side, and the Chancellor Nesselrode steered his master back to a waiting policy.

[22] 6 Apr. 1819, in *Portfolio*, IV, 282–301.

CHAPTER II

NEUTRALITY

1821–3

When the Congress assembled at Laibach in March 1821 was told that a Russian officer, an aide-de-camp of the Tsar, had crossed the River Pruth, with a handful of followers collected at the Russian army headquarters, and had invoked the power of Russia in aid of his feeble, ill-considered enterprise, Alexander I did not hesitate to disavow the raid as it seemed his duty to do: if he had any dangerous leanings, Metternich was at his side. At the same time he offered some prospect of mediation if order were restored, and showed a sympathy for Greek hopes which made his letter to the 'malefactor' Hypselantes far from reassuring to the Sultan.[1]

At Constantinople, the Russian ambassador, Stroganov, and his staff openly but not officially favoured the Greek cause. As soon as the news from Moldavia reached the city, he repudiated the revolt and persuaded the Greek bishops to pronounce anathema upon it; but the Russian consul at Bucarest did his best to conceal the fact.[2] The Turks, hardly restrained from declaring war on Russia at once, sent about 30,000 men to the Principalities and took some violent measures ending with the interruption of commerce, the imprisonment of the Russian Embassy's banker, and the execution of the Greek Patriarch. This last step, and especially the ill-usage of the body by the mob, did more than anything else to sanctify the cause in the eyes of every Greek. The Patriarch was of course no enemy of the *Hetaireia* and probably knew its secrets, but he had done the most that the Sultan could expect in publicly denouncing the revolt. The Porte claimed that he "subit le supplice mérité, et

[1] When no other reference is given, documents may be found, in order of date, in P. O. III–VI. For this and the following chapter, cf. Schiemann, I, c. 8, on 'Alexander and the Eastern Question, 1821–5'; and K. Waliszewski, *Le Règne d'Alexandre I, 1818–1825*, cc. 4–6.

[2] P. O. III, 58.

d'une manière exemplaire", and quoted the example of Peter the Great, who put his own son to death and abolished the office of Patriarch in Russia. The wholesale massacre of Turks at the beginning of the revolt in the Morea[3] roused the fury of the people of Constantinople. Stroganov brought to a head the unsettled disputes arising out of the Treaty of Bucarest, and demanded fulfilment of the treaties in general. Early in June relations were broken off, the ambassador retired to Buyukderé and then on board a Russian frigate; in July a new ultimatum of four points was presented, which, in addition to the points covered by the treaties, demanded a 'change of system' in regard to the Greeks generally. Stroganov, without waiting for a written answer,[4] left Constantinople, and war seemed certain. Russia claimed her right to protect the Greeks as Christians: the Sultan asserted his right to deal with them as rebels.

From this moment for the next two years the efforts of Metternich were devoted to separating the Russo-Turkish dispute from the Greek question, and so to preventing war. The danger was real; Alexander returned home in June and the scale at once began to turn. Society and the army clamoured for war, while Mme de Krudener, lately returned to the capital, preached a crusade. The voice of legitimist principle and even of common prudence seemed faint. Russia appealed to the Powers to prevent the "spectre of a religious war" by supporting her demands: she desired only to act "de concert et d'accord avec ses alliés", "d'assurer...l'affermissement du système conservatoire"; but Stroganov was told:

> si les excès auxquels se livrent les Turcs continuent, s'ils ne tendent qu'à exterminer la nation grecque, on sentira aisément que la Russie non plus qu'aucune autre Puissance ne saurait rester spectatrice immobile de ces profanations et de ces cruautés.

[3] Perhaps the most objective accounts (mostly from eye-witnesses) are those in the *Sketches of the War in Greece* (1827), by P. J. Green, English consul at Patras.

[4] The ultimatum (printed in *S.P.* 8, 1251) was drafted by Capo d'Istria, despatched 28 June and presented to the Porte 18 July; it expired in eight days, 26 July. The Turkish answer bore this date but was not presented until the last day of the month, when Stroganov was already on board ship, in some fear of his life; he refused to receive it so late.

The only extermination so far had been that of the Turks in the Morea, followed by isolated reprisals in Constantinople. The Porte, however, took credit "for not having used its right to exterminate the whole Greek nation".[5]

The Powers were not prepared to do anything in concert with so suspected an ally as Russia. Austria could never be sincerely her ally in the Eastern question until it should be time for an undisguised partition. Metternich steadily refused to do the one thing which the war party in Russia desired—to make the Greek revolt an excuse for a war of conquest, a war in which Austria was then in no condition to take part. In the Russo-Turkish dispute he would only agree to urge the Sultan to withdraw his troops from the Principalities and to concede the other points of strict treaty right. As to the Greeks, he independently pressed the Sultan to subdue the revolt without delay, to offer pardon on submission and to promise, for the future, privileges like those already granted to the Serbians; even if unsuccessful he wished to delay any general congress until the separate Russo-Turkish dispute should be settled. Above all he was anxious not to appear to countenance the rebels. Bernstorff on behalf of Prussia refused to join a secret pact with Austria or on the other hand to support the Russian view. Aiming at the rôle of mediator, he tried to appease Metternich's anger at the sympathy for the Greeks which had been cautiously expressed in a *Mémoire* by Ancillon, a Prussian official, and reproved the 'Philhellenic excesses' of the South German courts.[6]

The British Government was on different grounds opposed to any action by the Allies. On the subject of the Russian appeal Castlereagh told Lord Strangford, our ambassador at Constantinople, not to act with the Allies, but to prevent if possible a rupture between Russia and Turkey:

As far as we have had experience of the effect of conjoint representations upon the Ottoman ministry, they have invariably failed of pro-

[5] 28 June, 6 July, P. O. III, 89–92, 101.

[6] Ringhoffer, p. 6. Ancillon, originally a Lutheran pastor, a cousin of Gentz and once friend of Mirabeau, was at this time 'rédacteur' of the Prussian foreign correspondence—a man of 'cold rectitude'—Capefigue, *Les Diplomates Européens*, II. Cf. *Allg. Deut. Biog.* and Webster, *Castlereagh*, p. 363.

ducing a beneficial effect. The Porte has always looked upon the European Alliance as a league which they viewed with religious as well as political distrust.[7]

Castlereagh looked upon the revolt only as one more example of the unaccountable restlessness of Europe; the Porte was at least "exempt from the revolutionary danger". Strangford was told that "whatever the merits of the case you are accredited to the Porte and you must awaken it to the necessity of asserting its authority over an infuriated people".[8] But here as elsewhere in Europe Castlereagh refused to act merely on the ground of legitimacy. Strangford had proposed to summon the Greeks, on behalf of the Powers, to unconditional surrender; but Castlereagh made difficulties of form in order to avoid signing the joint declaration in that sense: it was consequently dropped, Russia of course refusing too.[9] He also rebuked the ambassador for telling the British admiral to assist the Turkish fleet.

He lost no time in defining the British policy as one of 'strict neutrality',[10] but this did not at first imply any recognition of the Greeks as belligerents. The High Commissioner of the Ionian Islands, like most of the officials on the spot, was strongly contemptuous of the Greeks;[11] he had already issued proclamations

[7] Castlereagh to Strangford, 13 July 1821, in *F.O. Turkey*, 97.

[8] Castlereagh to Strangford, 5 Aug. 1821, in *F.O. Turkey*, 97.

[9] Castlereagh to Strangford, 28 Oct., in *F.O. Turkey*, 97. Declaration in P. O. III, 167. Castlereagh quoted in *C.H.F.P.* II, 85.

[10] Castlereagh to Strangford, 20 Nov., in *F.O. Turkey*, 97. Bathurst to Maitland, 30 June, in *C.O. Ionian Is.* 20.

[11] There is an interesting *Life of Sir Thomas Maitland* by W. F. Lord, who, without attempting to whitewash his character, claims admiration for his strong points as an Empire-builder. Descended from a line of headstrong Earls of Lauderdale, Maitland was "born in the purple and totally uneducated". "Life to Maitland meant work...his diversion, his solace, was gross indulgence." Having tired of the bar and the army he entered Parliament as a "Friend of the People" in 1790 and spoke among the most violent of the Opposition until, in 1797, he was sent to treat with Toussaint l'Ouverture in San Domingo. Later as Governor of Ceylon (1805) he was occupied in repealing the experiments in land tenure begun by his predecessor, Sir F. North, whom he was afterwards to meet as Lord Guilford, the enthusiastic Philhellene and founder of Corfu University. As Governor of Malta (1813) and High Commissioner of the Ionian Islands (1817) he spent lavishly a princely salary of £13,000 a year, and the name of 'King Tom' was hated, feared and respected all over the Levant: a genial tyrant with a savage temper and no scruples, he combined the methods of a Turkish pasha

forbidding any interference by Ionians; but in spite of this more than 3000 Ionians found their way to the Morea, and the Turks complained that, although this was allowed, the Government asked for the return of a few Ionians serving in the Ottoman fleet.[12] At first the insurgent flag only was excluded from Ionian ports, but after October 29th, 1821, armed vessels of both parties were refused admittance.[13] Lord Strangford was loud in echoing

with the energies and abilities of a Scotchman. He died of apoplexy in January 1824 and was succeeded as High Commissioner by his deputy, Sir F. Adam, a soldier of a narrow official cast of mind, of whom an unpleasing picture has been drawn by the Resident in Cephalonia, the talented Charles Napier (*Life of C. J. Napier*, by his son; and his own book, *The Colonies*, 1833). On the eccentric Lord Guilford, see *Some English Philhellenes*, VI, by Z. D. Ferriman.

[12] Adam explained to Strangford, 5 Aug., that the islands were too near to prevent communication with the Morea; that as for the Ionians in the Turkish fleet, he had written to the Capitan Pasha only in order to satisfy opinion, with no intention of insisting upon their return—*C.O. Ionian Is.* 20.

[13] The Proclamations are in *C.O. Ionian Is.* 20. (For subsequent steps, see below, pp. 27, 37–8, 48.)

1821, Apr. 9th. Ionians forbidden to take part in commotions in Turkish dominions. May 7th. Turkish blockade of Morea must be observed. June 7th. 'Neutrality' proclaimed, i.e. Ionians again forbidden to take part. *S.P.* 8, 1282 ff. Sept. 5th. Banishment and confiscation of the property of those joining the insurgents after 18 July (forty days from 7 June). Oct. 29th. Neither belligerent to use Ionian ports. *S.P.* 8, 1284.

1822, Feb. 4th. Population disarmed. (In carrying this out there were six executions.) Apr. 2nd. Act confirming the decree of banishment and confiscation. *S.P.* 9, 1005.

Trikoupes admits that those taking part were bound to lose the status of Ionian citizens, but blames the confiscation of their property (I, 296). C. Metaxas (*Souvenirs*, c. 1) describes how in January 1821 he joined the *Hetaireia*, which was unknown to the primates of Cephalonia, and began recruiting in the island; the English resident, Napier, showed his complaisance by contenting himself with a friendly warning and allowing Metaxas to go to Zante. In May, 460 Cephaloniots sailed for the Morea.

Before the proclamation of 29 Oct. 1821, the Turkish fleet was twice received at Zante, but the Greeks attacked and killed the crew of an Algerine brig which had run ashore. This incident caused such enthusiasm and commotion among the islanders that it was judged safer to keep Turkish as well as Greek vessels outside Ionian waters up to four miles. The proclamation was less a concession to neutrality than a defensive act of the Government. Trikoupes says that it was afterwards unfairly enforced, and that Turkish ships were allowed to stay in the Bay of Myrto: but the Turks equally complained of unfair discrimination in favour of the Greeks (II, 73 ff., 153 ff.). Trikoupes also says that the Government offered an interview to an Argive deputy who came to suggest British protection for Greece, if the complaints of the Turkish ministers, whom he encouraged to summary measures in suppressing the revolt. He was a brilliant but somewhat erratic diplomatist, with a great knowledge of the East and a reputation for something too much of Eastern suppleness; he seems at least never to have been fully trusted either by the Foreign Office or by his colleagues.[14] The Russians complained much of his conduct on this occasion; on the other hand he was well fitted, as a devoted admirer of Metternich's principles and as a person in whom the Turks had confidence, to undertake the charge of obtaining concessions which would avert war with Russia.

Russia tried every means of turning the opportunity to account. The Tsar, unable to hope for a collective interference, first addressed to France (July 19th) a tempting offer of alliance, with the ultimate prospect of a French protectorate in the Morea. The French Government had already declared against taking any part: "L'insurrection grecque n'offrait des chances favorables qu'à la seule Russie....L'intérêt de la France était donc que les choses demeurassent en l'état". The Tsar's overture was not taken very seriously in Paris, for his mood was changing from day to day; but France, in her existing state of weakness and isolation, could not ignore the possible value of a Russian Alliance and the old lure of a revived prestige in the Levant under new conditions; the Duc de Richelieu admitted that "l'ancien système d'alliance de la France avec la Turquie et la Suède est devenu absurde...il serait utile que nous eussions dans la Méditerranée une escadre égale à celle de l'Angleterre".

In September the Tsar talked once more of an alliance of all the Powers, whose unholy object was hardly disguised—"il y a

he could get the signatures of the leading chiefs (II, 242). A paper blockade proclaimed by the Greeks, 25 Mar. 1822, was disallowed, but an effective blockade of Patras was soon afterwards tacitly admitted—*C.O. Ionian Is.* 20, 10 June 1822, and *S.P.* 9, 798.

[14] Strangford's *Selected Writings* show the versatile talents which he possessed. On the feeling about him, see Sch emann, I, 348 n.2; J. Krauter, *Ottenfels*, p. 90; also a phrase in J. Planta's letter t o S. Canning, 8 Aug. 1821, printed in Webster, *Castlereagh*, pp. 582–3. The whole letter is a good summary of moderate opinion in England, and a shrewd forecast of the future in Greece.

du Bosphore à Gibraltar de la place et du terrain pour tout le monde". Such characteristic projects met with little response, but he made yet another attempt to angle for French, for Prussian, and even for English co-operation. The French Government would take no active part for fear of Austria, but might be tempted, in return for some reward, to oppose a congress and to promote Russian interests by excluding other Powers from the settlement at the end of a Russo-Turkish war. But Castlereagh would not listen; on being told that, if Russia intervened, the first step would be the occupation of the Principalities, Castlereagh exclaimed: "That would be a new partition and a repetition of Poland"; and his conference with Metternich at Hanover in the autumn confirmed him in forebodings of revolution.[15] Prussia was equally unwilling to risk the displeasure of Austria.

Finding no encouragement, and fortified by the continued exhortations of Metternich, the Tsar did his best to restrain the war party in the army and in the Cabinet.[16] But the obstinacy of the Turks, elated by defeating the rebel Ali Pasha, was as great an obstacle to peace as the war fever in Russia. It was a gratuitous provocation to announce in a *Hatti-Sherif* (February 28th, 1822): "Il n'y a pas le moindre doute que c'est la Russie qui a encouragé les Grecs à la révolte. Lorsque leur rebellion éclata on me sollicita de les exterminer; n'écoutant que ma suprême clémence je m'y suis refusé". Such language was difficult for the most hardened legitimist to swallow. Even Strangford lost patience and (February 16th) told the Reis-Effendi (foreign minister) that he was "like the man who seeing his house on fire and all his friends hurrying up to put it out, sends them away saying, 'Don't trouble yourselves: if God wills the fire will put itself out: only give it a little time'".

In the first weeks of 1822 the scales turned more sharply

[15] Overtures to France, Isambert, pp. 99–105, 138–9. Pozzo to Nesselrode, 8 Oct., in Schiemann, I, App. IX. A. Sorel, *Essais d'histoire*, 'L'Alliance russe et la Restauration', pp. 95 ff. Overtures to England, in F. de Martens, XI, 323–5.

[16] Metternich interpreted one mood of the Tsar when he wrote "que l'Empereur Alexandre ne veut pas de la guerre et qu'il ne sait comment faire pour allier la conservation de la paix avec ce qu'il regarde comme étant de sa dignité"—to Lutzow, 5 Oct. 1821, in P. O. III, 206.

against war, and the campaigning season began instead with a special mission from the Tsar to Vienna; the Russian Government agreed to modify the four points in which its ultimatum had been defined, and not to seek the promise of the other Powers to recall their ambassadors from Constantinople unless the amended demands were rejected. But although the ultimatum was modified, the Greek question was reintroduced; the Powers were to take measures in common, first to end the war and assure tranquil possession to the Porte (by an act of amnesty), and then

> amener un arrangement au moyen duquel tous les habitans paisibles jouiraient du libre exercice de leur religion, possèderaient sans inquiétude leurs propriétés et verraient leurs biens, leurs personnes et leur existence comme placés sous une *garantie constante et réelle*.

Metternich objected to the last words as implying something more permanent than a simple act of amnesty, and he rejected altogether a third phrase which hinted at something less than full Turkish sovereignty over the Morea: "...complication qui renaîtrait sans cesse si l'on ne parvenait à établir entre les parties contendantes des *rapports nouveaux*". The Russian envoy spoke with two voices, being furnished with divergent instructions from the Chancellor and from the Corfiot, Capo d'Istria; he explained that the Tsar did not desire for the Greeks autonomy like the Serbians: "les Serviens comme les Moldaves et les Valaques forment des peuples, tandis que la Péloponnèse n'offre que des villes toutes en rivalité constante et indélible". Russia preferred "règler leur sort *comme sujets de la Porte*", a state of things which would arm Russia with a fertile source of complaints against the Turks at convenient seasons. After some bargaining Metternich agreed provisionally to the new formula, but he acknowledged privately that he was only gaining time.[17] The war party in Russia was for the time defeated or diverted to thoughts of intervention in Spain. The Tsar himself perhaps calculated that a Spanish crisis must either separate England

[17] Conversations with the special Russian envoy Tatishchev, 12 Mar. to 19 Apr. Metternich's agreement to recall his ambassador was conditional on the other Powers doing the same—P. O. III, 318 ff. The agreement was never ratified—Metternich's *Mémoires*, 621. Cf. Webster, *Castlereagh*, pp. 392 ff.

again from Austria or at least keep the Alliance busy in the West. Capo d'Istria offered to resign in May when he saw the instructions drawn up for the coming congress; his resignation was not formally accepted, but in August he was given unlimited leave of absence. He retired to Geneva and there became the centre of a large correspondence on behalf of the Greeks.

England, as Metternich no doubt expected, refused to take part in these proceedings, and used much stiffer language towards Russia. Castlereagh was determined not to interfere, if he could avoid it, in the Greek question: the arrangements proposed for the Greeks would have to be guaranteed by all the Powers concerned, binding England by new ties to the Alliance. Now this was just the course which he could never propose to Parliament. He had no desire to see a Greek State, but the aloofness of England was in fact the best chance for the Greeks. Strangford at Constantinople was surprised at Metternich's apparent surrender to Russia. The chief part in the negotiation was now entrusted to him. In all that concerned the Russo-Turkish dispute he acted practically under Metternich's instructions, and renewed the conferences, but without success. His only orders from home were not to meddle with the Greek question.[18] In the course of his conferences with Strangford the Reis-Effendi incidentally made confession of the Porte's perpetual dilemma about reform, when he said:

Vous connaissez assez l'organisation de notre Corps politique pour vous rendre compte de l'extrême difficulté de réformer les abus sans renverser les lois, dans un moment où les intérêts les plus opposés se trouvent en présence et les passions les plus violentes déchaînées....

But Metternich was in no hurry to withdraw his ambassador: the whole question was adjourned to the coming congress of all the Powers. Meanwhile, with the fall of Capo d'Istria, Metternich's ascendancy over the Tsar was complete. Nesselrode, the Chancellor, had professed a warm admiration for Capo d'Istria: only a year before he had declared, in contradicting a rumour that the Ionian was to lose his position, that "if he did, I should

[18] See Strangford's very familiar correspondence with Gentz, six letters from May 1823 to July 1824, in *Zur Geschichte*.

not remain an instant myself". But the two men were rivals in reality, and since the revolt Capo d'Istria had naturally inclined to the war party in Russia; Metternich believed that he had been actually in correspondence with Hypselantes. Nesselrode was an experienced German official, by nature cautious and opposed to violent measures; but his influence alone without that of Metternich could not have kept the Tsar in check.[19] About the same time, Mme de Krudener was dismissed from the capital, and died in 1824 in the Crimea.

When the Congress met at Verona, the Greek question was quietly but completely ignored. Russia demanded that plenipotentiaries should meet for the pacification of Greece, or else that the Porte should prove its sincerity "par une série de faits". This meaningless formula was adopted, as it involved no action. "Que la Porte enfin pacifie elle-même la Grèce"—a Turkish pacification being a pleasant euphemism for a retaliatory slaughter, as the massacre at Chios had just proved to the world. Solomon Rothschild, satisfied that the Tsar no longer intended war in the East, concluded at Verona the arrangements for a large loan to Russia, and was rewarded with the Order of Vladimir.[20] A deputation, which came to present its appeal and to declare that the Greeks would never accept a settlement in which they had no voice, was turned back at Ancona unheard.

Yet if the Greeks could hold their own they might be glad one day that their affairs had not been settled for them at Verona. Castlereagh and Canning took the only possible line, that of absolute neutrality; but Canning showed at once that he was even more suspicious than was Castlereagh of any settlement by

[19] Nesselrode, *Lettres et Papiers*, VI, 115 ff. His autobiography up to 1815 is in *Lettres et Papiers*, II. He was the son of a cosmopolitan eighteenth-century diplomat, who served first under Frederick the Great and then under Catherine. Born in 1780, Nesselrode had spent most of his career in Berlin until in 1811 he became Secretary of State and took a leading part in the coalition against Napoleon. Cf. Capefigue, *Les Diplomates Européens*. On Capo d'Istria's activities in retirement, see L. Oeconomos, *Essai sur la vie du Comte Capodistrias* (1822–8). Cf. *Les Rapports de Lebzeltern*, pp. 239, 350 ff.

[20] Corti, *Rise of the House of Rothschild*, p. 307; Waliszewski, p. 98.

congress, and therefore in appearance even less favourable to the Greeks. Castlereagh in his instructions to Wellington said that in view of the paralysis of the Turkish forces by land and sea and the progress made by the Greeks towards the formation of a Government, "it will be difficult, if a *de facto* government shall be established in the Morea, to refuse it the ordinary privileges of a belligerent". Wellington might offer his 'good offices' for submission upon condition of amnesty or for "the creation of a qualified Greek government" but was to make no engagement or guarantee. Canning's supplementary instructions, when he came to the Foreign Office on Castlereagh's death, rejected interference in any form whatever. "The Turks now appear to have the upper hand"; in any case "we cannot further interfere between Russia and the Porte or between the Porte and the Greeks". Supposing the Greeks first violated a settlement guaranteed by England, we could not help the Porte against them, and therefore in the opposite case we could not help them against the Porte.[21]

But there was soon a general impression that England favoured the Greek cause. The formal recognition of Greek blockades in March 1823 merely endorsed a practical measure already in force on the spot for the protection of commerce. Nevertheless, it was a step further than the other Powers would go towards conceding the rights of a belligerent to the rebel subjects of a legitimate sovereign. Strangford admitted that the Turkish minister made a thrust home when he asked whether Canning would allow the right of America to recognise Irish rebels as belligerents—a reference to Ireland was a favourite form of the *tu quoque* argument used by Continental statesmen in reply to lectures from Downing Street during the nineteenth century. In this case, Austrian shipping paid dearly for Metter-

[21] Castlereagh's instructions to Wellington, in *Despatches*, I, 284; Canning's, *ibid.* II, 369. For Canning's own explanation of his attitude at Verona, see below, p. 30. The Greek advance in the West had been checked at Petra (16 July 1823) and the regular corps discredited. In the following week the Turkish commander, Dramali, advanced through the Eastern Morea to Argos. He was forced (6 Aug.) to retreat with great loss to Corinth; but the defeat could have been retrieved if he had shown more energy.

nich's dogmatic attitude; by 1826 more than one hundred vessels had been captured or sunk by Greek privateers.[22]

In the same month of March 1823 the other Powers were disturbed by the rumour of conversations between the English authorities and the Greek leaders. Gentz feared a fateful decision by England to separate from the Alliance; even this might not mean intervention *against* the Turks, but if it did, Austria could do nothing against the English fleet.[23] At St Petersburg it was thought that Canning would be restrained by his colleagues, and it was even stated that he had been censured in Cabinet on April 30th for authorising such negotiations.[24] The truth was that Lord Strangford, on his return in January from Verona to Constantinople, found reason to believe that a large party in the Divan was ready to concede some privileges to the Greeks like those granted to the Serbs, and even to allow the guarantee of any Power other than Russia. Without waiting for the consent of his Government he wrote to Sir Thomas Maitland, asking him to make use of the information as he thought fit. Maitland on his own responsibility asked Mavrocordato to send a delegate, and deputed Captain Hamilton, of the frigate *Cambrian*, to explain the situation, without making any promises, to Mavrocordato and to the leaders of other Greek parties. Some of the islanders especially were at that time anxious to place themselves and their trading vessels under the protection of the Ionian flag, in fear of a descent by the Turkish fleet. The overture did not succeed; Constantine Metaxas describes an interview with Captain Hamilton at which Theodore Negris and another were present. According to this account, Hamilton spoke of a mediation by England for a status like that of the Principalities, but refused to put the suggestion in writing; the deputies, a little reluctantly, in turn refused to give any answer, and the Pro-

[22] Green (*Sketches*, pp. 288 ff.) prints two legal opinions (by Dr Lushington) on the effect of Canning's proclamation and of his letter to the Levant Co. (29 Apr.) which followed. On the piracies committed before the recognition, see *ibid.* letter of 24 Mar. 1823. P. O. to Gentz, 18 Sept. 1826, in *Aus dem Nachlasse*, I.

[23] To Ottenfels, 4 Mar. 1823, in *Zur Geschichte*, p. 1. Cf. *Dépêches inédites*, II, 188, 200; P. O. I, 194, 200.

[24] Schiemann, I, 331 and App. X, Nesselrode to Tatishchev, 22 May 1823.

visional Government approved their action; the people were infuriated at the bare rumour of compromise. A few weeks later the English consul at Patras sent on to Corfu an appeal, emanating from Petrobey of Maina and offering to place the Morea under the protection of England; Sir F. Adam, Maitland's deputy and successor at Corfu, returned "the same answer as before", a polite refusal.[25] The whole episode was over before it was known to the Foreign Office in London; it was in reality an attempt to discover on what terms the Greeks would submit, but it was differently interpreted by Greek hopes and by the fears of other Powers. After the autumn of 1821 British neutrality had been enforced on the whole impartially in very difficult circumstances by the Ionian Government; but Canning again insisted that it should be a real neutrality on equal terms and complained that "British subjects have been active in the Levant in their exertions in behalf of the Turks".[26]

These small indications of a change in British policy, added to the knowledge of Canning's views on South America, were enough to rouse the suspicions of the Turks and to awaken the jealousies of other Powers.

[25] Strangford to Canning, 10 Feb. 1823 (No. 8), in *F.O. Turkey*, 114. Maitland to Bathurst, 26 Mar., enclosing Strangford's letter to him, 1 Feb., and his own instruction to Hamilton, 8 Mar., and Adam to Bathurst, 12 Apr.—*C.O. Ionian Is.* 1090. Colonial Office Minute on the incident, 27 May, in *F.O. Turkey*, 119. In the same volume is a letter from Mavrocordato to Canning, 4 July (unanswered), and another, 14 Feb., from Luriottes (the agent for the loan) asking for an interview, which was refused. Metaxas, *Souvenirs*, pp. 110 ff. Capt. Hamilton, stationed in Greek waters throughout the revolution, was a candid but consistent friend of the Greeks and earned their gratitude by the energetic but tactful discharge of his duties. The *Cambrian* was afterwards wrecked in an attack on the pirates at Grabusa in 1828.

[26] Letter to Levant Co., 29 Apr. 1823, in P. O. IV, 18; cf. *C. and his Friends*, II, 181, 14 July 1823. Most of the merchants and consuls were strongly pro-Turkish. The interruption of British trade with the Morea was negligible compared with the disturbance to trade, in Smyrna and elsewhere, threatened by the Greek unrest. See complaints of Levant Co., esp. Aug. 1823, Jan. 1824, in *P.R.O., S.P. For. Archives*, 125. Sir T. Maitland hoped and expected that the revolt would be speedily crushed. See his letter to Wellington, 4 Dec. 1822, in P. O. III, 450, and *C.O. Ionian Is.* 20, *passim*.

CHAPTER III

BENEVOLENT NEUTRALITY

June 1823—*June* 1825

MEANWHILE Strangford returned to Constantinople and renewed his efforts to find a settlement between Russia and the Porte. He complained that Canning's policy had lost him the confidence of the Turks, but by September 1823 he had so far succeeded that the Tsar, after a meeting with the Austrian Emperor at Czernowitz (October), agreed to send a representative to Constantinople (for commercial affairs only) and to do nothing further about Greece without consulting all his allies. Canning's only anxiety was for the return of the Russian Embassy, in order to get the negotiation out of Strangford's hands: the Russians once back in Constantinople,

> I care not if they quarrel with the Porte to-morrow...had I been in office six months sooner than I was, so as to be in any degree master of the questions to be discussed at Verona and had I seen as clearly as I think I do now that in the prurient and tantalised state of the Russian army some vent must be found—in short that the Spanish war was the alternative of the Turkish—I should have preferred peace certainly, commercial peace, to any war, but deliberately the Turkish [war] to the Spanish.[1]

This suggests that he would have liked to prevent French intervention in Spain by a diversion in the East. After the meeting at Czernowitz Russia invited all the Powers to a conference at St Petersburg in the spring, and promised a *Mémoire* on the subject of Greece. Metternich accepted the proposal but intended to delay as much as he could; the Turks were expected to make a great effort to subdue the revolt the next year. Canning replied as before to the Tsar's invitation, and warned Bagot repeatedly to take no part until the conditions were fulfilled:

[1] Canning to Bagot, 20 Aug. 1823, in *C. and his Friends*, II, 197. Canning's silence hitherto had led Gentz to hope that after all England might not desert the Alliance, and to dream of a congress—the Austrian prescription for all ills—in the following year. To Metternich, 5, 11 Oct. 1823, in *Briefe*, III², 61, 69.

"when he has sent his mission I will talk Greek with him if he pleases", but "the allies must not be allowed to suppose that our difference from them is merely a feint to avoid conflict with public opinion"—a distinct reference to Castlereagh's apologies eighteen months earlier.[2]

In January the promised *Mémoire* appeared, proposing the division of Greece into three principalities, with a status like those on the Danube; the Turks would have an annual tribute and garrisons in specified fortresses.[3] This proposal, though far short of what the Greeks demanded, was a great advance on anything that had gone before: it was in fact the first *definite* scheme put forward. It gave the Greeks a much larger territory than they were ever likely to get by their own efforts, for the risings in Thessaly, Boeotia and Epirus had completely failed. From their point of view the scheme was not altogether to be despised; but it was not acceptable to the 'European' Greeks who saw in it the domination of Fanariot families with Byzantine traditions instead of the Western constitutional monarchy or the republic to which they looked forward; the 'Constitution of Epidaurus' had proclaimed the complete independence of Greece in January 1822. The effect of the *Mémoire* was to complete the disillusionment of many Greeks who had once staked their faith upon Russia; one of them wrote:

> I learn the real policy of the European Powers, particularly that of the Russian Court. I ask you a thousand pardons, Brother, for having hitherto disagreed with you in opinion. I now put faith in and humble myself in the name of Christ to England while I damn Russia from one end to the other, with all its inhabitants and noblemen.[4]

It would have been better if the Greeks had expected less from any of the Powers and had concentrated their attention on presenting Europe by their own efforts with a *fait accompli*. The

[2] Canning to Bagot, 22 Jan. 1824, in *C. and his Friends*, II, 218 and 221.

[3] (i) Morea (? + Candia), (ii) Thessaly, Boeotia, Attica, (iii) Epirus, Acarnania; the islands to have municipal self-government. Printed in *S.P.* 11, 819.

[4] Turturi to Gerostathi, 8 Mar. 1824, in *C.O. Ionian Is.* 27. This must have been founded on rumours, for the *Mémoire* was not published until May. See below, p. 36. Constitution of Epidaurus in *S.P.* 9, 620.

Mémoire was ill-received by the Powers, to whom it seemed a mere device for securing the predominance of Russia. Metternich answered cautiously in favour of the scheme *three months later*; he wrote to Gentz:

Que le comte de Nesselrode trouve les moyens: nous savons très-bien comme il faut traiter l'utopie grecque: à présent rendez-la possible!... Maintenant, quand un homme comme Strangford vient essayer de me prouver *que rien n'est possible*, je ne sais si je dois rire ou pleurer. La meilleure réponse serait: "V'là ce que je vous disais".[5]

In other words, Metternich was only waiting for the end: the Sultan's treaty with the Pasha of Egypt was already rumoured, giving him the Morea and Candia if he could subdue the revolt. In May, Strangford wrote to Gentz: "If Mehmed Ali Pasha does his duty we shall I doubt not escape from the infernal question at least in its present formidable shape".[6]

Canning still refused to have anything to do with a congress: "for Alliance, read England, and you have the clue to my policy".[7] In order to account for this horror of congresses we must not forget Spain and Portugal and South America. He was already in disgrace with the Alliance, and for that reason with the King and the ultra-Tory members of the Cabinet. The King complained that "the Jacobins of the world (now calling themselves the Liberals) saw the peace of Europe secured by this great measure and have therefore never ceased to vilify the principle of the Quadruple Alliance". The Tories could reasonably argue that our concern was not with the constitutions of other States but with the peace of Europe. But it was just in these two points that the Alliance had failed. It was based, in Metternich's view, on the principle of interference, and it chose to forego the best

[5] To Gentz, 21 June, in *Briefe*, III[2], 117. Gentz complained that Metternich underrated the importance to Austria of the Greek question, in comparison with which Spain mattered little; "hier handelt es sich um Leben und Tod", to Ottenfels, 3 May 1823, 25 Apr. 1824, in *Zur Geschichte*, pp. 7, 20.

[6] Mehemet was given the command on 26 Feb. On 4 Mar. Consul Salt at Cairo reported Ibrahim's preparations—*F.O. Turkey*, 126. The Egyptian fleet sailed from Alexandria on 19 July; among the transports were twenty-five sail flying the British flag, and thirty-five the Austrian—*C.O. Ionian Is.* 27, 16 Aug. Strangford to Gentz, 27 May 1824, in *Zur Geschichte*, p. 24.

[7] To J. H. Frere, 7 Aug. 1823; G. Festing, *J. H. Frere and his Friends*, p. 259.

prospect of peace for the sake of a theory. The new countries of South America, Spanish though they were in sentiment and civilisation, had little reason now to profess an obstinate loyalty to the King of Spain: to insist upon the abstract assertion was not to make for peace but to prolong civil war. Still less could the Greeks be expected to acknowledge again the absolute sovereignty of conquerors of different faith and, hitherto at least, of inferior intelligence. It needed no enthusiasm for the idea of nationality to see that, after the massacres of 1821, Turks and Greeks could never live peaceably together in the Morea. It was certainly no business of the British Government to stir up national or constitutional movements abroad, but it was equally no concern of England to prolong civil wars by refusing to recognise accomplished facts. Canning's policy was inspired not by 'Liberal ideas' but by plain common sense. But his strength in the Cabinet rested upon the outside support of 'Liberal' public opinion, to which he at times appealed to secure his object. For this reason he was branded as an opportunist alike by ultra-Tories and by Whigs, and the suspicion that he was among those who use sentiments to promote interests lay like a shadow across his career. His policy was attacked by Tories simply because it was approved by Liberals abroad and denounced by Metternich; it was disliked by the Whigs, who felt that he was infringing their patent on false pretences.

The case of Turkey in relation to the Alliance was indeed rather different from that of Spain or Portugal or South America. The Turkish dominions were not secured, even implicitly like those of other Powers, by the Congress of Vienna. It was argued therefore that England might well co-operate in this case with the Allies, since they were not bound in advance to support the Sultan's authority at all costs.[8] The distinction was fair in theory, but less clear in practice; one question cannot be treated in isolation from the atmosphere created by the rest. With the exception of Russia the parties were ranged nearly in the same camps as in the other issues of the time; the partisans of the sovereign Turks were to be found among the Legitimists, those

[8] Wellington's *Despatches*, II, 360, 1 Dec. 1824.

of the insurgent Greeks among the Liberals. It was not until after Charles X's accession that the French Government showed any partiality for the Greeks; the ministry of Villèle was strictly attached to the Alliance. Above all, Metternich, the mainspring of the Alliance, was the known enemy of any settlement which should seem to legitimise the revolt. But there was another special feature in the case of Turkey which made even the strictest Tories less inclined to co-operate with the Alliance. Castlereagh himself had given it as his opinion that collective threats had no effect upon the Turks and only made them suspect an alliance of Christendom against Islam. Wellington agreed that "our hands at Constantinople will be much weakened by becoming parties to this negotiation with other powers"; yet he pronounced in favour of attending the Congress, and alluded, in correspondence with Metternich, to the Cabinet's distrust of Canning. Metternich wrote full of hope: "Le cabinet commence à s'élever assez vivement contre Canning". Wellington, however incautious, was too loyal to be suspected of a foreign intrigue to overthrow his colleague; but his prestige must have led Metternich to underrate Canning's power in the country. The Duke himself had too much sense fully to share Metternich's doctrinaire notions of legitimacy: but his fear of ideas often blinded him too long to facts.[9]

Failing a congress, there remained isolation for England. It was for the present the strongest position. It did not preclude, if necessary, forcible resistance to Russian conquest, nor even isolated intervention on behalf of the Greeks. This last possibility, tempting as it seems in retrospect, did not perhaps occur to Canning at this time. It would have been a simple matter for a British squadron to have prevented the Egyptian fleet from leaving Alexandria for the Morea. Although the Pasha of Egypt was nominally a vassal of the Sultan, it might have been successful without a rupture with the Porte, considering what was

[9] Wellington to Canning, 10 Feb. 1824, in *Despatches*, II, 204. His correspondence with Metternich during 1824 will be found in the same volume. Metternich to Gentz, 30 June 1824, in *Briefe*, III², 131. Gentz to Metternich, 7 July, describing Wellesley's confidential laments over Canning, and setting forth the hopes of his fall, *ibid.* p. 135.

afterwards done at Navarin with impunity. And if it could have been done without war, it would have gone far towards settling the Greek question, for Metternich could not have delayed longer, with no prospect of the revolt being crushed. It would have been a stroke characteristic of Canning, but if it crossed his mind it must have been dismissed as impracticable. The Cabinet, already restless, would never have consented to such an enterprising policy.

Canning's ideas at this stage may be gathered (*cum grano?*) from the record of an interview with Sir John Bowring, the disciple and afterwards executor of Bentham, the editor of the Whig *Westminster Review*, and a leading member of the newly formed 'Greek Committee'.[10] To Bowring's suggestion that it would be a sound argument to create in Greece a barrier against Russia, Canning replied: "Yes, that would be a proper argument for English policy, but what language could we hold to Russia to obtain her consent, knowing as we do that she can conquer Greece and Turkey when she pleases?" Interference might involve the mediator in war. Canning then asked about the condition of the Greek Provisional Government and the prospects of the loan. Bowring said that the Greeks would reject the status of a Principality or of a tributary State, but might be willing to pay to the Porte a capital sum in compensation, if a loan could be raised for the purpose. (This was in fact the issue eight years later.) He complained of the conduct of our consuls in the East and argued that the Government should recover control by dissolving the Charter of the Levant Company—as was done in the following year for that and other reasons.[11] Canning thanked him for evidence about a consul having supplied the Turks,

[10] 16 Jan. 1824. See Bowring's *Autobiographical Recollections*, pp. 281–8. The account was probably written at the time and not in the light of later events, because the whole book consists of isolated notes and fragments posthumously edited. There is much interest in Bowring's notes on his travels in many countries and his conversations with famous men. They reflect the character of an active-minded, self-confident missionary of the Benthamite faith.

[11] On the dissolution of the Levant Co. and the reorganisation of the consular service, see an important memorandum by Consul-General Cartwright, 10 Oct. 1825, in *F.O. Turkey*, 135.

"because we can quote it at Constantinople where they speak of the interference of Englishmen on behalf of the Greeks". On the whole, Bowring came away with a very favourable impression of Canning's disposition towards the Greeks.

If isolation should fail in turn, a third course of policy remained, as yet remote—perhaps Canning's words, "I will talk Greek with him if he pleases", were the first hint of a separate understanding with Russia.[12] The conference at St Petersburg therefore languished: Bagot indeed attended its meetings but he was rebuked for misreading his instructions. Austria gave a vague general assent to the *Mémoire* of January, but refused to join in making it known at once to the Turks and the Greeks. Before any means of enforcing it had been settled, its publication in the Paris *Constitutionnel* on May 31st was practically the death-blow to the scheme. The Greeks at once repudiated the *Mémoire* and appealed to Canning for aid: that they should do so shows the reputation which he had already acquired abroad. His answer was not encouraging, but the mere fact of his answering at all implied another stage in the recognition *de facto* of the Greek Government (though not of independence). He denied any official knowledge of the Russian *Mémoire* and proclaimed once more the neutrality of England:

> Since we know that the two parties are equally decided to reject *every* conceivable arrangement, the hope of successful intervention becomes absolutely inadmissible at the present moment....Bound as we are to the Porte by established relations of friendship and by ancient treaty obligations which the Porte has not violated, it certainly cannot be expected that England should engage in hostilities unprovoked by this Power in a quarrel which is none of ours.

The conference broke up in June, and Bagot returned home.[13]

Meanwhile Strangford had been at work, and in June reported the full satisfaction of the Russian demands; he came home in the autumn, and for a year there was only a *chargé d'affaires* at Constantinople. The reality of his success was afterwards dis-

[12] See above, p. 31. Note the date, 22 Jan., a week after the interview with Bowring.

[13] Greek Provisional Government to Canning, 24 Aug., and Canning's reply, 1 Dec. 1824, in *S.P.* 12, 899.

puted, but at the time the Tsar accepted the result and nominated Ribeaupierre as his new ambassador at the Porte. The Turks, however, were in no hurry to see him, for that meant the re-opening of the Greek question, which public opinion would prevent the Tsar from dropping altogether. Their indignation at the *Mémoire* of January was unbounded; after one of his out-bursts, "the Reis-Effendi stopped here from perfect exhaus-tion".[14] They were equally angry at the proceedings of the Philhellenes, and could not understand how the Mayor and Corporation of London should be allowed to vote money for the Greeks if the Government professed friendship for the Porte. A *Hatti-Sherif* (September 16th) appointing the new Grand Vizir exhorted him to new efforts against the Greeks. Byron's arrival in Greece was the high-water mark of the Philhellene enthusiasm: in June the first instalment of the ill-fated loan arrived at Zante.[15]

The Greek leaders, made bold by so much encouragement, threatened to burn and sink as enemies any European ships hired by the Sultan for transporting troops or stores; but they were forced by the Ionian Government to withdraw their pro-clamation. The Greek 'fleet' consisted, for the most part, of armed privateers which took to piracy with or without formal commissions from the Provisional Government. The 'blockade' existed, except at rare intervals, only in name. Ionian trading

[14] The Ukase appointing Ribeaupierre declared that "de concert avec nos Alliés nous réussirons à terminer les malheurs qui désolent l'Orient". Lebzeltern to Metternich, 25 Aug., 31 Dec., in *Les Rapports de Lebzeltern*, pp. 165, 175. Strangford to Canning, 15 Sept., in P. O. IV, 125.

[15] The good faith of the Greek deputies who negotiated the loan in London may be measured by this extract from their letter to the 'Venerable Greek Government'. "With regard to the appropriation of the land [as security] we are of opinion the Government should not agree to it, or if it does, to allot them *barren unhealthy and mountainous* parts, giving them *ancient* and renowned names to make an impression on the Commissioners. Hume deserves such treatment, he alone having insisted on that article: by which means the Government fully satisfies all their demands"—13 Aug. 1824 (intercepted) in *C.O. Ionian Is.* 27. On the loan, cf. *Quarterly Review*, xxxv, 221 ff., Jan. 1827; *Cobbett's Weekly Register*, 28 Oct., 4, 11 Nov. 1826. A tradition that the Lord Mayor of London was almost as important as the Queen seems to have survived into the next generation at the Porte—Newton's *Life of Lord Lyons*, I, 172 (visit of Abdul Aziz in 1867).

vessels carrying provisions to the Turks in Patras had no right to pass a legitimate blockade, but were entitled to protection against the casual *mistico* which would shoot out from some creek, seize the cargo for the private use of these pirates, and perhaps murder the crew. Neutrality was less easy in practice than in theory, when the line between piracy and legitimate warfare was so uncertain. Austria, on the other hand, complained that British naval officers showed decided partiality to the Greeks.[16] Throughout the revolution, England was hampered both in framing and in executing a consistent policy by her delicate position in the Ionian Islands. But Philhellenes in England took little notice of these difficulties; the descent of the Ottoman fleet upon the island of Psará on July 4th had upon wide circles of opinion an effect like that of the destruction of Chios two years before, which had brought to birth the first 'Greek Committees' in Europe. On July 19th Ibrahim, Mehemet Ali's step-son, sailed from Alexandria with twenty-five ships-of-war and one hundred transports, carrying the Egyptian army which was to conquer the Morea; he joined forces with the Turkish fleet off the coast of Asia Minor. It was in this gloomy plight, in the interval between two civil wars, that the Greeks wrote to Canning repudiating the Russian *Mémoire.*

The Russians knew that without England conferences were of very little use. Each country felt that it could not tackle singly the question of the Greeks: alone, Russia dared not break from the Alliance and make war upon the Turks; alone, the English Cabinet would never have consented to risk a war by naval intervention. Both were tired of Metternich's delays: each was reluctant to make the first advances. In September Nesselrode wrote suspending all further communication with England on the Greek question, in the hope that Canning would

[16] Greek Proclamation, 27 May; modified 15 Aug.; revoked 3 Sept. 1824—*S.P.* 11, 828. A regular blockade of Patras and Lepanto proclaimed 26 Oct. was acknowledged by the Ionian Government, 17 Nov. 1824—*S.P.* 12, 903. A series of Admiralty orders on the subject of piracy, 1824–6, is in *Ad.* II, 1694; cf. *S.P.* 14, 784. Later, Hamilton described his own officers as being "almost without exception, violent anti-Greeks", to S. Canning, 7 Apr. 1827—*B.M.*, *Add. MSS.* 36566 (*Church Papers*).

be drawn out by the fear of being forestalled. But Canning was not anxious yet to 'talk Greek'. In October he was doubtful whether or not to join a new conference at St Petersburg early in the next year; the Prime Minister, Lord Liverpool, was on the whole in favour of doing so, with no commitment to intervention.[17] But on November 4th the Greek letter arrived, and its uncompromising tone convinced him that even mediation would be very difficult. Canning made this letter the chief ground for withdrawing after all from the conference, but the old condition for taking part in it was repeated with a new one added; not only must the Russian ambassador be actually back in Constantinople, but, further, Russia must make a previous and public disavowal of any intention to use force. Stratford Canning, sent to St Petersburg to watch the conference and on other business, drew up, at his cousin's request, a *Mémoire* in which it was said that England would welcome Greek independence if won by the Greeks' own efforts.[18] The sentiment was less of a mockery than it might seem. Putting aside the possibility of separate English intervention, it was certain that the conference would never do anything effective before Ibrahim's army should arrive in Greece: the Greeks, on the other hand, although none of their ships were large, could arm an almost unlimited number: if they could have been united in a scheme of defence they might have made it very difficult for Ibrahim to land; even when their commander, Miaoules, was left with only twenty-five sail, the rest having departed home, he succeeded once in turning back the expedition and in capturing several transports. It was only through the indifference or the quarrels of the Greeks that Ibrahim was able to reach Crete in safety at the beginning of December.

Metternich, too, was watching the expedition with some anxiety. He was committed to a conference, and it would be difficult to restrain Russia much longer. The 'sentiments

[17] Nesselrode to Lieven, 2 Sept., and F. de Martens, XI, 329. Liverpool, 18 Oct. and 2 Nov., recommending "a clear stage and no favour" in the contest, in Wellington's *Despatches*, II, 327, 329.

[18] Instruction to S. Canning, 8 Dec., in *F.O. Russia*, 144. Lane-Poole, *Life of Lord Stratford de Redcliffe*, I, 346; and 359, private notes for negotiation—"favourable to independence if to be had of itself".

chevaleresques' of the new King Charles X (Louis XVIII died on September 16th) were a fresh danger in France, and in England Canning's power was growing stronger in the country as it became more suspect in the Cabinet. Gentz wrote gloomily: "M. Canning sait trop bien qu'un ministre anglais qui a pour alliés le commerce, les journaux et les idées libérales n'est pas facilement culbuté". But there was no natural alliance between Canning's policy and Charles X's enthusiasm, which Canning called 'romantic ranting'; there had been no word hitherto between England and France on the Greek question.[19] Gentz put the dilemma thus: the Russian plan was out of the question; the Greek repudiation of it left only two alternatives—either intervention to subdue the Greeks, which public opinion made impossible, or a threat to recognise the independence of Greece as the only way to a settlement without war. Mavrocordato in a letter to Gentz pressed the arguments for Greek independence from an Austrian point of view: first it would be anti-Russian, and then it would be the prelude to an otherwise impossible friendship of the Greeks with Turkey. The second argument was of doubtful value because of the 'unredeemed' Greeks.[20]

Metternich decided to follow up these suggestions by a surprising change of front at the conference. The Austrian ambassador, Lebzeltern, was instructed to propose abandoning mediation and instead simply threatening the Porte with "l'admission éventuelle de l'indépendance des Grecs comme mesure de fait et de nécessité"—but merely as a weapon in negotiation; this would be enough to frighten the Turks at once into granting terms of their own accord to the Greeks, the only issue which would save the face of strict legitimacy. As Lebzeltern fastidiously pointed out, this method would avoid "une explication avec les Grecs,...la partie la plus scabreuse de la négotiation". This counter-proposal caused a sensation; Nesselrode was angry that the mere idea of independence should be

[19] Gentz, 15 Jan. 1825, in *Dépêches inédites*, II, 440. Canning to Liverpool, 21 Nov., to Granville, 8 Dec. 1824, in *Some Official Correspondence*, I, 203, 211.

[20] Gentz, 2 Nov., 1 Dec. 1824, in *Dépêches inédites*. Mavrocordato to Gentz, 17 Dec., in P.O. IV, 132 ff. Gentz's cautious indirect answer, *ibid.* IV, 139.

broached; he "could not conceive how such an idea could spring from Austrian soil...a Cabinet...the champion of correct principles". But there is ample evidence that Metternich's proposal was not seriously made even as a weapon of negotiation,[21] and it contained an obvious flaw. The Turks were to be forced to offer a settlement themselves; but what if the Greeks should refuse the terms so offered, just as they had repudiated the Russian *Mémoire*? Either the Powers must fall back on the forcible mediation which Austria wished to avoid, or the Greeks must be quickly subdued. This was in fact Metternich's expectation; on the day that the conference opened (February 24th), Ibrahim landed in the Morea the first division of his army of 10,000 Egyptians; and it seemed as if the end could not be far off.

It was soon clear that this second conference would fail like the first. Prussia, as before, tried to hold the balance between Russia and Austria. France alone gave any positive support to the Russian proposals, already fearing a separate Anglo-Russian agreement in the event of failure.[22] The conference dragged on for weeks, and then merely instructed the ambassadors at Constantinople to make a verbal preliminary attempt to persuade the Porte to *invite* mediation. The Turks naturally rejected these tentative 'good offices' of the Powers.[23] The Russian Cabinet did not even wait for the result, but sent a circular insisting on the necessity of coercive measures. Metternich would not admit it, foreseeing that in practice coercive measures would be aimed against the Turks alone. He was thoroughly satisfied with the meagre result of the conference: all that was necessary now was to humour the Tsar a little longer and to stave off any

[21] P. O. IV, 143ff.; *Dépêches inédites*, II, 435. Cf. Gentz to Metternich, 5 Aug., abusing Chateaubriand for stealing the idea of Greek independence with the difference that "he—wretched diplomatic charlatan—regards it as actually practicable"—*Briefe*, III², 227.

[22] Ringhoffer, pp. 28ff. and App. pp. 245–50. Gentz complained to Metternich, 8 July, of Prussia's independent attitude—*Briefe*, III².

[23] Protocol 7 Apr., in P. O. IV, 161: rejected in June. Since Strangford's departure at the end of 1824, England had a *chargé d'affaires* at Constantinople: Canning delayed sending an ambassador who would only have shared the odium of these 'good offices'. Cf. his instructions to S. Canning, 12 Oct. 1825.

action before the winter. In a short visit to Paris in March he believed that he had completely won over the French Government to his views. Even Canning seemed to have lost the will or the power to act. But Metternich was unduly optimistic and contemptuously ignored the power of 'public opinion', which easily made itself felt in the France of the Restoration in a case where the dreams of Republicans, Bonapartists and Royalists had a common centre and all parties saw in Greece a field of experiment. He felt sure that, once the Turkish fleet should arrive to co-operate by sea with Ibrahim on land, all would be over.[24] The Egyptians had already, by the end of July, overrun the whole of the Morea, although the armed bands of the Greeks kept up desultory attacks from the mountain districts. Missolonghi had been regularly besieged since April; but the Greeks, when they could assemble and pay enough ships for a short expedition, still kept some control of the sea, and were able to supply the town from that side. The islands kept up the spirit of insurrection, but only the incompetence of the Turkish fleet prevented the complete collapse of the revolt. In this deadlock, when the Greeks could do nothing by land, and the Turks could do nothing at sea, there was less prospect than ever of a speedy settlement. Piracy and loss to commerce increased, and a serious intervention from without became unavoidable. There was a general feeling of impatience and exasperation that four years had not sufficed to bring peace to the East.

[24] Metternich to Gentz, 13 July, 5 Aug., in *Briefe*, III², 197, 228; *Dépêches inédites*, 18 Apr., 6 May. Cf. Gentz to Metternich, 6 Apr., and (on Canning) 29 July. He had no fear that the Morea would remain in the hands of Mehemet Ali, who would be content with Candia: to Metternich, 17 July. But the Greek claim to a right of search at sea showed the impotence of the Austrian fleet to prevent, although it did not recognise, the right; and Gentz became less sanguine: to Metternich, 15, 31 July, 9 Aug. All in *Briefe*, III², under date. On the weakness of the Austrian fleet, cf. *Zur Geschichte*, pp. 175ff.

CHAPTER IV

THE RUSSIAN ALLIANCE

I

June—December 1825

WHILE the Conference dragged on at St Petersburg, the Russian minister, impatient of the solemn farce, kept his eyes fixed on England, without whom nothing really effective could be done. Discussion with England on the Greek question, already 'suspended' in September 1824, had been 'definitely closed' by Nesselrode (to Lieven, December 30th). The King and some of the Cabinet were alarmed at this new evidence of English isolation. George IV required his ministers to sign a joint profession of faith towards the Alliance, and noted on this document: "I am satisfied with these assurances provided they are *faithfully* fulfilled". Canning, at whom all this was aimed, offered to resign, but the King could not afford to lose him, and from this time made the best of it and showed him much more confidence.[1] The Russians found in Canning a possible ally; Princess Lieven, who had formerly abused him as a 'Jacobin minister', began to cultivate his friendship.

Stratford Canning, excluded by his instructions from the Conference, was unable to extract a word about Greece until he announced his intention of departing. Nesselrode thereupon consented to a separate discussion, wishing, not to break off abruptly, but only to draw England out. This discussion was fruitless, for Russia refused any undertaking not to use force, and Ribeaupierre had not yet started for Constantinople:[2]

[1] King's letter, 27 Jan.; Cabinet minute, 29 Jan.; Canning to King, 1 Feb.; interview of Sir W. Knighton with Canning, 27 Apr., in *C. and his Times*, pp. 437 ff. Cf. F. de Martens, XI, 329: according to this account the King told Lieven that he 'totally disapproved' of his own foreign minister's policy; Wellington, who was in the Cabinet, did the same. See *C.H.F.P.* II, 108.

[2] Canning refused to accept as equivalent to the full renewal of diplomatic relations the fact that the Russian commercial representative sent

Canning's two conditions were therefore not fulfilled. But Nesselrode was full of compliments for Canning and recommended him to place entire confidence in Lieven. Stratford, having departed from the capital, met the Tsar again in May at Warsaw, where there may have been some hints of a separate understanding in the future. On June 14th, when the failure of the Conference was certain, Nesselrode wrote to Lieven:

ce serait de notre côté un acte de véritable imprudence que de repousser la Grande-Bretagne....Plus le ministère anglais nous croira résolus d'aborder et de trancher cette grande question *sans* sa coopération, plus nous pourrons espérer de le voir se rapprocher graduellement de nos principes.

Lieven was to wait for confidential proposals on Canning's part. Canning was sick to death of congresses and was nearly ready for a new move. He was not blind to the elaborate trap which the Russians believed they were preparing for him. If he turned along a new path he did so with his eyes fully open. He told Lieven one day: "Nous voilà, les portes sont ouvertes".[3]

At the same time the activities of the different parties in Greece came to a head. Early in 1824 the Duke of Orleans sent an agent to Greece to propose the name of his son, the Duke of Nemours, as future sovereign of Greece; documents were circulated, including a 'protocol' in which Villèle was supposed to have given his consent. There was not much result at the time, but in 1825, after Ibrahim's landing, the same agent returned to Greece, followed by General Roche, who besides representing the Greek Committee in Paris was secretly acting for the Orleanist party. By bribery and propaganda he obtained a certain following, but his claims were denied by de Rigny, admiral of the French squadron. The Bourbon Government had in fact nothing to do with this intrigue, which only gave a fillip to the party which looked to England. Moreover the communications of General Roche with Ibrahim and with a number

early in 1824 had been made *chargé d'affaires* (11 Dec.). The Turks paid great attention to such points, as the barometer of Russian intentions.

[3] F. de Martens, XI, 334–5; and Metternich to Gentz, 30 June, in *Briefe*, III², 179. But there is no mention of a discussion at Warsaw in S. Canning's reports—*F.O. Russia*, 147.

of French officers serving with the Egyptians helped to discredit his offers in Greek eyes.[4]

In June 1825, a delegate, Spaniolacki, was sent to London to ask England to choose a sovereign, preferably Prince Leopold of Saxe-Coburg. A small Committee at Zante told the English Resident of General Roche's plans, and, with the knowledge but not with the direct authorisation of the High Commissioner, set on foot a rival appeal for English protection.[5] This Act of Submission, "drawn up", says Trikoupes, "in a foreign tongue and badly translated into Greek", announced that "the independent Greeks of their own accord solicit the Illustrious Protection (*τὴν σεβάσιμον ὑπερασπίσιν*) of Great Britain for all their several provinces to be comprehended under one permanent system of administration". It did not at first find much support; but at the end of June Ibrahim was advancing on Nauplia, the last fortified place in the Morea left to the Greeks. He met with a strong show of resistance at the mills of Lerna, but his sudden retirement may have been partly due to the approach of Captain Hamilton, who landed next day to confer with the Greek leaders. As to the appeal for Protection, Hamilton reported to the High Commissioner that he "told them I had no power to say anything about it, that it was out of my line, but that I would inform you of all they had said".[6] He was given a copy of the Act of Submission, dated June 30th and signed by Kolokotrones and about one hundred chieftains of the Morea. Another copy was signed on July 22nd at Hydra by Miaoules and the leading

[4] Debidour, *Fabvier*, pp. 278 ff. Col. Fabvier, proscribed from France for his assistance to the Spanish Cortes, had come to Greece in Dec. 1824 and was trying to organise a regular army. He disapproved of General Roche. Cf. Capt. Hamilton to S. Canning, 19 Apr. 1827, in *B.M.*, *Add. MSS.* 36566, f. 66.

[5] Trikoupes, III, 267 ff. Adam to Bathurst, 22 June, in *C.O. Ionian Is.* 33: the substance is—Count Roma (one of the Committee) is going too far in his proposals to Miaoules and Kolokotrones; Adam has warned him not to speak for the British Government. Cf. Kolokotrones, pp. 216–18.

[6] Hamilton to Adam, 9 July (enclosed in Adam's report, 4 Aug.), in *C.O. Ionian Is.* 33. The usual account, that Hamilton induced Ibrahim to retire by turning his guns on the town, cannot be true, for he says himself that Ibrahim had already retreated; and the American Philhellene, S. G. Howe, notes in his *Journal* Ibrahim's retreat on 28 June, and on the 29th, the "*Cambrian* and another frigate beating up the Gulf of Argolis".

islanders after much debate; Captain Hamilton was present but did not press for signature.[7] The Act was passed by the Provisional Government on July 24th and taken to London by the son of Miaoules. A public protest against it was circulated by General Roche and by an American called Washington, "a nonentity in an outlandish Hussar uniform", whose name was his only claim to represent his country. After the English refusal, Roche in turn obtained an offer of submission to France, but Villèle was no more ready than was Canning to be involved in such manœuvres. Later still there seems to have been made at St Petersburg a similar offer, which was likewise rejected.[8] Such were the amenities of foreign zeal in a land unrivalled for intrigue. Like Boswell on his tour in Corsica, innocent travellers among the rest were watched with suspicious eyes and provided matter for the solemn speculations of nervous consuls.

The Greeks hoped not only for political recognition but for the aid of the British fleet in stopping reinforcements from Egypt. In the meantime they laid plans for a large extension of organised privateering.[9] Captain Hamilton, unlike the Austrian squadron-commander, acknowledged the Greek right to lawful prizes and

[7] He said: "While there is a spark of hope, fight on! and when all is desperate, then think of foreign assistance"—S. G. Howe's *Journal*, 22 July. The originals of this 'Act of Submission' are in *F.O. Turkey*, 135. Two other copies were signed, at Athens on 26 July, and at Missolonghi on 6 Aug., making four in all. Each has about one hundred signatures, in three columns headed *κληροί, πολιτικοί, στρατιωτικοί*. The text (without signatures) is printed in P. O. IV, 176, and *S.P.* 12, 904. All the leaders signed except D. Hypselantes (brother of the Russian officer who began the revolt), Kolettes (of the French Party), Goura, and Konduriottes—Trikoupes, III, 273.

[8] Greek 'decree' appointing the Duke of Nemours hereditary sovereign, 20 Nov. 1825, in *S.C. Papers*, 17. Viel-Castel, XIV, 609. Another address, to the Duke of Orleans, 12 Feb. 1826, is quoted by Debidour, *Fabvier*, p. 292. On the offer to Russia, see Disbrowe to Canning, 18 Dec. 1826, in *F.O. Russia*, 159. According to this account, Andreas Luzzi came from Greece via Switzerland to St Petersburg, with an offer signed by D. Hypselantes, Kolokotrones and Niketas. The route chosen would be due, probably, to the presence of Capo d'Istria at Geneva. The American, Washington, was "presumably Lieut. William Thornton Washington of Virginia"—*Amer. Hist. Rev.* XVIII, 561. Cf. Hamilton to Adam, 1 Aug., in *C.O. Ionian Is.* 33.

[9] Greek Government to deputies in London, 18 July (enclosed in Adam's report, 1 Sept.), in *C.O. Ionian Is.* 33.

saw no objection to the scheme for privateers, but he was equally prompt to blockade Hydra in order to obtain the surrender of captains guilty of piracy. In August, possibly on his advice, but at the instigation of the Greek Committee in London, an agreement was signed for the services of the famous Lord Cochrane, on terms which promised a rich reward to that adventurer.[10] In the autumn of this year the growing interest of the New World in Eastern affairs was marked by the appearance of an American squadron in the Mediterranean.[11]

The 'Act of Submission', carried by young Miaoules, did not reach England until October;[12] but the news of it went before, and on September 29th the original delegate, Spaniolacki, with the London deputies Orlando and Luriottes, obtained an interview with Canning in order to discover what his attitude would be. The idea of a Protectorate was of course dismissed, and, in case of any doubt, a new proclamation of neutrality was published. Canning told the deputies that "there might be a point in the contest when Great Britain would promote a fair and safe compromise". The deputies replied that the Greeks would have independence or death; if the 'Act of Submission' itself seemed to belie their words, it was an act of faith in England rather than, as Metternich described it, a "renunciation of their political independence": at least they had not signed an Act of Submission to the Sultan. But it sufficed to remove

[10] S. G. Howe's *Journal*, 19–24 July. Mavrocordato to Hamilton, 1 Sept. (enclosed in Adam's report, 17 Sept.), in *C.O. Ionian Is.* 33. Later, Hamilton was disgusted with Lord Cochrane: to S. Canning, 19 Apr. 1827, in *B.M., Add. MSS.* 36566. Correspondence relating to Cochrane in *B.M., Add. MSS.* 36461–36464 (*Broughton Papers*). Copy of the agreement with Cochrane, 36461, f. 224, 16 Aug. 1825.

[11] Gentz talked of the 'monstrous intervention' of America, to Metternich, 13 Sept.—*Briefe*, III², 249. In answer to a Greek application, the United States had expressed themselves sympathetic but unable to interfere: Papers laid before Congress, 31 Dec. 1823—*S.P.* 11, 287 ff. J. Q. Adams refused to subscribe even privately to the Greek Committee, as a 'breach of neutrality'—*Memoirs*, 10 May 1824. The object of the Mediterranean squadron was to protect American merchants at Smyrna, and to obtain, if possible, a commercial treaty with the Porte—*ibid.* 6, 26 May 1824.

[12] A. Miaoules' account of his arrival and reception by Planta at the Foreign Office is in an intercepted letter to Zante, dated 11 Oct.—*C.O. Ionian Is.* 33. The bearer was not Trikoupes as stated in *C.H.F.P.* II, 594.

Canning's previous objection to a mediation, namely that *both* parties repudiated it. His objections to a combined mediation remained: "French intrigues and Austrian partiality" made its success more than doubtful.[13]

But the way was now clear for England to offer mediation, preferably alone, or if that failed, with Russia for an ally. Canning, who was embarked on a complicated voyage of diplomacy and wished to keep both courses open, despatched his cousin Stratford Canning to Constantinople with instructions to urge the Porte to accept mediation before Russia should force the issue.[14] If this separate intervention were successful, Canning hoped to win prestige for England and still more for himself, leaving Russia with no excuse to make new demands. But the chances of success with either party in the struggle were small at best, and he did not neglect the second possibility, the daring policy of controlling Russian aggression by joining her as an ally. He therefore sent Strangford at the same time to St Petersburg with instructions to deplore the continued silence of Russia and to say that "whenever H.I.M. shall think fit to relax that resolution, H.M. will be disposed to meet confidence with confidence".[15] In the long battle of waiting, Canning was the first to break silence. The Russian Cabinet was no less anxious to secure his aid, trusting to escape in the end from any ties which England might seek to impose as the price of co-operation. Everything was so disposed as to frighten Canning, if he could not be cajoled, into an alliance.

[13] Interview, in Wellington's *Despatches*, II, 507. Proclamation (30 Sept.), in *S.P.* 12, 525. Metternich, 9 Sept., in *Mémoires*, 781–2. Canning to Wellesley, 27 Sept., in *Despatches*, II, 503.

[14] Stratford Canning had made his name at Constantinople in negotiating the Treaty of Bucarest in 1812 between Russia and the Porte. He began with an ardent sympathy for Greece, tempered by doubts: "Are terms of accommodation recommended by other Powers likely to embrace the independence of the Greeks, which could never be won from the Porte without a war? I speak of probabilities...as a matter of humanity, I wish with all my soul that the Greeks were put in possession of their whole patrimony, and that the Sultan were driven bag and baggage into the heart of Asia" (Sept. 1821)—Lane-Poole, I, 307. Instructions, 12 Oct. 1825, in *F.O. Turkey*, 133.

[15] Canning to Strangford, 14 Oct., in *F.O. Russia*, 149.

The news of the Greek offer determined the Russian minister to lose no time. On October 2nd Lieven reported that his wife, a 'dépêche vivante', had just arrived from St Petersburg with Nesselrode's 'petit billet'; that he, Lieven, was ready to act but had made no sign as yet; and that he would soon meet Canning at Seaford, where the foreign minister was preparing his instructions for Constantinople and St Petersburg.[16] There, on October 25th, Lieven told Canning that the Court of Russia had positive information that Ibrahim was to keep whatever part of Greece he should conquer, "and that *his* plan for disposing of his conquest is...to remove the whole Greek population, carrying them off into slavery in Egypt or elsewhere and to repeople the country with Egyptians and others of the Mahometan religion". Stratford Canning afterwards heard a like rumour on his way to Constantinople, and reports of it appeared in the press. Even if no good evidence for this outrageous plan was ever forthcoming, it was true that Ibrahim had lately begun a new system of terrorisation; such a positive statement of the rumour was perhaps made by the Russian minister in order to act as a spur upon the English Cabinet.[17]

On the same day, Canning wrote to Granville in Paris: "I begin to think that the time approaches when *something* must be done". On the 30th Lieven reported: "Nous sommes, M. Canning et moi, sur le chemin des confidences". Yet Canning

[16] Tatishchev to Nesselrode, 10 Sept., in Schiemann, I, 610. Lieven to Nesselrode, 2 Oct. *ibid.* I, 612. Princess Lieven's *Diary* (ed. Temperley), pp. 95–100. The meeting was at the house of Canning's friend Charles Ellis, at that time member for Seaford, and in the next year (1826) promoted through Canning's influence to the House of Lords as Lord Seaford. He was a cousin of George Ellis, the friend of Scott and Canning and part author both of the *Rolliad* and of the *Anti-Jacobin*. The family of Ellis won great advantage from the patronage of Canning, and he from their support as leaders of the 'West Indian interest'.

[17] Memo. of conference, 25 Oct., in Wellington's *Despatches*, II, 547; cf. *C. and his Times*, p. 474. The same report, attributing the plan to Soleiman Bey (Col. Sève), is mentioned in a despatch from the Russian consul at Corfu to Nesselrode (22 Nov.)—*C.O. Ionian Is.* 33. Stratford, 16 Dec., in Wellington's *Despatches*, II, 581. Report unconfirmed—*ibid.* III, 82, 119, 284; but Mehemet Ali told Consul Salt (Alexandria) that he was determined to "punish Hydra and Spezzia", whatever amnesty might be granted to the Morea and Rumelia—*ibid.* III, 121.

was by no means yet persuaded to abandon the strong position of isolation; on the 31st he wrote again to Granville: "Things are not yet ripe for our interference; for *we* must not (like our good Allies) interfere in vain. *If* we act we must finish what is to be done". And again on November 8th: "The Turks may so receive Stratford's overture as to make another move useful or practicable. But in whatever direction that move is made, to do any good we must make it *alone*".[18] Not only Lieven and the French but even the Austrian ambassador professed to look to England for the next step.[19] From the tone of Canning's private letters it is abundantly clear that he was influenced by the alluring prospect of a personal triumph in a field where his rival Metternich had failed, of a national triumph where the Alliance had failed. He would prefer to succeed alone; but it seemed that Russia would not give him time to do so.

Alexander was deeply mortified by the Greek offer to England, which revealed how utterly the old prestige of Russia was discredited by the self-imposed shackles of the Holy Alliance. In September he travelled southwards, on October 13th the old points of dispute between Russia and Turkey were revived at Constantinople, and there was every appearance of warlike preparation. Wellington began to feel alarmed about the probable consequences of war.

The establishment of a new Power in Europe which must be founded on the principles of modern democracy and therefore inimical to this country which must be continental at the same time and maritime... would under any circumstances be no small subject for consideration. ...But the establishment of a Greek Power in Europe by means of...

[18] Lieven in F. de Martens, XI, 336. Canning to Granville, in *C. and his Times*, pp. 466, 446, 467.

[19] Charles X looked to England and Russia to devise a plan: France would co-operate later. Huskisson to Canning, 17 Oct., in *Some Official Correspondence*, I, 303. Esterhazy, quoted in *C. and his Times*, p. 448 (Canning's account of an interview with the King). Prince Esterhazy, the Austrian ambassador, was heir to one of the largest estates in the Empire; he found it already heavily mortgaged and by his fantastic extravagance reduced himself to bankruptcy after raising new loans amounting to 23 million crowns. He was a favourite of George IV—*Allg. Deut. Biog.* Canning was strengthened by the unwonted friendliness of the King; Gentz to Metternich, 9 Nov., describing a conversation with Sir W. Knighton, the King's secretary, in Vienna—*Briefe*, III², 266.

a Russian army is quite a different case from that of a Greek power established by its own unassisted exertions against the Turks....I would recommend you then to connect yourself with Austria and France as the best mode of preventing the Emperor of Russia from carrying out his supposed measure....

He recommended a joint declaration of the three Powers against Russian aggrandisement, thus dividing the unpopularity of saving the Turks.[20] But Canning was not to be daunted by such forebodings. The Russian ambassadors, who had been asked for their opinion on the situation, advised the Tsar to bold measures. Russia, wrote Pozzo, has been patient long enough: she must occupy the Principalities once more, making a public declaration that she is doing so in order to relieve those provinces from the exactions of Turkish occupation [actually about 1500 police who could not do in a year the damage done in a week by a Russian army]: but must avoid the inconvenience of self-denying promises. Lieven's answer was rather different:—if Russia is in her present position next spring, war will be necessary. But—"déjà l'Angleterre nous recherche: telle combinaison que la prévoyance humaine ne saurait calculer peut s'offrir à nous:... l'empereur saura la juger et en tirer parti". Both Pozzo and Lieven were more aggressively disposed than Nesselrode himself, and in all that followed they took the leading share.[21]

During December the Lievens and Canning stayed once more at Seaford and there the project of a separate and secret understanding with Russia took shape. The only account of the discussions is from the Russian reports, which said that Canning was the first to make the proposal, but this has been contradicted.[22] Lieven is represented as saying that they must act on a plan and not desist until success should be reached. Canning replied that he could not have undertaken anything of the kind

[20] To Canning, 22 Nov., in Wellington's *Despatches*, II, 568–70.

[21] The Tsar's circular letter of 6 Aug. declared once more "qu'il croit désormais inutile d'entrer dans les nouvelles explications avec ses Alliés sur les affaires de Turquie". Pozzo's and Lieven's answers (16, 30 Oct.), in *Recueil* (1854), pp. 4ff.

[22] F. de Martens, XI, 337–8. Schiemann contradicts this, saying that Russia, not England, was the suitor—*ibid.* I, 348. He warns his readers against the inaccuracy in general of Martens' summaries of Russian diplomatic correspondence.

six months ago. So far there was no real understanding. Then came the news of the Tsar's sudden death at Taganrog on December 1st. The succession was uncertain, and on it seemed to hang the question of peace or war. Metternich's opinion was that Constantine would be peaceful and would concentrate on much-needed administrative reform, and that he took no interest in the Greeks. "L'*histoire* de la Russie va commencer là où vient de finir le *roman*." But if the young soldier Nicholas is to be Emperor, "il serait impossible de tirer un horoscope quelconque du nouveau règne".[23] Nicholas had the character of a martinet, but he had mixed much at Berlin in a society of liberal ideas and of Philhellene enthusiasm. That which found vent among Germans in subscriptions for material relief was likely with him to take the form of militant nationalism. On Christmas eve Constantine's letter definitely renouncing the crown reached St Petersburg. Two days later the Decabrist mutiny was put down, and Nicholas was firmly in the saddle. Five of the leaders were executed and more than a hundred sent to Siberia. This was the fate of those who hoped for Constantine and perhaps unwarrantably connected his name with reform. If Metternich was disappointed, Berlin was decidedly pleased.[24]

Before the news reached England, Canning had decided to follow up the Russian overture, but only if the separate mediation, of which he was anxiously awaiting news from Stratford, should fail. He explained his policy to Granville in a single sentence: "I hope to save Greece through the agency of the Russian name upon the fears of Turkey, without a war".[25] His justification against conservative suspicion lay in assuming that Russia meant war, at Christmas 1825, only if she could not get the English alliance. The other view was that only when Russia had got the English alliance would she dare to make war; but

[23] Metternich to Ottenfels, 18 Dec., in P. O. IV, 193.

[24] See pp. 2–3 above. One of the conspirators, Prince Trubetzkoi, was brother-in-law to Lebzeltern and tried to hide in his house. The Austrian ambassador was horrified, but the scandal led to his recall.

[25] Canning to S. Canning, 9 Jan. 1826: "I am not one jot abated of my preference for separate intervention"—Lane-Poole, I, 395. To Granville, 13 Jan. 1826, in *C. and his Times*, p. 471. Wellington to Canning, 9 Dec. 1825, in *Some Official Correspondence*, I, 346.

in that case inaction would mean endless anarchy in Greece and piracy on the seas. Perhaps even a Russian war was preferable. His justification against radical impatience was that a Russian war by itself would not benefit Greece, and would bring new misery to the Principalities on the Danube. Canning was therefore prepared for either issue, for peace or war between Russia and Turkey. England in any case would use her navy only.

Some have argued that the whole action of Russia was a gigantic piece of bluff, designed to lure England into an alliance for Russian objects. Nesselrode told the Tsar that he was now "the arbiter of this great question", and he wrote to Lieven: "Nous ne pouvons dès lors qu'aller au devant des communications ultérieures qu'il [Canning] vous a promises".[26] Canning was supposed to have been won over by the prospect of personal glory and by the persuasive tongue of Princess Lieven to a course which his better judgment would have disapproved. His enemies at home fostered this version of the story, which is much too melodramatic for real life. The war party in Russia was very strong and very much in earnest. He would have been a bold man who counted on the Russian Cabinet being able to draw back if the new Emperor should declare for war.[27] Even if Russia was suspiciously anxious for the shackles which Canning hoped to impose, and if in all that followed, Russia rather than England led the dance, yet Canning probably found the right solution. He never pretended that an Anglo-Russian alliance for a special object was desirable in itself or easy in execution, but only that in the circumstances it was the best escape from a dilemma. The air of secrecy with which the affair was surrounded was due to the probable opposition of the rest of the Cabinet. This was to be the first *positive* departure from the system of the European

[26] 1 Nov., to Alexander (who died without reading it), in Schiemann, I, 614. To Lieven, 6 Jan. 1826 (intercepted), in *P.R.O.*, *Howard de Walden Papers*, 4. Cf. précis of the historical sketch presented to Nicholas on his accession, in *Recueil* (1854), p. 235.

[27] Nesselrode told the Austrian ambassador that Alexander had really meant war. Strangford to Canning, 17 Jan. 1826, in *F.O. Russia*, 157. See too an account by Schöler of Alexander's last plans, in Schiemann, I, 495–6. He thinks that Alexander expected a war which would liberate Greece and strengthen the Empire, but that he did not intend to make new conquests.

Alliance: the separation of England had already made it ineffective; the creation of a separate understanding now challenged its very existence. Outside the Alliance there was no recognised means of settling difficulties, and the breach with it must mean a return to tortuous diplomatic fencing. In the questions of South America and Spain, Canning had appealed directly to public opinion; in Eastern affairs the appeal was more dangerous, because public opinion either was indifferent, or, once aroused and knowing little of the real conditions, might be too ready for an indiscriminate crusade. The chances of successful intervention without war were doubtful at best: intervention which appeared to be based on religious grounds would be doomed to failure from the first.

II

January—April 1826

At the end of December 1825 Canning proposed and George IV reluctantly agreed to send the Duke of Wellington to St Petersburg to congratulate the new Emperor (whichever it should prove to be) on his accession, and at the same time to follow up the new policy. Canning could count on the Duke's loyalty and hoped to "soften his prejudices" about the Tsar, while his absence might remove obstacles at home.[28] He instructed him to inform Russia of Stratford's separate negotiation, and to avoid a general conference "by multiplying conditions". The awkward paradox was this: Stratford's lever of negotiation with the Turks was admitted to be the prospect of a war with Russia: yet Wellington, so far from admitting the right of the Tsar to make war, was to obtain if possible an undertaking from him not to do so. The new understanding with Russia was to be introduced on the ground of Ibrahim's barbarities. If these reports were verified, England with Russia would use force to cut his communication between Egypt and the Morea. This would lead on to a general settlement

[28] The King disliked the choice, regarding the Duke as a kind of sentinel over Canning—F. de Martens, XI, 338. Canning to Granville, 13 Jan., "I am perfectly satisfied and so I believe is he; he with my intentions, and I with his disposition to execute them not only fairly but strenuously"—*C. and his Times*, p. 471.

of Greece as a tributary vassal State guaranteed by the Powers concerned.[29]

Canning had been hoping for news of the separate negotiation with the Turks before Wellington's departure, but Stratford was detained on the voyage and was then unable to secure an interview before the middle of March. Wellington, therefore, not only had to set out in ignorance of Ibrahim's real intentions and of Stratford's success or failure, but actually signed the Protocol of April 4th without any news from Constantinople. But before he left England came news at least of Stratford's communication with the Greeks, making failure with the Turks almost certain. On January 10th, on the way to his post, he had a discussion with Mavrocordato and Zographo on board ship near Hydra. They admitted in private conversation that many leading Greeks were ready to accept an arrangement which should secure autonomy and removal of all the Turkish population, without releasing them from tribute and the sovereignty of the Sultan. But the only answer which they were authorised by the Government to make was still—death or independence. Mavrocordato, whose eyes were fixed on the diplomacy of Europe rather than on the condition of Greece, was much elated by the death of Alexander, and convinced that Russia would go to war. But the old admiral Miaoules was depressed. He was afraid that the ill-paid sailors would rather surrender the islands than face a real attack by the Turkish fleet. He remarked that the resolution of a man who had nothing to lose was not surprising; this was the feeling of many of the native Greeks towards the Fanariot families who boasted of their European outlook. The islanders in fact had very little to gain by continuing the war; but they

[29] Instructions to Wellington, 10 Feb., in *Despatches*, III, 85–93; cf. Wellington's own Memoranda 26, 29 Jan., *ibid.* III, 73, 77. Cf. Canning to S. Canning, 10 Jan. 1826, in *F.O. Turkey*, 140, and a private letter which describes Ibrahim's conduct as "the foundation of a new mode of speaking *if not* acting...and one which I confess I like the better because it has nothing to do with Epaminondas nor (with reverence be it spoken) with St Paul". Canning to S. Canning, 9 Jan., in Lane-Poole, I, 395–6. Charles X, not to be left out, talked of "uniting squadrons to settle the Eastern Question", Jan. 1826—F. de Martens, XV, 52. Cf. a French semi-official *Mémoire* recommending an independent Greece, 15 Jan., in *Despatches*, III, 94.

were not fair to Mavrocordato and his like, who had really more to expect in power and influence if Greece should achieve a vassal instead of an independent status; for the power of the Fanariots rested on their influence at the Porte.[30]

Stratford's account of this interview enabled George Canning to frame the heads of an agreement with Russia, and when in April the Assembly held at Epidaurus wrote after all inviting mediation,[31] the terms which they were ready to accept were not substantially more exacting than those which had, unknown to them, already been embodied in the Protocol of April 4th. But meanwhile Stratford had no concessions to offer to the Turks, who would certainly never grant independence unless compelled by force. As to the reported projects of Ibrahim, the Reis-Effendi angrily denied any knowledge of them; and there was no evidence for an actual plan to deport the population. But there was little doubt of the conqueror's temper; a visitor to his camp found every village, house or hovel destroyed from Kalamata to the gates of Tripolitza. Ibrahim exclaimed: "I am determined to put them down....Everything shall be destroyed and the inhabitants in the mountains must perish whether of cold or hunger". Yet he received very few submissions. The traveller had to get a safe conduct not from the Egyptians but from the Greek chief Petrobey: "the communication of the entire Morea is in Greek hands....The Pasha is master but of the spot his army occupies".[32]

The Turks were irritated by these inquiries as well as by Stratford's defence of the action of the Philhellenes; and their leisurely habits were outraged by his haste to arrive at a result for Wellington's benefit. The personal influence of the Sultan,

[30] For this interview, see Lane-Poole, I, 398 ff.; more fully in Wellington's *Despatches*, III, 121 ff., with several letters of Mavrocordato.

[31] 29 Apr., in P. O. IV, 259. D. Hypselantes protested (24 Apr.) against the invitation, and was dismissed from the Government. This 'Congress of Epidaurus' was controlled by Kolokotrones and the two primates Zaimes and Londo—Trikoupes, III, 1 ff. Proclamation of the Assembly, 28 Apr., in *S.P.* 13, 1062.

[32] Letter from Lieut. R. Smart of H.M.S. *Cambrian*, enclosed in S. Canning to Canning, 20 Mar., with reports of an interview with the Reis-Effendi, in *F.O. Turkey*, 141.

always opposed to concession, was stronger than ever. Finally, they daily expected news of the fall of Missolonghi, the last garrison apart from Athens left in Continental Greece, and the focus for months past of sympathy in Europe. The Greeks were in a desperate position; their agents and sympathisers fed the newspapers of Europe with comfortable lies, but the same people confessed in private letters that "the Peloponnesians behave as if the war no longer existed: the government is powerless outside Nauplia, and anarchy is unchecked".[33] The fall of Missolonghi (April 22nd) after a year's siege had been delayed partly by the real heroism of the garrison on this occasion and partly by the jealousy existing between Ibrahim and the Turkish general Reshid. The attack was encouraged by Austria: soon after Stratford visited Hydra, the Austrian consul at Prevesa was dining with Ibrahim and discussing his plans: "As soon as Missolonghi has fallen, Ibrahim and the Capitan Pasha will attack Hydra and then Nauplia by land and sea".[34]

Nothing was to be expected in Greece or at Constantinople: the only ray of hope left was at St Petersburg. Wellington's mission could not pass unnoticed in political circles; it was supposed that he "was not going to St Petersburg only to make his bow". The general impression in England was that he had gone to negotiate for the *independence* of Greece, but Gentz doubted any result from the overtures to the Greeks. Wellington himself was at last convinced that general conferences were useless and that we must aim at qualified independence. Passing

[33] Cf. intercepted letter, 3 Jan., from Zante to Greek deputies in London announcing the death of Ibrahim and recovery of Tripolitza: and another letter—"perfect harmony now reigns". Intercepted letter from the deputies to Gerostathi asking for some good news to revive the sinking credit of Greece, and to raise a new loan, 9 Jan. Letter from Gerostathi quoted in the text, 23 Feb.; and 10 Aug., telling his friend to believe nothing in the newspapers. All in *C.O. Ionian Is.* 37.

[34] Intercepted letter from the Austrian consul, 26 Feb., after a conference at Missolonghi; cf. Austrian admiral, 23 Dec. 1825, "Missolonghi ere this it is to be hoped has fallen to the Turks"—*C.O. Ionian Is.* 37. But Gentz, who hated nationality, as any Austrian must, felt its power more clearly than Metternich. He saw that the Greek revolt would not die with the fall of this town or that; it came of too deep-rooted a spirit which could not be exorcised; to Ottenfels, April, in *Zur Geschichte*, p. 122.

through Berlin he found war feared and expected; his arrival at St Petersburg was "hailed by all descriptions of persons here with much exultation". But he found to his surprise that the new Emperor, though determined to settle once for all the Russo-Turkish disputes, seemed indifferent to the Greek question and inclined to let it drop. Lord Strangford approvingly wrote: "the young Emperor Nick does not care a straw for the virtuous and suffering Greeks. He considers armed intervention or indeed any intervention at all as little better than an invitation to his own subjects to rebel".[35] The Tsar's ministers did not speak quite so decidedly, and tried to explain away his too definite promises. They had no intention of dropping the Greek question, but they were willing to let the Tsar give that impression so long as he did not commit himself. Although Nicholas involved himself in contradictory statements, Wellington was not critical of the words of Majesty, and believed all that he was told. He was much puzzled by the inconsistency of the Tsar's declarations with those of Nesselrode, but thought that the minister's influence must be gone, and that the Tsar leant on some secret adviser. Strangford too was deceived, and the Austrians believed that the Greeks were abandoned and Canning discomfited.[36]

Wellington therefore accepted the Tsar's assurances and concentrated on toning down the language of the new Russian ultimatum to be sent to Constantinople.[37] It was drafted before

[35] Lyttelton to Bagot, 31 Jan., in *C. and his Friends*, II, 328. Greville's *Diary*, 12 Feb., I, 78. Grey to Holland, 10 Feb., in *Lord Grey*, p. 227. Gentz, 3 Mar., in *Dépêches inédites*, III, 96. Wellington to Bathurst, 17 Feb., in *Despatches*, III, 113. Bathurst disagreed, 2 Mar.—*ibid.* 142; he was responsible for the Ionian Islands. Sir D. Bayley (consul at St Petersburg) to Bagot, 22 Feb., *C. and his Friends*, II, 333. On the speculations at Berlin about the Duke's visit, see Ringhoffer, p. 46. Strangford to Bagot, March, in *C. and his Friends*, II, 337.

[36] Wellington to Canning, 5 Mar. to 14 Apr., in *F.O. Russia*, 154–6; *Despatches*, III, 164, 179. Cf. Lane-Poole, I, 405 ff. For the Russian side, see Schiemann, II, c. 4. For the Austrian, see Gentz, *Dépêches inédites*, 16, 26 Mar., 16 Apr. Lebzeltern to Metternich, 11 Feb., in P. O. IV, 215. Comte de Clam to Metternich, 2 Mar., *ibid.* IV, 217. Metternich to Ottenfels, 14 Apr., *ibid.* IV, 232. Cf. Metternich's *Mémoires*, 805.

[37] The points were (i) complete evacuation of Principalities, (ii) release of Serbian deputies, (iii) plenipotentiaries to meet and discuss the still disputed points of the 1812 treaty. Wellington secured that (iii) should not

his arrival, shown to him on March 10th, and sent off with one or two changes on March 17th, but he was not informed of this until four days later. On the same day (21st) Lieven arrived upon the scene of action and the Greek question was suddenly brought forward once more. Being the prime mover in the affair, he had come on leave from London at the Tsar's command in order to complete the work. Yet Wellington still seems to have believed that the Emperor was not serious, and he wrote complacently to Stratford on March 27th, assuring him that if once the Turks accepted this ultimatum there would be no fear that Russia might go to war for Greece. Actually the Russian policy was very different. Having despatched the ultimatum, Nesselrode asked for Wellington's proposals about Greece. The knowledge of the ultimatum made Wellington anxious to get an agreement signed; the knowledge of the agreement in the background made the Turks in turn more willing to accept the Russian demands and eventually to sign the Convention of Akkermann. On March 25th the heads of an agreement were drafted. Wellington tried to make the 'self-denying' clause as binding as possible; Nicholas assured him that he had no intention of adding "a single village" to his dominions, but Nesselrode refused to put this in writing, and there was some controversy about a satisfactory form of words. On the 31st a second draft was discussed. Nesselrode would not undertake to send an ambassador to the Porte unless England would promise her good offices for the ultimatum. On April 2nd a mutually self-denying clause was agreed upon, but the second difficulty remained at a deadlock. Wellington therefore proposed that a settlement about Greece should come before both these questions, and at last a protocol was signed.

Taken by itself, this Protocol of April 4th, 1826, was a very tentative document; but unlike the protocols of the Allies it was the work of two parties who meant to act upon it. The offer of mediation was grounded, not on Ibrahim's proceedings, as

be, in the last resort, a *sine qua non*, and also that the Turks should be given six weeks' instead of four weeks' grace to comply. The ultimatum, presented 5 Apr. to the Porte, is printed in *S.P.* 13, 1056.

Canning had suggested (for there was not yet any confirmation of them), but on the Greek invitation to England.[38] The protocol proposed to make Greece a tributary dependency of the Turkish Empire, autonomous but allowing to the Sultan "a certain share" in the nomination of its rulers: all the Turks were to be removed from the territory concerned and the Greeks to buy out their properties. Nothing was said about the Turkish fortresses, or about boundaries, except that the two Powers would settle later the details to be proposed. The Greek letter of April 29th did not define the boundaries which they expected to obtain, but made a general claim to all the districts which had been under arms, whether subdued or not, referring especially to Euboea and Crete. The full claim would have included most of Thessaly and Epirus and territory even further north, where risings were suppressed during the first months of the revolt in 1821. But about the same time Trikoupes, afterwards foreign minister of Greece and historian of the revolt, wrote for Stratford a memorandum on the possible boundaries. He pleads first for a large territory, but passes on to suggest that "si moyennant quelque grand sacrifice en argent, il serait possible d'y comprendre aussi Négropont [Euboea] ce ne serait que plus heureux": possibly in exchange for Acarnania and Aetolia, "qu'on regardera peut-être trop obstinément comme pays réacquis et soumis....A pis aller, que les Monts Cythéron et Parnès fassent les dernières limites de la domination Turque". The letter ends with a not too confident plea for including Athens at least. This shows that the Greeks' expectations were then very modest.[39] The other points in which the protocol fell short of the Greek offer were that the latter gave no share to the Turks in the nomination of the governors, and said nothing about compensation to the Turks for their properties; it also demanded the guarantee of Great Britain as indispensable. The last point was afterwards conceded in the form of a guarantee in general terms: the other two

[38] This was not yet strictly true; but Stratford's interview (10 Jan., p. 56) gave reason to expect that the Assembly would make the invitation which was sent in fact on 29 Apr. Protocol, 4 Apr., in Temperley, *Foreign Policy of Canning*, App. VII, with Lebzeltern's comments.

[39] *S.C. Papers*, 13.

differences were not unbridgeable.[40] In the most important of all, the question of boundaries, the Greeks were likely to take whatever they could get. The whole offer was of course based not on their desires but on what the leaders thought practicable after their interview with Stratford. The protocol made it quite clear that mediation was to be offered to, not forced upon, the Turks—"the arrangement to be proposed to the Porte, if that Government should accept the proffered mediation". There was in the protocol no mention of force: but although both parties clearly disclaimed any views of aggrandisement, the possibility of a Russo-Turkish war was not definitely excluded:[41]

> If the mediation offered by H.B.M. should not have been accepted by the Porte and *whatever may be the nature of the relations between H.I.M. and the Turkish government* Great Britain and Russia will still consider the terms of the arrangement specified in this first article of the Protocol as the basis of any reconciliation to be effected by their intervention *whether jointly or separately* between the Porte and the Greeks.

In other words, even if Russia should go to war, the agreement would not necessarily be dissolved. Those words "soit en commun, soit séparément" led afterwards to much recrimination; the Russian ambassador at Constantinople said in February 1827: "cette parole 'séparément' est russe, elle n'est pas anglaise".[42] Wellington was not alive to these subtleties, but in any case he would never have obtained from Russia an absolute disclaimer of force, the only argument in the last resort to which the Sultan would listen.

The protocol therefore contained by implication an effective *threat* of force on the part of Russia; there was no hint of force on the part of England, but in conversation the idea of a 'pacific blockade'[43] was mentioned in connection with Ibrahim's sup-

[40] For the comparison, cf. Canning to Lieven, 29 Aug., in P. O. IV, 305; and Wellington's *Despatches*, III, 393.

[41] The Russian ministers would never have signed an agreement on those terms. Cf. Nesselrode to Lieven, 6 Jan. 1826, in *H. de Walden Papers*, 4.

[42] P. O. V, 35. See below, pp. 73–4, 104.

[43] The phrase was used. T. E. Holland (*Studies*, p. 131) attributed its invention to an international lawyer, M. Hautefeuille, in 1849.

posed plan. The last paragraph of the protocol was the most unsatisfactory: it provided that

> H.B.M. and H.I.M., desiring that their Allies should become parties to the *definite arrangements of which this Protocol contains the outline*, will communicate this instrument confidentially to the Courts of Vienna, Paris and Berlin, and will propose to them to guarantee in concert with Russia the final transaction which shall reconcile Turkey and Greece, as that transaction cannot be guaranteed by H.B.M.

Wellington afterwards explained that he regarded the protocol as an eventual arrangement not immediately applicable; but if it was to be communicated to the Powers with a proposal to guarantee, it needed further definition without delay, otherwise unfriendly critics might make "the very natural reflection, how can we engage to guarantee, we know not *what*".[44] He did obtain a verbal promise that it should not be communicated until Lieven's return to England, but as soon as he was gone, a copy was sent to the Russian ministers at each capital, who took care that it was seen. When Wellington reached London with the protocol on April 27th, the Austrian ambassador had known it forty-eight hours earlier from Paris. On May 8th the text was printed in *The Times*, possibly by Russian design; there was now no going back.

[44] Canning to Granville, 8 Aug. 1826, in *C. and his Times*, p. 278; he added: "The Protocol I need not observe to you is not very artistically drawn". Metternich's question, "What is Greece?" was not yet answered. Metternich once drew attention to the inconvenience of the word 'Greek', as it was used indiscriminately to signify a territory, a race, a language, or even a religion—*Weisungen nach London*, 247, 21 Sept. 1829.

CHAPTER V

THE TREATY OF LONDON

I

April—December 1826

CANNING did not wish to go back: but he seems to have wished that Russia had either gone further or not so far. It is difficult to interpret his real intentions, but at least he made it appear that he would not be altogether sorry if Russia made war after all. He wrote to Granville: "I do not know any more than you do on what the Duke of Wellington grounds his hopes that the peace between Russia and Turkey will not be interrupted", and again, on the question whether the Russian ultimatum had been sent according to the original text or modified in accordance with the Duke's suggestions: "For many reasons I hope the former".[1] Esterhazy found him "more surprised than alarmed" at the Russian ultimatum, and exclaiming that "it would be impossible to pity the Turks if they were given a good chastisement".[2] It is likely that Canning, disappointed at the apparent abandonment of the Greek question, wanted to make "the agency of the Russian name upon the fears of Turkey" so formidable as to secure the success of Stratford's negotiations, if possible "without a war"; but he knew that he was using a two-edged weapon, and perhaps he did not regret it. He told his cousin "to insinuate that we may join with Russia hereafter if the Turks will not come to some understanding". Stratford too was asking: "would it be impossible to enlist the Viceroy of Egypt...by holding out to him the prospect of a pashalik in Syria?" Missolonghi had fallen and it seemed as if delay might make all interference too late. But Canning's anxiety for the

[1] 14, 18, 25 Apr., in *C. and his Times*, pp. 473–4. Compare his letter to Bagot, Aug. 1823, quoted on p. 30, above.

[2] Esterhazy to Metternich, 16 Apr. 1826, in *Austrian Extracts*; cf. Maltzahn to King of Prussia, 18 Apr., in *H. de Walden Papers*, 4.

moment was to delay the execution of the protocol until he could persuade France to take part, and perhaps even Prussia, which was more and more inclined to escape from subservience to Austria. The French Government was offended at being left out, but made the best of it in the hope of taking part later.[3]

Metternich poured scorn upon the protocol as "une œuvre pleine de faiblesse et de ridicule", done to save Wellington's face and impossible to execute without war; he spread it about that the Greeks had definitely refused the English offer of mediation and that Canning had wanted to disavow Wellington's performance altogether. From such misleading rumours he painted a lurid picture of the situation—"Nicholas alléché de sang Mussulman, le Grand Turc brandissant le cimeterre et rugissant comme un lion de désert: les Grecs, autant de Léonidas et de Thémistoclès, et enfin la voix du peuple russe formant le chœur de l'ancienne Tragédie".[4] Metternich's much-vaunted policy of peace did a real service in the years of exhaustion immediately following the Napoleonic wars; but it was artificial, and at bottom dictated only by Austrian interests. It was the natural policy for the Austrian Empire; but to represent it as the moral duty of all Europe was mere humbug. Its unconscious hypocrisy is nowhere more clearly shown than in one of his letters about this time:

> Nous voulons la conservation de la paix politique, non que nous ayons épousé les utopies de l'Abbé de S. Pierre, mais parce que le jour où cette paix serait interrompue, la meute libérale se jettera sur les puissances. En un mot nous voulons toujours et une fois pour toutes le contraire de ce que veulent nos ennemis. Le jour où ceux-ci voudront la paix, nous nous demanderons si le moment n'est pas indiqué pour la guerre.

As for the King of Naples, no language was too strong for his disagreeable conviction that the "powerful influence which

[3] Canning to S. Canning, 26 Apr.: and S. Canning to Canning, 4 June, in Lane-Poole, I, 409. Ringhoffer, pp. 48 ff.

[4] To Ottenfels, 19 May, in P. O. IV, 244; cf. Gentz, 31 May, 1826, and 30 Jan. 1827, in *Dépêches inédites*, III, 137, 211. Metternich to Esterhazy, 7 June, in *Austrian Extracts*.

England must thus acquire must greatly contribute to uphold and propagate the diabolical principles of Liberalism".[5]

The Russians on their side were in no hurry to carry out the protocol until their own demands were satisfied. The Tsar spoke of it apologetically as signed merely to humour England and as unlikely to come to much. He was distracted by a peasants' revolt, and was feverishly pushing on plans for the settlement of military farm colonies on the great estates. The navy too was being hurriedly recreated after the destruction wrought by the great floods at Cronstadt in November 1824. The Turks accepted the ultimatum a few days before it expired, and sent delegates to Akkermann; while the negotiations were proceeding, the Russians, in order to secure their own point, kept the Greek question in the background and practically gave an undertaking that it would not be revived.[6] They assured the Turks that in any case the protocol contained an absolute disavowal of force. The Sultan can hardly have put much faith in such phrases, but in any case he was bound to yield. As soon as this was fairly clear, Russia had no more need of caution and began to force the pace. Her anxiety was increased by the revolt and destruction of the Janissaries in June. A week of slaughter, during which corpses could be seen floating down the Bosphorus past the windows of the British embassy, was hailed by the friends of Turkey as the beginning of a real reform. Mahmud drilled his Regulars with the enthusiasm of a child who has been given a new toy. All the ambassadors urged the Turks to yield, if only to avert worse evils.[7]

The Convention of Akkermann was signed on October 7th, 1826, confirming the treaty of 1812, especially the articles of whose non-execution Russia complained, and legalising the seizure by Russia of some forts on the Asiatic frontier. It

[5] Metternich, 12 May, *Mémoires*, 809. King of Naples to Ludolf (Neapolitan ambassador in London), 18 May, in *H. de Walden Papers*, 4.

[6] "Une négociation amicale dans la pure intention d'écarter de leurs relations mutuelles tout sujet de différend ultérieur"—P. O. IV, 290. S. Canning, 14 June, in *F.O. Turkey*, 143.

[7] S. Canning to Canning, July–September, in *F.O. Turkey*, 144; on the drilling, 8 Sept. Convention of Akkermann printed in *S.P.* 13, 899, with Treaty of Bucarest (1812) and extracts from earlier treaties.

secured new advantages for Serbia, where no Mussulmans except the garrison were to remain, and for the Principalities, where the alien Greek *hospodars* (governors) were to be replaced by native *boyars* (nobles). There was not much in this to excite the fears of any but a 'Russomaniac'; but the Russians admittedly regarded it merely as a prelude. Their next object was to obtain through the Greek question an excuse for war; for this purpose it was necessary to have a promise from England of resorting to force if necessary, and if possible to throw upon England the lead in negotiation. Ribeaupierre at last set out for the post at Constantinople to which he had been nominated two years before.

Lieven returned to London in August, and at once addressed to Canning a number of questions, to which he did not reply for a month and then only with great caution. There was no evidence for Ibrahim's plans: Stratford Canning, having failed alone, was to tell the Turks that he expected Russian support: finally, if this joint mediation failed too, they would resort *with the consent of the other Allies* to a withdrawal of ambassadors and a *threat* of recognising Greek independence. This seemed like a return to the congress system and to Metternich's "worn-out and delusive policy".[8] Canning was forced to make this concession by the opposition of the rest of the Cabinet. He told Lord Granville:

> We must proceed in this Greek business with caution and good heed, for I have considerable *difficulty* in my way: not the least of which arises with the signer of the Protocol himself. I see my way, however, and will get through to the end, but it must be as old Lord Chatham used to say, *gradatim*.

He wrote to Stratford promising instructions: "I shall have more difficulty in *grecizing* them with others than with Lieven". The first step was merely to communicate the protocol to the French ministry (August 20th), which gave a general approval. The reply to Lieven's questions was not made until September

[8] Canning to Liverpool, 21 June, urging that on Lieven's return there should be no delay, in *Some Official Correspondence*, II, 59; cf. Princess Lieven to Lieven, 8 May, 27 June, in *H. de Walden Papers*, 4. She was over-hopeful when she wrote: "M. Canning a tué l'Opposition". Lieven to Canning, 1 Aug., in Wellington's *Despatches*, III, 358; Canning to Lieven, 29 Aug., 4 Sept., in *ibid.* 393–6, and *S.P.* 40, 1208. Sir R. Gordon to Gentz, 4 July, and Gentz's reply, 23 July, in *Zur Geschichte*, pp. 135 ff.

4th, after undergoing considerable alteration in the Cabinet. Lord Bathurst (Colonial Secretary) complained to Wellington: "I know it has long been a great object with the Foreign Office to take a part for the Greeks as being a very popular cause among a large description of well-meaning people, as well as with all democrats".[9]

In spite of these difficulties with his colleagues, Canning did not change his attitude towards the struggle in Greece. During the summer the Greek pirates became more active than ever. The merchants at Smyrna complained of the misuse of the right of search; the Greeks demanded tribute of the rich traders of Syra who had never joined the revolt, and on refusal bombarded the town. Neutrality became more than ever difficult in execution: orders were sent to deal sternly with pirates, but *not* to follow the practice of the French and Austrian admirals by refusing recognition to the Greek flag altogether.[10] Canning ingeniously made the principle of legitimacy recoil upon itself by arguing that Powers which denied a national existence to the Greeks should seek compensation for piracy from the Porte, which was responsible for keeping its subjects in order. This was not mere sophistry but a real argument, and the only one which seems to have made some impression upon the Turks themselves.

[9] Canning to Granville, 7 Aug., in *C. and his Times*, p. 477; to Stratford, 4 Aug. (private), in *S.C. Papers*, 12. Cf. 15 Aug.—next step still doubtful —*F.O. Turkey*, 141. Bathurst, 5 Sept., in *Despatches*, III, 402, quoted in *C.H.F.P.* II, 94.

[10] S. Canning, 9 June, 22 Aug., in *F.O. Turkey*, 143, 144. Capt. Hamilton found nineteen pirate boats in the Euripus, where a score of European ships were plundered during three weeks—4 June, in *S.C. Papers*, 15. *Ad.* II, 1694; 4, 23 July. Canning to S. Canning, 4 Aug., in *F.O. Turkey*, 140. The Greek Government did something to co-operate: ditto, 9 Oct., in *S.C. Papers*, 15; and Greek proclamation, 8 June, in *S.P.* 13, 1066. Metaxas, sent by the Greek leaders to punish the pirates, had a private letter from one of them, advising him not to "pursue those who by piracy would force the European powers to recognise the independence of Greece"—*Souvenirs*, p. 270. Canning to Granville, 22 June, in *C. and his Times*, pp. 475–6. Consuls were warned on threat of dismissal not to connive at the carrying of Turkish supplies under simulated papers; Circular, 15 July. Consul Salt (Alexandria) on the difficulty of enforcing this, 2 Oct., in *F.O. Turkey*, 147; he was told in reply not to interfere with merchants running honest risks or to make inquisition beyond asking for a declaration: 10 Jan. 1827, *ibid.* 160. There is a collection of correspondence on piracy, 1824–8, in *C.O. Ionian Is.* 293.

It was certain that the Turkish fleet could never pacify the Archipelago: there was no reason why England should do so indefinitely on its behalf.[11] The increase of piracy was in fact only one more argument for a speedy settlement which should enable pirates, or force them, to resort to a more honest means of livelihood. Wellington wanted to arrest Lord Cochrane, who was notoriously fitting out a steamer to join the Greek service; but Canning successfully contested the point of law, and Cochrane was tacitly allowed to sail.[12] The merchants of Smyrna again expressed their fears that he would attack the town; but, although Cochrane was a bold adventurer, he did not achieve against the Turks what was expected from his reputation in Chile, and certainly did no damage to any European merchants.

Forced by the Cabinet to take this step in retreat, Canning escaped from the difficulty by enlisting the aid of France. As soon as the Cabinet dispersed, he travelled to Paris and remained there for nearly six weeks (September 18th—October 25th). Charles X was enthusiastically anxious to co-operate in naval measures; he was determined not to be left out, and wanted to outbid Russia for the alliance of England. If Canning could convert the protocol into a treaty with the addition of France, he need have no fear of Austrian 'co-operation'.[13] Meanwhile the English answer to Lieven's questions had been referred to St Petersburg, where it found no favour. Nesselrode replied that even though Ibrahim had not been convicted of the scheme of depopulation, his continued occupation of the Morea meant a gradual extermination of the people: Canning must be convinced that "his own earlier suggestion" of a pacific blockade

[11] See draft letters to S. Canning, 2 Aug., with Wellington's objections, in Wellington's *Despatches*, III, 355 ff. The Turkish fleet left the Dardanelles in July and returned in November, having done nothing. S. Canning, 29 Nov., in *F.O. Turkey*, 145. Urquhart's conversation with the Cadi of Arta, *Spirit of the East*, I, 173.

[12] The arms being sent separately from the steamer, there was no legal proof of her destination and purpose. Cf. Canning to S. Canning, 3 July (private), in *S.C. Papers*, 12. Draft to S. Canning, 2 Aug., in Wellington's *Despatches*, III, 355.

[13] Canning to Liverpool, 16 Oct., in *C. and his Times*, p. 484; to George IV, 20 Oct., in *B.M.*, *Add. MSS*. 38568, f. 136 (*Liverpool Papers*). Pozzo to Nesselrode, 22 Dec. 1826, in *New Portfolio*, I, 127 ff.

would be easy to execute: Russia had foregone her opportunity to make war, and confined herself to the modest demands of Akkermann: "si après de tels sacrifices la Russie n'obtenait pas au moins l'arrangement définitif de la Grèce,...quel rôle le Cabinet de S.M.I. aurait-il joué?...S'il entama la question grecque c'est pour la résoudre".[14]

These were almost the words of Canning a year before: "If we act we must finish what is to be done". He hoped still to restrain Russia from war, but he was ready to run the risk for the sake of a settlement. Russia was pressing for a promise of force if necessary: Canning was ready for a strictly limited coercion, but the Cabinet was uneasy. (The question of sending troops to Portugal was a new cause of division.) Wellington wrote to him: "your refusal to go to war cannot be too peremptory", and complained that Lieven was already going beyond the terms of the protocol.[15] On November 19th Lieven wrote to Canning, assenting in the first place to the proposed plan of co-operation with other Powers by a threat of withdrawing ambassadors and of recognising the Greeks as independent; but in a separate letter of the same date he wrote: "the Emperor only enters the Greek question with the firm determination of deciding it.... He has authorised me to *concert with Your Excellency the ulterior measures* which it would become indispensable to adopt". Canning replied to the first letter (which was to serve as the joint instruction to Ribeaupierre and Stratford Canning) that if the other Allies refused to withdraw their ambassadors, England and Russia should drop the measure; he said nothing of further measures in case of failure. But in a separate reply to Lieven's other letter he said that, though the co-operation of the Allies was to be obtained if possible, "refusal ought not to alter the stipulations of the Protocol and we are prepared in this case to pursue with Russia alone this work of conciliation and peace... sparing no effort to bring it to a satisfactory conclusion". Lieven,

[14] Nesselrode to Lieven, 29 Sept., in *F.O. Russia*, 161; part quoted in F. de Martens, XI, 347.

[15] Canning to Granville, 12 Nov., in *C. and his Times*, p. 486; and 22 Nov., in *F.O. France*, 347. Wellington to Canning, 8, 12 Nov., *Despatches*, III, 446, 455. C. Arbuthnot to Liverpool, 5 Sept. 1826, in *Life of Liverpool*, III, 395.

reporting this assurance to Nesselrode, described how Canning hesitated for a fortnight before finally giving it; even if it was still a little vague, Lieven was sure of Canning's good faith: allowance must be made for his difficulty with the Cabinet and for his anxiety to include France before moving forward.[16]

Wellington afterwards showed Lord Sidmouth a letter written in the spring of 1827, objecting to the project of a treaty; in 1829 he recalled having told Lieven at the time, that as a member of the then administration he would never agree to it; and in 1830 he wrote:

> I did everything I could to prevail on Mr Canning not to enter into the treaty and he certainly negotiated it as far as negotiation went before the secession of Liverpool [February 1827] without the knowledge of any of his colleagues except myself. But they and we all are highly blameable for having suffered the negotiation to move at all.[17]

It appears then that Wellington might have threatened to resign when it came actually to signing a treaty, if other events had not already thrown him out of office. The Whigs, on the other hand, were getting impatient. Russia had just declared war on Persia, and Lord Grey wrote to Princess Lieven: "I congratulate you on your Persian successes and on your peace with the Turks. I had rather it had been the other way, that you had accommodated matters with Persia, and were engaged in a laudable endeavour to drive these miscreants out of Europe". But the Whigs recognised the difficulty of Canning's position and his success in separating England from the Alliance.[18]

A new and tempting opportunity of detaching Mehemet Ali from his conquest had to be rejected. Asked if he would be

[16] Lieven to Canning, 19 Nov., in P. O. IV, 309; separate letter, in *Portfolio*, IV, 554. Canning to Lieven, 20 Nov., in Wellington's *Despatches*, III, 460; separate letter in *Portfolio*, IV, 572. Cf. Canning to S. Canning, 22 Nov., in *F.O. Turkey*, 140. The separate letter and reply are also in *F.O. Russia*, 161, which thus confirms the accuracy of the *Portfolio* documents. Lieven to Nesselrode, 27 Nov. (secret), in *Portfolio*, v, 80.

[17] *Diary of Lord Colchester*, III, 547 (Feb. 1828). Wellington's *Despatches*, VI, 145 (8 Sept. 1829), and VII, 170 (15 Aug. 1830).

[18] Grey to Princess Lieven, 12 Nov., in *Correspondence*, I. Hobhouse on Burdett's hatred of Canning, in Broughton, *Recollections*, II, 160. Russian declaration of war on Persia, 28 Sept. 1826, and papers relating thereto, in *S.P.* 13, 1045.

willing to promote the mediation or at least not to put obstacles in the way, he told Consul Salt that he was tired of the war and had purposely ordered his son to "loiter about in the interior":[19] that he could easily have taken Hydra and Nauplia, but would not be ordered about by the Turkish admiral. There was an old feud between them, for Chosrew Pasha had been supplanted as ruler of Egypt by the man who was once an obscure adventurer under his orders. Mehemet had no mind to make more sacrifices for a jealous Sultan, he was ready to mark time until the spring, and then to withdraw from the Morea if England would help him to develop his navy and give written leave for him to "aggrandise himself towards Arabia". "Mehemet Ali is little but he will be free."[20] These schemes, set on foot by the zeal of Stratford Canning, were dismissed by Wellington as "inconsistent with our neutral character,...the worst description of war against the Porte". The objection on the ground of principle had not much weight: Mehemet's allegiance to the Porte was so shadowy that he could almost be regarded as a third Power called in, by treaty with the Sultan, to conquer Greece.[21] The Turks were too apt to claim sovereignty over countries for whose behaviour they refused responsibility: just as they made no attempt to deal with the Barbary pirates, yet complained loudly when France undertook to subdue the Bey of Algiers. A more conclusive objection against buying Mehemet out was that Europe, and England in particular, had no desire to see a maritime Arab power in the Mediterranean. Mehemet himself knew that England would not let him keep the Morea, but he still hoped for Syria. Six years later Palmerston was faced with the same

[19] P. J. Green (Consul at Patras) confirms this, writing in September 1827: "Upwards of 18 months have elapsed and Ibrahim has not struck a *single blow*"—*Sketches*, p. 258.

[20] S. Canning to Consul Salt (Alexandria), 10 June; Salt's conversations with Boghoz (the Armenian chief adviser of Mehemet), 16–26 Sept., in *F.O. Turkey*, 147. A. G. Politis, *L'Hellénisme et l'Égypte moderne*, t. I (1929), emphasises the influence upon Mehemet Ali of the Greeks in Egypt.

[21] Wellington to Canning, 27 Nov., in *Despatches*, III, 469. Observations of Lieven, Mar. 1827, in P. O. v, 48. Prokesch v. Osten's attempt (in his book *Mehemet Ali*) to paint the Pasha as the loyal subject of the Sultan, misunderstood by his enemies at Constantinople and by the whole of Europe, is hardly convincing.

question in a more critical form. Yet these overtures at least revealed that not much force would be needed to drive Ibrahim from Greece.

On November 26th Gentz felt confident that the whole edifice of the protocol was collapsing. Two days later the other Powers received a formal invitation to take part in the work, but Metternich was very suspicious, and said that Canning was trying to bring them into a new Alliance on his own terms: Austria must beware of a Concert which would belie its true function by putting Turkish *suzerainty* for full *sovereignty*. He addressed to Russia and to England a number of questions designed to find out exactly what was the settlement in which he was invited to take part. Canning's answer pointed to a total separation of Turks from Greeks in the Morea and the islands at least, and made it plain that he intended to persevere with or without the co-operation of the Alliance. Neither he nor Lieven told Esterhazy in London anything of their plans: Canning had now the support of the King, who defended his policy against the Austrian ambassador's insinuations.[22] His sudden landing of troops at Lisbon and his great speech on Portugal in December made Metternich still more angry and even alarmed the Russian Cabinet.

At the end of the year Austria refused to take part in the Greek settlement in view of the coercive measures proposed, but promised to bring pressure upon the Turks. For the present Metternich contented himself with advising the Sultan to forestall mediation by offering a plan of his own. The Sultan's pacification was to take the form of a new expedition from Egypt, the form which Metternich really welcomed most. "Le gant est jeté entre M. Canning et moi", he wrote at the end of the year. Prussia gave a non-committal promise of support, but refused to take part in a treaty without Austria; France agreed provisionally, but again proposed turning the protocol into a treaty.[23]

[22] Gentz, 26 Nov., in *Dépêches inédites*, III, 187. Questions and answers (according to Esterhazy), in P. O. IV, 311–17. Esterhazy to Metternich, 11, 18 Dec. 1826, in *Austrian Extracts*.

[23] Austrian refusal, 22 Dec., and Metternich to Ottenfels, 30 Dec., in P. O. IV, 319, 329. Metternich to Esterhazy, 26 Dec., in *Austrian Extracts*.

Villèle suggested a guarantee of Turkey after the settlement, but Russia would have nothing to do with "a manœuvre directed against us". Canning was equally unwilling to do what the Alliance itself had not undertaken at the Congress of Vienna; but he was half inclined to waive the prevailing objection of England to such commitments, in favour of "a guarantee limited in object and common to all the powers", *not* of Turkey, "but of our work in Greece".[24]

II

January—July 1827

At the beginning of 1827 Canning had passed the blind alley of a settlement under the auspices of the Alliance, and had little now to fear from Metternich; he still had to spur on the unwilling horses of his own team, and here too he triumphed; but in the hardest task of all, to keep in friendly company with that runaway coach the Russian Cabinet, he did not live to show his mettle. It was the Emperor's cue to make England appear to the Turks to be the leading spirit in the negotiation. Nesselrode therefore instructed Ribeaupierre to tell the Turks that he was bound to follow Stratford's lead, since Russia must fulfil her engagements with England. In a separate despatch he explained that England was becoming half-hearted: "as we cannot admit the indefinite prolongation of the Levant troubles, we should be obliged to terminate them separately according to the very letter of the stipulations of the Protocol". The last words referred to the unfortunate phrase "soit en commun, *soit séparément*", which was now brought forward as proving the right of Russia to settle the question by herself if necessary. Nesselrode added: "As soon as Great Britain has seen in us the sole arbiter of the destinies of Greece she has never failed to offer a

Prussian answer, 4 Jan. 1827, in Ringhoffer, p. 63; French answer, Damas to Granville, 8 Dec., in *F.O. France*, 352.

[24] Pozzo to Nesselrode, 22 Dec. 1826, in *New Portfolio*, I, 127 ff. Nesselrode to Lieven, 21 Jan. 1827, in *Portfolio*, v, 438. Canning to Granville, 22 Dec., in *C. and his Times*, p. 486.

co-operation which thenceforth became zealous and sincere".[25] Ribeaupierre did not conceal from the Austrian the nature of his instructions: "je suis l'organe de la force: cette parole 'séparément' est russe, elle n'est pas anglaise, car nous avons bien l'intention d'y aller seule, quand même l'Angleterre ne voudrait pas". But he succeeded in making the exasperated Turks believe that England was leading the way: he "described Great Britain as the sworn enemy of the Porte", wrote Stratford, "and me as little better than a Greek". Stratford well understood the Russian policy and asked the Austrian Internuncio to enlighten the Turks: but, tired of the latter's "more than Turkish dissimulation", he was soon clamouring for more active measures and asked that, if the treaty were not speedily signed, he might be recalled.[26]

The negotiation in London proceeded slowly.[27] On January 19th France offered a draft treaty, but without any mention of the means by which it was to be enforced except the sending of consuls to Greece. Before it had been fully considered, Lord Liverpool's sudden illness and retirement threw everything into confusion. The struggle long impending between Wellington and Canning was fought out, and on April 10th Canning became Prime Minister with Lord Dudley at the Foreign Office; Wellington resigned his seat in the Cabinet and his command of the army. Canning's triumph had come at last: momentous issues hung on the result, not least among them the fate of the Greek treaty. The reputation of Canning in Greece is illustrated by this confused tribute: "The new English government is for nations in general and not for Aristocracy alone".[28] In March the Russian draft had appeared, proposing a naval blockade if the Turks would not yield, and in the background 'ulterior measures'—

[25] Nesselrode to Ribeaupierre, 23 Jan. 1827, in P. O. v, 18; and 23 Jan. (secret), in *Portfolio*, III, 128. Cf. circular letter to Russian envoys, 21 Apr., *ibid.* VI, 6, and Nesselrode to Minciaky, 24 Dec. 1826, *ibid.* v, 236.

[26] S. Canning, 15 Mar. 1827, in *F.O. Turkey*, 152. Ottenfels misrepresented him as having wanted to back out of the Russian Alliance altogether —to Metternich, 7 Mar., in P. O. v, 34ff. See above, p. 61, and below, p. 104.

[27] Drafts in *F.O.* 97/233, with comments of ministers, and in *F.O. Russia*, 168, as exchanged with Lieven; cf. F. de Martens, XI, 348–55. Granville to Canning, 19 Jan., 10 Feb., in *F.O. France*, 363–4.

[28] Archbp. Ignatius to Viaro Capo d'Istria, 25 May, in *C.O. Ionian Is.* 43.

presumably a Russo-Turkish war. Wellington objected to the whole of this article, but only succeeded in putting for "moyens ultérieurs dont l'emploi *serait* nécessaire", the words "*pourrait devenir*": Canning himself added the words "without taking part in hostilities". He seems to have hoped even now that Austria would come in on his terms; but Metternich would agree to no sanction except a threat of rupture in the name of the five Powers, refusal not necessarily to imply an actual rupture. The Turks must retain their fortresses in the Morea and full sovereignty over Greece, and the Turkish dominions must be solemnly guaranteed for the future. The best comment on this is a letter of Gentz to Metternich a fortnight earlier: why not draw up a *fourth* plan and so increase the confusion—"plus les ténèbres seront épaisses, plus tôt les médiateurs sans mission se briseront la tête".[29] France was very reluctant to join without Prussia at least. Von Bülow in London was anxious to take part, and the Prussian King was unwilling to offend his son-in-law the Tsar, but Bernstorff would not consent, though he agreed to support the preliminary note to the Porte.[30] At the beginning of May an amended draft was submitted by France, including this time the additional article. After many delays raised by Polignac, yet another draft was produced by England and Russia; in deference to France the withdrawal of ambassadors was dropped. In June Nesselrode wrote twice, insisting that there must be no more delay and threatening to act alone if the naval measures were not made really effective; the Russian fleet left Cronstadt for the Mediterranean.[31] But the French insisted on one more useless effort to invite Austria and Prussia to take part.

[29] Canning to S. Canning, 19 Feb., in *F.O. Turkey*, 151. A long *Mémoire* containing the Austrian proposals (? Jan. 1827) is printed in *Les Rapports de Lebzeltern*, 439–64. Metternich to Esterhazy, 25 Mar., in *Mémoires*, 856; Gentz, in *Dépêches inédites*, III, Mar.; and in *Briefe*, III², Feb.–Mar. Esterhazy to Metternich, 27 Mar., in *Austrian Extracts*. Pozzo to Nesselrode, 2 May, in *F.O. Russia*, 168.

[30] Ringhoffer, pp. 64 ff. He does not mention the very strong pressure from Vienna against Prussian action—*Dépêches inédites*, III, 277.

[31] Nesselrode to Lieven, 21 June, in Wellington's *Despatches*, IV, 42. The fleet sailed 22 June, reaching Portsmouth 8 Aug., the day of Canning's death. This short voyage revealed such defects in the newly fitted ships that all the tackle had to be renewed, involving a fortnight's delay—Schiemann, II, 196.

At last, on July 6th, the Treaty of London was signed:[32] its terms were ostensibly almost the same as those of the Protocol of 1826, with one or two modifications introduced at the desire of France; in the preamble, the Greek invitation to France as well as to England was made a ground of intervention, besides commercial interests and the spread of piracy: England no longer refused to guarantee the settlement, but did not promise to do so. A step towards recognising the claims of the Greeks to be heard was made in the provision that the boundaries should be negotiated between the Allies and the *two contending parties*; by the protocol the Allies were simply to have decided what boundaries they would propose to the Porte.

The important part of the treaty was the additional article, which provided that in case the Porte should not after one month accept the mediation, the Allies would at once send consuls to Greece: if either party should refuse the preliminary armistice, "the High Powers will jointly exert all their efforts to accomplish the object of such armistice, without, however, taking any part in the hostilities between the two contending parties". Conditional instructions to this effect would be sent to the admirals. In case of obstinate refusal, the Powers "will nevertheless continue to pursue the work of pacification" as the Conference in London might decide. These expressions were vague enough: and they were made little clearer by the instructions sent to the ambassadors and the admirals a week later. The armistice was first to be notified to both parties; if the Turks should refuse, the admirals were to treat the Greeks as friends, and to unite their squadrons for intercepting supplies from Egypt or the Dardanelles; but they must take "extreme

[32] Text and drafts in Temperley, *Foreign Policy of Canning*, App. VIII. Instructions of the Conference, etc., in *Parl. Papers*, 1830, XXXII. Schiemann says that the secret article was not signed until 13 July, but the letter (in his Appendix) from Lieven to Nesselrode of that date clearly refers only to the complementary instructions to the ambassadors and admirals, which were sent on 14 July—II, 194, 429. Gentz said that Canning left the negotiation to underlings, Dudley being inexperienced—*Dépêches inédites*, III, 273. This is not true of the earlier drafts, but it is likely that, absorbed in forming his ministry, he did not supervise the wording of the instructions to the admirals, which were certainly not satisfactory.

care to prevent the measures which you shall adopt against the Ottoman marine from degenerating into hostilities" and "...not to make use of that force unless the Turks persist in forcing the passages which they [the admirals] had intercepted". It was obvious that a naval encounter could not be completely barred; but it was equally obvious that no effective force could be used against either party by land. The treaty was, perhaps inevitably, a compromise between a strictly impartial mediation and an open intervention on behalf of the Greeks; but it led to a great deal of sophistry and puzzled the admirals not a little. What were they to make of their instructions "to watch over the maintenance of the armistice without taking part in the hostilities"? But the general sense was clear enough: to cut off Ibrahim's supplies and to set the Greek Government on its legs.

France signed the treaty in order to keep England and Russia in check, just as England had signed the protocol in order to restrain Russia. The French had delayed the signature and the execution of the treaty in every possible way. It suited Austria to exaggerate the jealousies and to minimise the goodwill of the new allies; but those jealousies were real enough. In a sense the mutual suspicion of the Powers was the Greeks' best security: no one of them was concerned to make Greece an independent State (Canning himself gave no clear indication of it) but each was driven in that direction by the fear of allowing the other an excuse for further interference. The native Greeks cared little for their diplomatic status so long as the Turks were excluded from their midst; the interests of the Powers more than the enthusiasm of the people eventually made Greece into an independent kingdom. After the first years of real struggle, the part of the Greeks was the negative one of keeping the problem alive by continued disorder. With a little more perseverance and stability they might have won a privileged but vassal position already: but their very failures set them on the path of complete independence. Independence had practical and financial drawbacks which for a compact self-contained community might have outweighed its sentimental value; but national sentiment was the very life-blood of a people which from the first laid claim to some further extension, and already dreamed of almost indefinite expansion in the future. The 'European' Greeks with ambitions for the future recognised this and built upon it; Metternich saw it too, but without the same satisfaction. He ridiculed the treaty's lack of precision and prophesied that the naval squadrons *could* not follow their instructions without hostilities.

It was easy for unfriendly critics to attack the treaty point by point and to accuse it of uncertainty, inconsistency, and even of partiality: but the alternative offered by Metternich was not a better treaty, but no treaty, nor any other useful suggestion to end the six years' misery.

CHAPTER VI

NAVARIN

I

April—August 1827

THE treaty was published, including the secret additional article, in *The Times* of July 12th. This, with the Russian *Mémoire* of January 1824 and the protocol of 1826, was the third document which found its way prematurely into the press, in the last two cases at least to the advantage of the Russian policy.[1] The Turks of course would know of the treaty officially before long, but the knowledge of the forcible methods threatened in the secret article would make the risk of desperate resistance even greater. The news in Greece, though long expected, caused the greatest joy and excitement; even in Corfu (an island under British protection and officially discouraged from taking too much interest in the fate of Greece), "men went mad with joy. The bells were rung, the Christians gave thanks to God, old men danced,...a day of resurrection".[2] Greece indeed seemed very nearly dead. At the meeting of the National Assembly in April the party feuds had been composed only by the appearance of Lord Cochrane and Sir Richard Church, who were thereupon elected as commanders-in-chief by sea and land. Capodistrias was elected President for seven years in the face of some opposition from the islanders, who did not want national union. There were some fears too of the disapproval of England, but Stratford in spite of doubts encouraged the Greeks to choose him.[3] Kolo-

[1] The published copy contained mistakes which appeared only in the final drafts sent to each party before correction and signature. The betrayer must have seen all three copies and must therefore have been one of the signatories or their secretaries. Dudley to S. Canning, 30 July, in *S.C. Papers*, 16. Cf. Hertslet, *Recollections of the Old Foreign Office*, pp. 40–2. Schiemann says that Canning was responsible, but gives no evidence—II, 195.

[2] Viaro Capo d'Istria to his brother, 28 July, in *C.O. Ionian Is.* 43.

[3] Lane-Poole, I, 443. On Capodistrias' acceptance and activities during the rest of the year, see below, pp. 132 ff. The change in spelling of his name was his own from this date.

kotrones was at first opposed, but having resigned his own command in favour of Church he told the politicians that they in turn ought to give way to Capodistrias. He went to ask the advice of Hamilton, who was so exasperated at the party strife that he would only say: "Take C. or any other devil you like, for you are quite lost".[4] These were high-sounding appointments, but outside the Assembly and even within it the Greeks were losing heart. The new commanders were not easy partners. Cochrane was a headstrong adventurer, imperious and too impatient of Greek indiscipline and intrigue to judge coolly the chances of success; Church, who had some experience of suppressing brigands in the kingdom of Naples, understood and won the affection of the Greek irregular bands, but he too was impulsive and not strong enough to impose his will upon Cochrane.

Their attempt to relieve the Acropolis of Athens failed miserably: the Greek troops were demoralised by the disgraceful scene at the Monastery of St Spiridion, when a party of Turks who had surrendered were put to death. Church, who saw it all from the harbour, makes it clear that it was not a cold-blooded massacre, but the outcome of an attempt to disarm one of the prisoners, whose pistol went off in the process. A Greek shot him dead, and the leaders were unable to prevent a general *mêlée*. The Greek chief Karaïskaki was opposed to Cochrane's plan of attacking across the open ground; he wished instead to cut off from the north the supplies of the besieging force. General Church agreed with him, but when Cochrane threatened to depart if his own plan were not followed, they surrendered their judgment.[5] Finally, on the eve of the attack, Karaïskaki was killed in a chance encounter, and the camp was thrown into confusion by his loss. The attempt next day was a complete fiasco, and on June 5th the garrison capitulated, although the state of their

[4] Kolokotrones, pp. 245–50. Kolokotrones was a *klepht*, who had some training in an Ionian regiment before the revolt. His difficult temper was responsible for many feuds.

[5] *B.M.*, *Add. MSS.* 36563. (Church's *Narrative*, I–XXII.) The *Narrative* seems to show that Finlay's account is prejudiced against Church. Hamilton distrusted Cochrane, but was friendly with Church, "a fine fellow, but a complete Irishman". Hamilton to S. Canning, 7 Apr. 1827, in *Add. MSS.* 36566, f. 62; and Capt. Charles Fallon's *Diary*, *ibid.* f. 1.

supplies perhaps hardly warranted the surrender of this, the last fortress north of the Isthmus. There is an attempt elsewhere to translate one of the Klephtic ballads on the death of Karaïskaki, who survived deservedly in tradition as one of the few Greek captains of real energy and devotion.[6]

Church's camp was soon broken up, and he remained with a small force holding the Isthmus. The *capitani* on the borders began to think of making terms with the Turks;[7] in the Morea some of the long-enduring peasants were driven for the first time to submission. The islanders made no effort to prepare against the new Egyptian fleet which was coming to destroy Hydra and Spezzia. The Government, according to an English observer, consisted of a boy, a sailor, and a cuckold. The editor of the Greek gazette wrote to a friend: "If I knew that by telling untruth I could be useful to the country, I would not have written truth to anybody; but our situation is known to all the world".[8]

But the Greek leaders' inactivity was due partly to their hopes of intervention; if the Powers were going to save them, there was no need to bestir themselves. They forgot that intervention was not intended to conquer territory from the Turks, but to impose an armistice. Consequently they took no trouble to keep at least an appearance of a footing beyond the Isthmus, and Church's efforts to organise expeditions all fell through.

Canning's advent to power was very welcome to the Russians, who dreaded the hostility of Wellington.[9] Their belief that he would allow England to be used for Russian objects was mistaken: he had entered the alliance for a definite and limited purpose; if he had lived to see that accomplished, Russia might have found in him thenceforth an opponent less irritable but

[6] See Appendix IV(*a*).

[7] Submission of Acarnania, Arta, Lepanto, Negropont (with Salona, Thebes and Athens), and Triccala, addressed to the Greek patriarch, in P. O. v, 113. Patriarch's interview with Reis-Effendi, 25 Sept. But Stratford wrote to Codrington, 29 Sept., "The Porte has lately taken measures concerted with the Patriarch for the purpose of *representing* Greece north of the Morea as having submitted"—*S.C. Papers*, 17.

[8] May 1827, in *C.O. Ionian Is.* 43. George Lee (from Nauplia), 22 July, *ibid.* 44. Church's *Narrative*.

[9] Princess Lieven, *Letters*, p. 98.

more formidable than the Duke.[10] If a Russo-Turkish war became inevitable there is little doubt that he would have replied by promoting the full independence of Greece; he was moving, as he said, '*gradatim*'. The Duke himself was driven in the end to the same course, but in a moment of panic and without conviction. The Cabinet took many weeks to form, but at last Canning was free of that suspicion from colleagues under which he had suffered for so long. The King was quite reconciled to his policy, and indignant at Wellington's behaviour in the crisis; he told Esterhazy that he never expected that the Duke would look to be Prime Minister, or resign his command rather than serve under Canning, whose conduct was free of all the low intrigues imputed to him. The attacks upon Canning from Whigs and ultra-Tories alike were more violent than ever, but he was in a position to meet them. Early in July a friend wrote to Stratford: "If your cousin does but keep his health (of which there is every chance, for he is delightfully well now) I think he will in the end triumph over all opposition". A month later Canning was dead. Princess Lieven wrote: "*We* have just lost Canning. The Mercantile class is in dismay, the people in tears, everybody who is not Metternichish is in despair".[11] Metternich did not conceal his joy, and prophesied the return of Wellington after an interval of confusion. The makeshift government of Goderich and Dudley was in doubt about Eastern and most other affairs. Lord Grey, a possible successor to power, was decidedly hostile to the treaty, as his letters to Princess Lieven show: "What you say does not satisfy me as to the expediency of a combined naval operation....I must view with considerable jealousy any arrangement which may have a tendency to place Greece in a state of dependency upon Russia".[12] Wellington was now commander-in-chief once more, and reserved a very

[10] The same opinion comes with surprising force from the Austrian *chargé d'affaires*, a year after Canning's death. Neumann to Gentz, 8 Aug. 1828, in *Zur Geschichte*, p. 181.

[11] Esterhazy to Metternich, 22 June, in *Austrian Extracts*. Planta to S. Canning, 10 July, in *S.C. Papers*, 16. Princess Lieven, 10 Aug., in *Letters*, p. 104.

[12] Grey to Princess Lieven, 2 Sept., in *Correspondence*, I. He spoke against the treaty in Parliament.

questionable right of differing publicly from the Cabinet upon political matters. But Bathurst wrote to him: "We cannot recall our stipulations with France and Russia and it seems therefore desirable that this crusade should be executed by those who have advised it".[13]

II

August—October 1827

When Canning died (August 8th) the treaty was fairly launched; Stratford was ready to act on August 3rd, but he had to wait for his colleagues' instructions. On the 16th the ambassadors delivered their first declaration to the Reis-Effendi, who received it jocosely, refusing even to read it in their presence. They were supported by a note from Prussia, but the Austrian Internuncio withheld even the unofficial support which had been promised; although his action was afterwards disavowed by Metternich, he can hardly have mistaken his instructions on so important a point. The term for acceptance had been shortened to a fortnight in view of the violent manifesto published by the Turks before the treaty was even signed. On the 31st the second declaration was presented, and final instructions to the admirals followed. The limits of the blockade were important, as they would inevitably be taken by the Greeks as the minimum boundary favoured by the Powers. They were fixed by the ambassadors so as to extend from the Gulf of Volo on the east to the mouth of the Aspropotamos on the west, with the "contiguous islands" —and in addition Samos, and perhaps Candia "if in a fit state to enjoy it". A month later Codrington was told not to blockade Candia for the present. Stratford was at this time in favour of *excluding* Acarnania so as to "leave a large portion of the coast opposite our Islands in Turkish hands". This was the very cause of Wellington's anxiety afterwards; but the fact that a year later the Greeks had re-established themselves in the province rightly outweighed in Stratford's mind the doubtful objection of policy. It was another instance of the awkwardness

[13] 12 Aug., in Wellington's *Despatches*, IV, 81.

of combining our 'protection' over the Ionian Islands with our Greek policy.[14]

The blockade was to prevent neutral as well as Turkish vessels from bringing supplies to the Turks. But in deference to Austria, Dudley relaxed this provision on October 16th; her ships did a brisk trade with the Turkish armies under convoy of her men-of-war. Her position was that, not recognising any "prétendu droit des gens naturel" and having no special convention with the rebel Greeks, she must observe a "neutralité de fait". In other words, Austrian subjects must commit no acts of war for either side, and could only pass an effective blockade at their own risk. But the Austrian naval commanders were told to give convoy whenever possible to vessels trading with the Turks, and in that case not to submit to any right of search. Dudley's concession was made because the Law Officers could find no legal ground for interfering with such convoys of a neutral power, when the allies were themselves not belligerents. The complications of a 'pacific blockade' were indeed subtle.[15]

The Turkish and Egyptian transports were to be encouraged by the allied commanders to return home; as to those which, being already in Navarin or Modon, "may persist in staying there, they must, like the fortresses, incur all the chances of war". Privately Stratford wrote to Admiral Codrington that "although the measures...are not adopted in a hostile spirit,...yet the prevention of supplies...is ultimately to be enforced, if necessary, and when all other means are exhausted, by cannon-shot". Codrington repeated this phrase to all his captains. The sailor's view of the matter was simple: "I have never felt a wish to see another war until now, and I really think it might prove a more

[14] For conferences and reports, Constantinople and London, see *Parl. Papers*, 1830, XXXII. S. Canning's despatches in *F.O. Turkey*, 155–7. Metternich's disingenuous conduct is clearly exposed in memoranda (10 Dec. 1827, 1 Jan. 1828) circulated to the Cabinet—*H. de Walden Papers*, 3. Turkish manifesto, 9 June, in *S.P.* 14, 1042. On the blockade, see conference, 4 Sept., in *Parl. Papers*. On Candia and Acarnania, S. Canning to Codrington, 8 Sept., in *F.O. Turkey*, 156; and 18 Oct., in *S.C. Papers*, 17.

[15] Metternich to Esterhazy, 31 Oct., and Dudley's reply, 28 Nov., in *Parl. Papers*; and *Ad.* I, 4241.

humane way of settling affairs here than any other. One strong act of coercion would place the Turks at our mercy and we could then settle the whole matter as we chose and take Candia ourselves into the bargain". He felt very uneasy about pitfalls in executing the treaty: "how can we coerce the Turks without hostilities?"[16]

Codrington's first duty was to persuade the Greeks to accept the armistice, but meanwhile his opinion was "that the Greeks should work hard to do all that is possible before the armistice".[17] The French admiral, de Rigny, was a man of steady judgment, without any Philhellenic sympathies. His attitude towards the Greeks was mid-way between the decided partiality of Codrington and of Captain Hamilton and the animosity of the Austrian naval commanders. But he too was writing: "One must serve them in spite of themselves. It is necessary too, I repeat, to leave to those whose life depends on warfare some corner to carry it on without bad consequences". After much discussion the Greek Government formally accepted the armistice on September 3rd; but the Rumeliot troops, backed by Church and Cochrane, Fabvier and Kolokotrones, tried to prevent it and in fact took very little notice of it. Having failed all through the summer to act, Cochrane was able, now that an armistice had been accepted, to organise without difficulty an expedition to the west coast. As the Turks had refused the armistice, and the Powers could only enforce it by sea, the Greeks could not be expected to fold their arms while Ibrahim ravaged the Morea; but in any case the Government at Nauplia had no check on the activities of the chiefs. A last effort to prevent the new Egyptian fleet from sailing had failed: as soon as Stratford had unofficial news of the treaty he had written to Codrington (July 26th) suggesting that his appearance off Alexandria might stave off the blow, but the French ambassador objected. An officer, Colonel Cradock, had also been sent out from England to detach

[16] S. Canning to Codrington, 19 Aug., 1 Sept., 18 Oct., in Lane-Poole, I, 449, and *S.C. Papers*, 17. Codrington to his wife, 28 July, in *Life of Codrington*, I, 395.

[17] Codrington to his wife, 20 Aug., in *Life of Codrington*, I, 242. Greek acceptance, 21 Aug., in *S.P.* 14, 1048.

Mehemet Ali if possible from his allegiance to the Sultan; but when he arrived at Alexandria on August 8th, the fleet had already sailed three days before. Having no authority to offer either definite threats or definite promises of protection to the Pasha, he got no satisfactory answer: Mehemet only recommended that the admirals should invite Ibrahim to be tractable and leave the rest to him.[18]

At the end of August Codrington left Smyrna and sailed to the island of Hydra, which the Egyptian fleet was expected to attack first. He did not receive until September 8th the instructions authorising him to act on the Turks' final refusal. The French admiral was nowhere to be found, having mentioned three different *rendez-vous*; actually he had returned to Smyrna, writing that he proposed to stay there until the Russian fleet should arrive. He showed the greatest reluctance to risk an encounter with the Egyptians, who had a number of French officers among them. The Egyptians were equally anxious not to force an issue; their fleet, after leaving Alexandria, wasted a whole month, sailing first to Rhodes, and then (August 22nd) to the north coast of Africa. It was not until September 10th, when news came that it was actually on its way to Navarin, that de Rigny at last left Smyrna. On the same day Codrington sailed from Hydra in order to intercept the Egyptians with his squadron alone; but when he came in sight of the bay on the 12th he found them already anchored there, three days earlier, beside the Turkish fleet. He decided to stop all supplies even of provisions to the Turkish fortresses, and thought that, if Cochrane intended to attack the Turkish fleet, "I may perhaps be out of the way". This was certainly straining the letter of his orders in favour of the Greeks: but Stratford at Constantinople was getting impatient too; he wrote to Dudley urging him to "change your present neutrality with folded arms into a French neutrality with both hands out...one little monosyllable would end the matter". Sir F. Adam, asked by Codrington for advice, defined the position in cryptic words: "The Greeks having accepted the

[18] Col. Cradock's Mission, in *F.O. Turkey*, 182. There is an account in *E.H.R.* xv, 277, by A. Stern.

armistice and the Turks refused it, the Greeks are at liberty to commit hostilities, but we are not at liberty to allow hostile collisions".[19]

Here were sophistries enough to bemuse even a diplomatist, and the temper of the fleet was impatient of such subtleties. On September 19th Codrington served a notice on Ibrahim, inviting him to return under convoy to Egypt: no answer was given, but on the 21st the Egyptian fleet put out to sea, probably for Hydra. Codrington determined to oppose it alone, although his flagship *Asia* was badly manned and his tackle was poor: but at this moment the French admiral appeared, and the two commanders now sent a joint letter to Ibrahim pointing out the consequences of resistance. "Our orders are such that we will go to any extremities rather than abandon the object....If then a single cannon-shot were fired against our flags, it would be fatal to the Ottoman fleets." A warning was also sent to the Austrian transports in the harbour that they could not be treated otherwise than as Turkish vessels. In face of the two squadrons, the Ottoman ships all returned to the harbour by the evening of the 24th. The French admiral had a separate interview with Ibrahim, and professed to be convinced of his good faith; but it was harder to count on the Turkish admiral, who was disposed to resist, and suspected Ibrahim's loyalty.

On the 25th there was a conference between all the four commanders; three accounts exist, by Codrington, de Rigny and Ibrahim, but no written agreement was signed. Ibrahim promised to remain in the harbour, and to suspend operations on land until a courier should bring orders from Constantinople within twenty days. Ibrahim says that he only promised not to attack Hydra, and that he was given permission to provision Patras, but the other accounts deny this: the explanation is perhaps to be found in de Rigny's version—"I will not enter into a detail of the objections and arguments he put forward, when, after his promise had been given, the conference *ceased to be*

[19] Codrington to Sir F. Adam, 16 Sept., in *Life of Codrington*, I, 470. Sir F. Adam to him, *ibid.* I, 464. S. Canning to Dudley, 16 Sept., in *S.C. Papers*, 18, first part quoted in Lane-Poole, I, 448.

official". Ibrahim's long expostulations are described in a letter sent home by Codrington's young midshipman son, who was also present. Ibrahim may have lied or he may have misunderstood; but it is hard to believe that Codrington, after his expressed intention to the contrary, should have given leave for the supplies to a Turkish fortress. In return Codrington promised to prevent Cochrane from raising a commotion in Albania.[20]

Next day a dragoman came from Ibrahim, asking leave to stop Cochrane from entering the Gulf of Patras, but Codrington answered that the gulf was not, like Albania, beyond the existing theatre of war. "Within it, the Greeks having accepted our mediation, I had no authority for interfering with their operations."[21] This was again a very doubtful interpretation of his instructions, but no interpretation of them was convincing. It was really the Philhellene volunteer, Captain Hastings, who had entered the gulf, and on September 29th he sank nine Turkish ships in the Bay of Salona. Hastings was an ex-officer of the Royal Navy, who now commanded the steamboat *Karteria*, and had trained there the only disciplined and effective gunners in the Greek service.[22] Codrington had, after the conference on the 25th, sent the *Philomel* with a letter for Cochrane, warning him not to attack Albania; but the letter was delivered to Hastings instead, and not until October 6th, a week after the action in Salona Bay.

Ibrahim, when he heard of this exploit, was naturally furious, and set out in company with the Turkish fleet in order, as he said, to provision Patras. The allied squadrons had departed, leaving

[20] Accounts of the interview by Codrington and de Rigny in *Parl. Papers*, 1830, XXXII. Ibrahim's version, as related to Capt. Pujol nine days after the battle, in Wellington's *Despatches*, IV, 141. Cf. Prokesch v. Osten, *Aus dem Nachlasse*, under date 9 Apr. 1828. Letter from Codrington's son, in *Life of Codrington*, II, 14.

[21] Answer to Question 7 of F.O. inquiry, in *Life of Codrington*, II, 126ff.

[22] See the account of an eyewitness in D. Urquhart's *Spirit of the East*, I, 22–31. The *Karteria* had appeared in Greek waters in the autumn of 1826 and caused great astonishment. She was, probably, the first steam vessel used in warfare, sailing whenever possible, but using her engines in action so as to outmanœuvre the enemy. Capt. Hastings invented the use of hot shot heated in the fires, carried up on deck and rammed down the muzzle of the gun—a slow and perilous proceeding. See his *Memoir on the use of shells, hot shot, etc.* (1828).

guard-ships to watch the bay. Codrington, coming out from Zante, met the Turks on October 2nd, and turned them back. Two days later they again set sail, and owing to stormy weather passed unmolested to the mouth of the gulf, where they anchored under Cape Papas. But on the 6th, Codrington reappeared and warned them to return: he fired several shots across their bows, and towed away one boat which was carrying provisions ashore. When the wind allowed, they began to return; on the 10th the Russian fleet was at last sighted and they all, blockaders and blockaded, proceeded back to Navarin. The time agreed upon for Ibrahim to get his orders from Constantinople expired on the 15th. Prokesch v. Osten, on behalf of Austria, advised him to follow the orders of the Porte whatever they should be, and gave as his opinion that the admirals had no authority to fire.[23]

But there was now little doubt about the issue. In spite of Ibrahim's promise, his captains went on ravaging the country, especially round Patras and Vostitza. The Egyptian fleet had brought 5000 more men and 400 cavalry; after destroying the currant crops, they burnt and cut down the olives, enslaving any Greeks who fell into their hands. The admirals' report of Ibrahim's conduct has been sometimes represented as a mere pretext for the battle, unsupported by real proof. It is true that the British consul at Patras, writing in September, said that Ibrahim had not struck a single blow for eighteen months: that "several Capitani have submitted and received pardon,...districts as far as Kalavryta have returned to their former allegiance": and Greeks were cultivating their vineyards at Vostitza with Egyptian soldiers quartered upon them. But it seems that Ibrahim, exasperated by the appearance of the fleets, began a new system; Prokesch v. Osten, an unimpeachable witness, declares that he was acting on express orders from Constantinople. On October 17th it was reported that Ibrahim, after the arrival of a courier from Constantinople, had led a column in person towards Messenia: his proclamation to the Messenians was intercepted and sent to the admirals by Kolokotrones. A letter sent into the bay by the admirals was not delivered to Ibrahim; and a frigate, which

[23] *Aus dem Nachlasse*, 3 and 9 Oct. 1827.

sailed down the coast to inspect, returned next day having "observed by the clouds of fire and smoke that the work of destruction was still going on". The officers had landed and distributed bread among some of the starving people.[24]

Codrington made no secret of his intention to fight; he wrote to Wellesley in Vienna: "There His Highness' fleet will terminate its hostile career". The Russian Admiral Heyden was "ready, perhaps too ready, to go all lengths"; he told Codrington that in his opinion the Emperor had already declared war.[25] Only de Rigny was less keen, for France was already cultivating the friendship of Mehemet Ali. It was indeed a curious situation. Inside the bay, the Turkish and Egyptian fleets, mutually suspicious, together with many French officers and a number of Austrian transports. Outside, the three allied squadrons, also a little suspicious in such unwonted co-operation: the coasts infested with Greek pirate boats, so that the admirals could not even promise safety to Ibrahim's courier: and, cruising not far off, the famous Lord Cochrane, commander-in-chief of the Greek navy, deliverer of Chile and once an admiral of the British fleet against the French.

The admirals held a conference on the 18th and laid down three possible courses. First, to maintain the blockade; but this would be expensive and difficult in winter: secondly, to anchor in Navarin and remain there; but such a situation could not last long in a confined space: or thirdly to "proceed to take a position with the squadrons in Navarin in order to renew to Ibrahim propositions which entering into the spirit of the treaty were evidently to the advantage of the Porte itself". Codrington afterwards explained that these propositions were simply that the Egyptian fleet should return home, but they were never actually made before entering the harbour, because Ibrahim was nowhere to be found, and no sooner were the squadrons inside than the battle began.

[24] Church's *Narrative*. P. J. Green, *Sketches of the War*, Sept. 1827. Prokesch v. Osten, *Aus dem Nachlasse*, 26 Oct. Kolokotrones, p. 270.

[25] Codrington to Wellesley, 11 Oct., in *Life of Codrington*, II, 45; 17 Oct., *ibid.* II, 56; to S. Canning, 16 Oct., in *S.C. Papers*, 19.

Codrington seems to have originated this plan of sailing into the harbour: Heyden at once agreed, and de Rigny acquiesced without much trouble; the British admiral, who was the senior, took command and allotted positions. On the day before the battle he wrote in ambiguous oracles to his wife: "Well, this day has gone by with all preparation and no fight...we must now take the chance of what to-morrow produces. My own squadron will think it a pity if it all ends in smoke. Such, however, is my own expectation". The allied fleets were inferior in actual numbers but had far more guns than the Turks. It was common prudence to enter the harbour absolutely prepared, but there is little doubt that the admirals meant to fight on the smallest pretext. The 'Order of Battle', issued on the 19th, contained this sentence: "If time allows, the allied squadrons will, before the Turkish fleet takes any hostile action, cast anchor with spring cables. No shot must be fired before a given signal, so that it may be the Turks who open fire".[26]

Codrington's account of the way in which the battle began next day (October 20th) is confirmed by, perhaps taken from, the log of the *Dartmouth*, the vessel which was chiefly concerned. At 12.30 her captain answered the signal to prepare for battle, at 1 o'clock the signal to close. At 1.23 a Turkish boat came alongside the *Asia* as she entered the narrow mouth of the bay, in order to ask (as Codrington reported) that the fleets should not come in. Meeting with a refusal, the Turkish officer went ashore to a tent on the hill, where a gun was fired and a red flag hoisted. The fleets entered and anchored without firing a shot. A fireship was lying near the mouth of the harbour, and men were seen actively at work on board. *Dartmouth* was ordered to remove it, and a boat was manned to carry out the order; as they rowed up, bearing a flag of truce, they were fired upon and several men were killed. *Dartmouth* returned the fire with musketry, and the French flagship joined in. This French ship was in turn greeted with cannon-

[26] Schiemann, II, 202. This 'Order of Battle' is not quoted in the English *Parl. Papers* or in the *Life of Codrington*, from which our narratives come. The best short account of the battle itself is in Clowes, *The Royal Navy*, VI, 251–62. There is a painting of the battle reproduced in the frontispiece, and at p. 192 a view of the flagship *Asia*.

shot from the nearest Egyptian, and thereupon, "the action became general". This is not the place to follow the battle, if it can be called a battle, to its conclusion: before nightfall the Ottoman fleets were destroyed.

III

October—December 1827

Rumours of the battle reached Stratford at Constantinople on October 29th;[27] the Reis-Effendi, asked whether he would consider a collision as establishing a state of war, answered enigmatically: "When a woman is with child, which of you can tell whether she will bring forth a boy or a girl?" The official news came on November 1st, both to the Turks and to the ambassadors in the form of the admirals' reports, and was followed a week later by news of an attack on Chios by the French Philhellene Fabvier, supported by Lord Cochrane. The Sultan would have declared war at once if he had dared, but order was preserved in Constantinople and none of the Christians were molested. The Turks at first refused to see the allied ambassadors and demanded, through the Austrian Internuncio, that the Powers should drop the Greek question altogether, acknowledge Navarin as an unfortunate mistake, and pay compensation for the loss of the fleet.[28] They laid an embargo on all shipping in the Straits. But they knew the risk of a war with half Europe and, as the Reis-Effendi told the ambassadors privately, were ready to do anything short of openly accepting mediation or a public recognition of the Greeks: they would order an armistice, so long as it was not publicly declared; they would remit all the arrears of the Greek *rayahs'* capitation tax and even an extra year into the bargain, but—"the meanest Mussulman would prefer death to the ignominy of a connection with the Greeks". After this

[27] From a Capt. Cotton, who wrote from Smyrna on the 23rd, that he had fallen in with a Greek captain who was on board the *Asia* on the 19th, and found "everyone at his post", and on the next day heard "long continued firing and numerous explosions" from the direction of Navarin—*F.O. Turkey*, 157.

[28] Porte to Ottenfels, 9 Nov., in P. O. v, 131.

there was nothing more to be said: the ambassadors refused to admit, by writing for new instructions, any doubt as to the enforcement of the treaty, and prepared to depart. On the last day of November the Turks repudiated the Convention of Akkermann signed a year before; in a Grand Council at which the Sultan, all the Ulemas and nearly five hundred officials were present, foreign intervention was declared contrary to Mohammedan law. On December 8th the French and English ambassadors sailed for Corfu, and Ribeaupierre for Odessa a few days later.

To Metternich, celebrating his second marriage in the country, the news of the battle was a blow palliated only by a grim satisfaction in prophecy fulfilled. He called it a "frightful catastrophe"; the Emperor declared it to be an assassination: expressions beside which the "untoward event" of the King's Speech seems mild enough. Metternich hoped to seize the moment for a close alliance with Prussia against the three Powers, but opinion in Berlin swung right over to Russia, and Prince William was sent to reassure the Tsar. To meet the reproaches of public opinion for not sharing in the good work, the Prussian King was anxious to publish his instructions to Constantinople, and Bernstorff agreed, though he thought it a dangerous precedent.[29] In Paris all parties were pleased, especially the Liberals, who were helped at the elections by the feeling aroused, and forced the King to accept a more Liberal ministry. It is hardly necessary to say that St Petersburg was delighted; orders were given to Wittgenstein, in command of the southern armies, to be ready to forestall an Austrian occupation of Wallachia.[30]

Meanwhile the English ministers had been genuinely anxious to pursue Canning's policy, but they were regarded by everyone, themselves included, as a stopgap administration; they had not enough skill or confidence for skating securely on such thin ice. Lord Dudley, the most indolent and eccentric of foreign ministers, was soon confronted with the paradox of the situation; when

[29] Metternich to Werner, 16, 27 Nov.; Bernstorff to Maltzahn, 2 Dec., in Ringhoffer, pp. 85–100.

[30] Schiemann, II, 210. The correspondence of Gentz with the hospodar of Wallachia had just fallen into the Tsar's hands, and the *Dépêches inédites* end abruptly.

Russia called another conference on September 10th, to propose as 'ulterior measures' a blockade of the Dardanelles and Bosphorus, so as to isolate Constantinople, the French envoy was ready to agree in case the Turks should refuse mediation, but Dudley was non-committal: "the measure implies war and cannot be adopted unless we are disposed altogether to throw away the scabbard".[31] But inaction could not prevent the Russians from making war if they chose; a blockade of the Dardanelles was a measure in which the British fleet could take part, and so perhaps keep a controlling voice. The Turks would never listen to threats, but they were always ready to acknowledge the argument of force. Once a Greek settlement was forced upon them, the British fleet would be there to prevent a Russian war of aggression. It was admittedly a difficult game. But the one certain way of bringing on a Russo-Turkish war was to leave the question unsettled: yet this was what the ministers did. Russia was soon proposing a much more dangerous 'sanction', the occupation of the Principalities. Dudley took refuge in an appeal to the delusive help of Austria: Metternich, by persuading the Porte to yield to the allies, could give "les moyens de nous arrêter avec honneur". Metternich interpreted this conversation as an appeal for *Austrian* mediation, and persuaded the Vizir to ask for it in a letter repudiating the *allied* mediation, which was passed on to England.[32] Dudley pointed out that he had never gone so far behind the backs of his allies, but he was inclined at first to pursue the opening if Austria would disclaim a formal mediation. The Vizir's letter soon undeceived him, and led him to speak of the "sinister policy of Austria" in fomenting the resistance of the Turks.[33] Lieven was disgusted at this and

[31] To Granville, 20 Sept., in *F.O. France*, 362.

[32] Esterhazy to Metternich, 18 Sept., in *Austrian Extracts*. Metternich to Ottenfels, 3 Oct.; Vizir to Metternich, 24 Oct., in P. O. v, 118 ff.

[33] Dudley to Granville, 15, 20, 27 Nov., in *F.O. France*, 362. Austrian opposition to the treaty had taken refuge in a vigorous press campaign carried on at Smyrna in the *Spectateur Oriental*, which was suppressed more than once, but reappeared in Jan. 1828 as the *Courier de Smyrne*, and was for long a thorn in the side of Capodistrias. It was disliked by the Turkish authorities because it urged voluntary concessions to avoid worse evils, and by the Greeks because it exposed their helplessness and faction; cf.

at the delay in sending further instructions to the admirals. At a conference on October 2nd, Dudley had proposed a blockade limited to ships sailing under the Turkish flag: draft instructions were ready on the 6th, but they were delayed by the English ministers until the 16th, and finally contained no decision about the blockade, nor any indication of a way out before the winter. The controversy was cut short by the news of the battle, which reached England on November 13th. The Duke of Clarence at the Admiralty at once recommended Codrington for a G.C.B., which was given without consulting the ministers.[34] Dudley was puzzled and alarmed. Lord Grey, though a friend of Greek independence, thought the whole proceeding unwarrantable and likely to bring reprisals, but he and other critics all exculpated the admiral. Even the rejoicing of the Liberal press was cautious, and the Conservative papers were soon lashed to indignation at this attack on a friendly power in time of peace. Reports from Russia described the Russian army as prepared to enter the Principalities at a moment's notice. Just as in the autumn of 1825, the Tsar travelled southward and war was expected. All the English ministers were agreed on the necessity either of advancing or else of retreating, but they could not agree

Michaud, *Correspondance d'Orient*, I, 217. The *Courier* was edited by a French merchant, Blacque, under the direction of Prokesch v. Osten who took care not to be compromised—*Aus dem Nachlasse*, 1827–8 *passim*. Gentz wrote to P.O.: "The freedom of the press which brings such evil upon Europe may serve as your protecting aegis if you have need of it on the coast of Asia for the cause of truth and right"—*ibid.* 18 Nov. 1828. Capt. Hamilton believed Blacque to be an agent of the French admiral, and directed by their consul at Smyrna—to S. Canning, 7, 19 Apr. 1827, in *B.M.*, *Add. MSS.* 36566. M. Blacque may have been receiving subsidies from both parties. He was afterwards editor of the *Moniteur Ottoman*, and one of the props of the anti-Russian propaganda carried on by Lord Ponsonby and David Urquhart. See the latter's *Reminiscences of William IV* (1891), containing private correspondence of Ponsonby with Urquhart 1834–6. Also *Opinions of the European Press on the Eastern Question* (1836), edited by David Ross of Bladensburg.

[34] On his recall the following year, see below, p. 115. Later Codrington petitioned for the "usual head-money" for distribution to his crews, quoting the £100,000 paid to Lord Exmouth after the attack on Algiers in 1816; but his application was refused—Wellington's *Despatches*, v, 613. Codrington estimated the enemy losses at Navarin at 6000 men, a third of the whole naval force.

on a policy. The news from Constantinople made it clear that the ambassadors would soon be gone. At one moment Dudley seemed ready for vigorous action. "This conduct on the part of the Porte if unaccompanied by any explanations may not improbably turn out to be the prelude to actual hostilities"; the allies must agree on the speediest means of attaining the object of the treaty: "among those means are—pecuniary aid to the Greeks, a blockade of the Dardanelles, and ultimately invasion of the Turkish dominions by the Russian army". He did not seem to see the possibility of forestalling the last by hastening the first expedients. After a Cabinet meeting on the same day he wrote that "the tenour of the last accounts from Constantinople makes it probable that the Allied Powers will soon be placed in a state of war with the Ottoman Empire".[35] The following days were spent in an effort to bind Russia in advance against a war of conquest. Lieven made difficulties, but on December 12th signed a protocol disclaiming all interested views and confining the allied action to the Treaty of London.[36] Nesselrode had already written (December 5th) advising this course; he was no doubt sincerely anxious to avoid a war of conquest, but the war party surrounding the Emperor was hard to contain, and the English ministers by their delay were playing into the hands of this party. Esterhazy thus described the Cabinet divisions: Huskisson, Lansdowne and Tierney in the front rank for pushing on, then Dudley, Goderich and the Chancellor, with the rest reluctant or rebellious.[37] On December 14th Goderich offered to resign, but soon returned unwillingly at the King's bidding.

Princess Lieven awaited the issue of the crisis with some confidence; as a Russian she judged rightly that "Mr Huskisson is the strong and important feature of the Cabinet", and hoped that Lord Holland would obtain office. The best comment on this is to be found in letters to Wellington that Huskisson was ready to follow Russia to war, and that there was a movement to include in the administration Brougham and Lord Holland—

[35] Dudley to Granville, 7 Dec., in *F.O. France*, 362.
[36] F. de Martens, XI, 361; cf. numerous drafts, 8–12 Dec., in *F.O.* 97/233.
[37] Esterhazy to Metternich, 15 Dec., in *Austrian Extracts*.

which meant war. Princess Lieven may have been carried too far by her hopes, and the Duke's friends by mistrust of political opponents, but there was some colour for their expectations.[38] Such was the position at the end of the year.

The battle itself brought no immediate relief to Greece. The only positive result was to make it impossible for the diplomatists to go back; but it did not prevent them from standing still and protesting. Given the policy of the treaty, it was not the battle but the inaction following it which made the Russo-Turkish war inevitable. The opponents of the treaty afterwards pointed to the fact that Russia had tried before to cross the Balkans, but never succeeded until the Turkish fleet had been destroyed. Those, on the other hand, who were willing to see Constantinople fall at all costs, forgot that movements for independence must come from within, if the people are not to exchange one conqueror for another. If England had joined Russia after Navarin in war against Turkey for undefined objects, it is likely that Constantinople would have fallen and a partition would have followed in which Austria would have claimed a share. But in fact no one in England advocated such an adventure. If the Treaty of London was a crusade, it was a mistake: as a crusade it was attacked by its opponents. It is possibly true that the Powers could have pacified the East more speedily by abandoning the Greeks altogether, as Metternich wished; it was not the forces on the spot, but European opinion which prevented that. But the chief author of the treaty did not look on it as a crusade; he justified it on other grounds as a practical necessity, and if he had lived he might have justified it more completely. His course of action was never laid down in advance; but it is hard to see what course remained open, except to create a Greek State as soon as possible, and, if Russia still threatened war, in the last resort to force the Dardanelles and use the British fleet both to coerce Turkey and to protect her. It would have been a risky policy, for Russia might have accepted the challenge, and England was not yet convinced that a war with Russia was one day inevitable.

38 Princess Lieven's *Letters*, 20 Oct. 1827. Hon. F. Lamb to Wellington, 14 Dec., and Bathurst to Wellington, 19 Dec., in *Despatches*, IV, 168–9.

CHAPTER VII

THE DUKE'S DILEMMA

I

January—May 1828

A WEAK administration like that of Goderich and Dudley had no alternative but inaction and reliance on that prophecy of Joseph Planta—"The Turks will hold the Russians a long Tug before the latter get to Constantinople". But the beginning of 1828 brought the Duke of Wellington upon the stage. Here at least was a man who could not be accused of weakness, and might be expected to call a halt in the interval before the Russian campaign could begin in the spring; but he too was forced to stand aside and watch events. The Duke might be a novice in domestic policy, but in Europe he had a great reputation not merely as a soldier but as a statesman. Like Canning he was no doctrinaire but an opportunist. Both men based their policy on English interests, but differed in their conception of those interests and in their method of upholding them. The one, supple, genial and sarcastic: the other, courteous and rather impulsive, but often suspicious and abrupt. The Duke was unable like Canning to clothe his opportunism in a phrase, to strike the imagination and bring a glow of excitement into the conduct of business. He relied, not upon far-reaching combinations backed by timely appeals to public opinion at home, but upon the assurances of a few public men in Europe whom he knew personally and understood—and, for the rest, upon threats and complaints. It was tempting to admire his terse outright expressions of opinion, to believe that a frank and honourable soldier was bringing a draught of fresh air into the stuffy corridors of diplomacy. But in reality the best ventilated Palace of Truth is not always a Palace of Peace; tactful people avoid causing unnecessary draughts. The Eastern difficulty above all needed handling with both caution and good-humour; and in dealing with other nations the Duke was suspicious, irritable and uncompromising. A passage from *Coningsby* is no bad introduction to the following chapters:

> The Duke of Wellington has ever been the votary of circumstances. He cares little for causes. He watches events rather than seeks to produce them. It is a characteristic of the military mind. Rapid combinations, the result of a quick, vigilant, and comprehensive glance, are generally triumphant in the field: but in civil affairs, where results are not immediate; in diplomacy and in the management of deliberative assemblies, where there is much intervening time and many counteracting causes, this velocity of decision, this fitful and precipitate action, are often productive of considerable embarrassment, and sometimes of terrible discomfiture. It is remarkable that men celebrated for military prudence are often found to be headstrong statesmen.[1]

On taking office, the Duke agreed reluctantly to keep Dudley at the Foreign Office, on Dudley's condition that they should abide by the treaty although "interpretation might differ". These words were ominous; the Duke could hardly keep his pledge with a good grace, and he treated Dudley from the first as a cipher. His situation was admittedly difficult, for he disapproved of the treaty; yet he had signed the protocol of 1826, and with Liverpool and Canning had shared uneasily the secret of the negotiations for the treaty.

His policy now of continual delay and resistance was the worst that he could have chosen. Instead of deciding at once to retreat upon ground where he could stand firm, with a mere skirmish perhaps at the intervening positions, he was driven back step by step, announcing at each stage his irrevocable determination to yield no more, and then with growing irritation finding his position forced or turned. In other words, he refused to concede at once such a settlement for Greece as might satisfy Russia, and to join with her in forcing it upon the Porte: with the result

[1] *Coningsby*, I, c. 7. For Wellington's administration, besides his own *Despatches*, Ellenborough's *Political Diary, 1828–1830*, is illuminating, especially on Eastern affairs, in which Ellenborough, as President of the Board of Control, had a lively if not always judicious interest.

that in the end Russia alone dictated the settlement at the Peace of Adrianople, leaving the Greeks to feel that she was their real protector and Great Britain a false friend. The steps which led to this result must now be traced.

On January 29th Parliament met. The famous sentence in the King's Speech must be quoted once more:

...a collision, wholly unexpected by H.M., took place....Notwithstanding the valour...of the fleet....H.M. laments that this conflict should have occurred with the naval force of an ancient ally: but he still entertains a confident hope that this untoward event will not be followed by further hostilities.

In the House of Lords, Lord Holland was almost alone in decided approval of the battle: he criticised the expressions 'ancient ally' and 'untoward event', which Wellington in turn defended; the first could be justified by precedent, and the second was explained as meaning merely 'unfortunate'. The words were in fact intended less for the ears of Parliament than to soothe the warlike feelings of the Sultan. In the Commons there was stronger language: Lord John Russell spoke of Navarin as "a glorious victory and as honest a victory as was ever won", and Brougham "rejoiced in the event". Morpeth thought *untoward* "an injurious and shabby epithet". On both sides almost all the speakers took care to exculpate Codrington personally; Lord Lansdowne remarked that "it was childish to expect armed interference without some risk of war". The ministers themselves were non-committal on this point, and they gave little indication of their future policy except a general assurance that the treaty would be carried out faithfully.[2]

Their minds must have been troubled by the decision which would be necessary on the despatch from Nesselrode handed to them by Lieven the previous day. The measures which it proposed were an occupation of the Principalities in the name of the allies, to be restored at the peace: a blockade of the Greek coast to intercept supplies: and a blockade of the Bosphorus and Dardanelles, or better still, since the three Powers would be at war

[2] Hansard (3rd ser.), XVIII, 9ff. Wellington might have quoted some expressions used by Canning himself, p. 36, above.

with the Porte, "to penetrate even to Constantinople, there to dictate peace under the walls of the Seraglio". Late as it was, the ministers might well have consented at least to the first two measures, and to the proposals for a settlement of Greece: that the allies should reply to the Vizir, requiring the immediate evacuation of Greece and free navigation of the Bosphorus for trade: that the ambassadors from Constantinople should meet in the Aegean and make a settlement in two months, that consuls should be sent to Greece and that measures should be taken meanwhile to remove Ibrahim. Russia offered to guarantee a third share of the loan of £2,000,000 proposed by Capodistrias. This despatch contained in its original form a long *résumé* intended to prove that England had taken the initiative in all the events leading up to Navarin, but Lieven was persuaded to omit this from the official version shown to the London Conference. He also discreetly kept back the fact that the Emperor intended to annex the Black Sea ports, Anapa and Poti, which would have been a new offence to the ministers, already alarmed by the Russian conquests in Persia and by the delay in concluding peace.[3]

In the East, war was generally expected. The British consuls struck their flags, on Stratford's advice, except in Egypt and Albania and at Bucarest. Although British shipping was not detained, there were forced sales of some British and Russian cargoes. While the Russian armies were assembling for the campaign, the Conference was silent for some weeks. The new ministry in France, which had won the election partly on the news of Navarin, accepted the Russian proposals at once. La Ferronays wrote to Wellington that energetic action in pursuance of the treaty was the safest policy. But Wellington counselled delay; when the Government was pressed for papers in Parliament, he said that he would not now go into the difference between his protocol and the treaty, but the treaty would

[3] Nesselrode to Lieven, 6 Jan. 1828, in *Parl. Papers*, 1830, XXXII, 199. *Résumé* in Wellington's *Despatches*, IV, 230–50. Peace with Persia was arranged in Nov. 1827, but not signed until 22 Feb. 1828, at Tourcmantchai: printed in *S.P.* 15, 669. The Russian boundary was advanced to the Araxes.

be executed loyally.[4] He at once rejected the French proposal for an expedition to the Morea, now first officially put forward, though there had been talk of it in the previous autumn.[5] Charles X's speech from the throne (February 5th) referred to Navarin in terms very different from those put into the mouth of George IV.

Meanwhile (February 23rd) Lieven produced the Sultan's proclamation of the end of December, which was used as the *casus belli*. Although it was not intended for foreign eyes, being in the form of a circular to local governors (*ayans*), it contained the remarkable admission that the Convention of Akkermann was signed only in order to gain time, and foretold a holy war for the existence of Islam: "Remember that the Infidels once possessed the whole Earth, yet since the time when the All-Powerful revealed the law of our Great Prophet, our brothers... have slain in many wars hundreds of thousands of Infidels and conquered so many countries".[6] Dudley replied truly enough that it was not a formal declaration of war: allowance must be made for the natural suspicions of the Turks excited by the armies assembling on their frontiers: "We can afford not to stand on a point of honour with a feeble power like the Porte". At the same time he answered coldly, after two months' delay, Nesselrode's note of January 6th. The British Government could not admit measures of general war by land and sea. Action should be definite and limited: isolation of the Morea only, for the limits proposed by the ambassadors in September 1827 were not unanimously agreed; a blockade by sea, the Greeks to co-operate on land; and an invitation to other Powers to join in the demand.[7] But it was hopeless to expect that the Greeks could deal with Ibrahim alone, and Navarin had done nothing to improve the position.

[4] S. Canning to Dudley, 10 Feb., in *F.O. Turkey*, 165. La Ferronays, 21 Feb., and reply 26 Feb., in Wellington's *Despatches*, IV, 270, 274. Hansard, XVIII, 260, 11 Feb.

[5] Palmerston says that in Nov. 1827 he himself proposed to Goderich a joint expedition—Bulwer's *Palmerston*, I, 250.

[6] Turkish proclamation, 20 Dec. 1827, in *S.P.* 14, 1052.

[7] Dudley to Disbrowe, 7 Mar., in *F.O. Russia*, 171. Dudley to Lieven, 6 Mar., in *Parl. Papers*, 1830, XXXII. F. de Martens, XV, 60.

At a Cabinet meeting[8] on March 9th Wellington proposed that the Porte should name a ruler for the Morea and Islands, which were to pay a tribute of £200,000 and compensation of £1,500,000, sums which would cripple an infant State ravaged by war and reduced in population. The Conference at Poros afterwards recommended a maximum tribute of about £60,000, to be reached by gradual stages. The compensation eventually paid was less than half a million sterling, although the boundaries were enlarged. Palmerston strongly objected to the proposed boundaries; he was supported by Grant, and by Dudley whose despatch three days before must have been dictated by Wellington. Peel himself would have preferred independence to a suzerainty which would only be an excuse for Russian interference;[9] Wellington was ill-pleased to find Peel a partisan of Greek independence, which Bathurst had described as "a very popular cause among a large description of well-meaning persons as well as with all democrats". He refused to see that policy if not principle must lead to independence.

In face of these divided opinions, it was decided that Dudley should merely sound Lieven and Polignac about the limited boundary; accordingly, at the Conference which met on March 12th, instructions were drawn up for the admirals to continue blockading the coast from the Gulf of Volo to the mouth of the Aspropotamos, with the proviso that the limits were not definitely settled. After this decision Lieven produced a new note from Nesselrode dated February 26th, which had already reached him on March 9th. In this note the complaints of Russia against the Porte were set forth, and her intention to declare war announced. The Emperor would not make peace without freedom for commerce, protection for the *rayahs* and an indemnity for the loss and expenses of the war (an indemnity which could hardly be paid except in territory). His right to make war was based on grounds independent of the Treaty of London, but in any case

[8] This and following accounts of Cabinet meetings are taken from Palmerston's Journal in Bulwer's *Palmerston*, I, 229–52, and from Ellenborough's *Political Diary*.

[9] The same argument is elaborated in the conservative *Quarterly*, July 1828 (XXXVIII, 190).

he appealed to that unfortunate phrase in Wellington's Protocol "soit en commun soit *séparément*" (in a sense in which Wellington certainly had not suspected that it would be used).[10] As to Greece, if his allies would consent to the Russian proposals of January, the Emperor would still abide by them; if not he would execute the treaty consulting only "ses intérêts et convenances".

The effect of this ultimatum was that the instructions to the admirals were not sent; the Conference was suspended without deciding anything, and was not resumed until June. The Duke and Ellenborough would have liked to take this opportunity of withdrawing from the treaty, or at least of declaring Russia to be excluded from it, but they found little support in the Cabinet. Palmerston and Huskisson were both inclined to act with Russia in spite of war.[11] On March 25th Dudley replied to the last Russian note, deploring the Tsar's resolve but not contesting his right to declare war, and announcing that combined operations of the fleets would no longer be possible. The protest was bound to be ineffectual, but nothing was done to hasten a settlement of Greece. There were two rival plans in the field. Metternich, seeing that something must be done, proposed, in a circular of March 15th, to "invite the Porte to recognise the autonomy of the Morea and Islands only", and on refusal "to recognise their entire independence" and act accordingly with the fleets and if necessary an army. It might be done without war with Turkey, which would thus at least know the limits of what it had to fear; but if not, things could not in any case be worse. This, unlike the proposal made by Metternich in 1825, was seriously put forward as his counsel of despair. Since the triple alliance was not to be dissolved, England had better act quickly. But Wellington would not hear of Greek independence, not so much from an abstract attachment to the principle of legitimacy as from a dislike of anything which would encourage the English and Continental Liberals. The Tsar, as in 1825, professed great indignation at Metternich's proposal: "I detest, I abhor the Greeks, I consider them as revolted subjects and I do not desire their

[10] See above, pp. 61, 73–4.
[11] Ellenborough's *Diary*, 4 Apr., 11 May.

independence; Austria has abandoned her principles. My grievance is against the Turks' conduct to Russia". In fact the Russian Declaration of War was grounded on reasons independent of the Treaty of London, which had been signed only in order "to put an end to a contest which was no longer compatible with the security of the seas, the necessities of commerce, and the civilisation of the rest of Europe". The Turks replied in an equally long and reasoned Declaration, reviewing the encroachments of Russia since 1812. Metternich's only success lay in persuading Solomon Rothschild not to take part in a large loan to Russia, but as the money was found elsewhere the financier lost more than the Chancellor gained.[12]

The French meanwhile insisted on their plan of sending troops to the Morea, and pressed for wider limits. In answer to a note from Dudley, La Ferronays pointed out that the limits suggested by the ambassadors in September 1827 "were notorious in the Archipelago", and added the plea of sentiment that there would be "a cry of grief and indignation" if Athens were left out. An armistice must be enforced before deciding upon the tribute and upon the nature of the government. The French counter-proposals were similar to those of Russia—for a joint loan, consular agents and a conference in the Aegean; and finally a joint expedition of 12,000 men.[13] The French Government could not in fact turn back, even if it had desired to do so; but once the treaty was signed, Charles X was as enthusiastic as the rest of the country in the Greek adventure. La Ferronays, the new foreign minister, had been ambassador at St Petersburg and was a strong supporter of the alliance with Russia. Dudley, again at Wellington's dictation, declined to discuss this note, and, in order to justify the refusal to send troops, said that Capodistrias had threatened to resign if a single foreign soldier landed. It may

[12] Report of Esterhazy, 28 Mar., in P. O. v, 186. Gentz to Prokesch v. Osten, 19 Apr., in *Aus dem Nachlasse*. Tsar's interview with Zichy, 24 Apr., in P. O. v, 204. Russian manifesto, and Declaration of War, 26 Apr., in *S.P.* 15, 655, 658. Turkish Declaration, June 1828, *ibid.* 15, 914. Corti, *Rise of the House of Rothschild*, p. 404.

[13] Dudley to Polignac, 5 Apr., in P. O. v, 235. La Ferronays to Polignac, 28 Apr., 9 May, *ibid.* v, 237, 251. Cf. A. Sorel, *Essais d'histoire*, pp. 95 ff.

well be that the President, who disliked all foreigners in the country as a source of intrigue, was reluctant at first to resort to foreign troops. But there is no reason to believe that he ever made such a threat officially. At first he asked only for money and a strict blockade, but wrote at last in June to the French Government begging for an expeditionary force.[14]

At every point in the Greek affair Wellington found himself at odds with the Canningites in his Cabinet, and opposed by the whole weight of French and Russian influence, with even Metternich counselling retreat. Moreover the King, who had not forgiven Wellington for his conduct to Canning in 1827, lent some support to the Canningites. Princess Lieven thought him friendly to Russia, and later reported him as having said "King Arthur must go to the devil, or King George must go to Hanover". The Tsar took the same line in a conversation with Lord Heytesbury, and spoke with emphasis of "the King my friend", attributing "all he had hitherto considered unaccountable...to the difficulties of its [the ministry's] parliamentary position". The Russians naturally made the most of any indications; the King was no Russophil, but he objected to Wellington's stubborn tactics. That the Duke was able to resist so long was due to his overwhelming prestige in the country, giving him an absolute indifference to opposition, which would be heroic if it were not so unwise. He had nothing to fear from public opinion in the Greek question, because the public had lost interest in it, and he had that prestige at his back when it came to a deadlock in the Cabinet. Princess Lieven reported him as saying: "I am the most popular Minister that England has ever seen; take my word for it, I am very strong".[15]

There was much discussion over the degree of independence for Greece. Peel would have preferred it unqualified, but failing that, argued at least against making the new Greece follow its

[14] Prokesch v. Osten, 22 June, 19 Aug., 18 Sept., in *Aus dem Nachlasse.* Capodistrias, 15 May, in *Correspondance*, II, 87; and Church's *Narrative*, *B.M.*, *Add. MSS.* 36563.

[15] Lieven to Nesselrode, 28 Mar., in F. de Martens, XI, 373. Princess Lieven, *Letters*, 19 May, 22 Aug., 28 Nov. 1828. Heytesbury to Aberdeen, 11 Aug., in *F.O. Russia*, 173.

suzerain Turkey in questions of peace and war. At last Wellington, finding the sense against him, proposed leaving it open, and in Dudley's despatch of April 5th it was suggested that the Porte, instead of choosing a governor for Greece, should only have a power of veto on the President up to the first two choices.[16] All these questions could more properly have been left to the conference of ambassadors in the Aegean proposed by Russia in January: and when finally the conference was arranged, its instructions were necessarily of the vaguest.

Another dispute arose over the question of naval co-operation with the Russians. Wellington was opposed to combining the fleets, even if Russia would remain neutral in the Mediterranean; but, unlike Aberdeen, he was, by the beginning of May, ready to renew the Conference in London. Even this was some advance. La Ferronays wrote to Nesselrode: "Le duc de W. ne marche pas encore très vite, mais il commence à se mettre en mouvement, peut-être finirons-nous par lui faire prendre notre pas". On May 16th came a definite offer from Russia, but the wording was certainly open to suspicion, in view of what happened later. The old phrase from Wellington's protocol was, surely with intentional irony, brought up this time in support of combined operations: 'séparément' having done duty in one argument, 'en commun' was now cited for an opposite purpose. The offer made was that on receipt of fresh joint instructions, Admiral Heyden should suspend his belligerent rights and "not enforce them save in the case of an urgent necessity or of an attack on the part of the Turks". On May 18th Wellington was still opposed to co-operating.[17] The next day Princess Lieven wrote that the French expedition was still held up by him. He is said to have exclaimed that "if the French send a single soldier to the Morea, I shall declare war with France". A vote authorising a loan of 80,000,000 francs and calling up 60,000 men of the 1827 class had been passed in the French Chamber on May 13th. The preparations were

[16] Palmerston's Journal, 2, 4 Apr., and *Parl. Papers*, 1830, XXXII.

[17] Dudley to Lieven, 25 Mar., and Wellington's *Despatches*, IV, 315. La Ferronays, 1 May, in Nesselrode, *Lettres et Papiers*, VII, 10; and in the same vol., his letters, 28 May, 1 June; and Lieven to Nesselrode, 30 June, 15 July. Wellington's memoranda for Cabinet, 18 May, in *Despatches*, IV, 444.

certainly on a scale to excite alarm.[18] The differences in the British Cabinet could no longer be concealed. Then came the resignation of Huskisson over a trivial dispute, which was merely the occasion of a long-impending split. Even at the end of March Grant had been thinking of resignation, and the other Canningites were prepared to follow him. On May 22nd, in the middle of the crisis, Palmerston wrote: "The Cabinet has gone on for some time past as it had done before, differing upon almost every question—meeting to debate and dispute, and separating without deciding".[19]

II

June—July 1828

The resignation of all Canning's followers broke up the Tory party and left the Treaty of London almost without a supporter in the ministry. Wellington was now dictator, and he still made no secret of his disapproval; holding this opinion, he was certainly in a very embarrassing position. But for the moment, the change in the ministry seemed to clear the air, and strangely enough was soon followed by Wellington's yielding on every point which had been in dispute. It illustrates the vehement personal way in which he treated disagreement with his policy. He was accustomed to command, and discussion only made him angry and unyielding: once rid of the tiresome wrangling in the Cabinet, he began to face the facts; like a true military commander he made no difficulties about sudden changes of front.

The new Foreign Secretary, Lord Aberdeen, was a warm admirer, and during this ministry grew to be a personal friend of the Duke. Lord Dudley, who suffered from unbusinesslike habits, had been reluctant to continue in office, and Aberdeen describes himself as having been "coadjutor, jure successionis" even before Dudley's resignation. 'Athenian' Aberdeen had travelled in Greece fifteen years before, and had taken a keen interest in the struggle. At the very beginning, in 1821, when Castlereagh sent him the draft of a despatch to warn Russia

[18] Princess Lieven, *Letters*, 19 May, 30 June. Viel-Castel, XVII, 505 ff.
[19] Palmerston's Journal, 28 Mar., 22 May.

against going to war or in any way encouraging the Greeks, he replied:

The existence of the Greek insurrection would give an entirely new character to a Turkish war....The cause itself would be in a measure sanctified. It is quite impossible that we should expect the Greeks to enter into general views of preserving the tranquillity of Europe, or to participate in our dread of commotions and our love of peace, in the blessings of which they have no share whatever....Is it impossible to avert these consequences by taking part in a settlement which sooner or later will surely be effected, and which if effected without our aid can at best, if accomplished by the Greeks alone, earn us no goodwill and which if carried out by Russian arms may seriously imperil our most vital interests?

Castlereagh sarcastically answered that he was

much more ready to adopt a plan of Greek regeneration prepared by Lord Aberdeen than one framed by the mongrel minister [Capo d'Istria], but he did not think it prudent to occupy his time in Downing Street by taking with his own hands the initiative in such portentous experiments.[20]

Aberdeen began by attending a meeting in favour of the Greeks and subscribing to the cause, but as time went on and the cause came to be associated with that of the Liberals all over Europe, he shrank from shocking his friends further, and relapsed into silence. Now that he was involved in the 'portentous experiment', he seems to have forgotten his own wise counsel, or at least to have resigned his judgment to that of his leader. For almost every despatch of the following years there is a draft memorandum, preserved in Wellington's correspondence, and often embodied with just the necessary diplomatic wrappings from which his own peculiar telegraphic style was so refreshingly free. Ellenborough, disappointed in his hopes of the Foreign Office, occupied his leisure as Lord Privy Seal in criticising Aberdeen's diplomacy, and, succeeding to the Board of Control in September, found new reasons for fear and suspicion of Russia.

The first step in the Duke's retreat was taken at once (May 29th) with the invitation to Stratford Canning to return to the

[20] Lord Stanmore, *Aberdeen*, pp. 70–2.

Aegean. If Wellington was anxious to curtail the limits and the independence of Greece, the ambassador who had publicly recommended the wider limits in September 1827, who had advised Codrington to enforce the blockade if necessary by cannon-shot, who was a devoted admirer of his cousin's foreign policy, was the last man to carry out the Duke's views.[21] Moreover Stratford had urged an expedition to the Morea and he objected to Codrington's recall. On his way home he wrote from Ancona: "without efficient support and financial assistance Capodistrias will be utterly unable to realise the hopes of his countrymen". On his return to London, he reminded the ministers of the threat veiled in Dudley's own despatch to him of November 18th: Navarin was not to alter the position as to the Greek question, and "His Majesty will sincerely rejoice if by timely acquiescence the Porte should avert extremities never to be resorted to without regret". This despatch had reached him at Corfu after leaving Constantinople: he had embodied its substance in an instruction to the interpreter, dated January 2nd. In due course the Dutch ambassador (who was acting for England at Constantinople) reported that these threats might have had effect two months earlier, but since the Speech from the Throne and the debate in the Lords the Sultan's confidence was overweening.[22] It is true that Stratford was the obvious man for the post, and it would have been difficult to replace him. But even that could not have had worse consequences than to send him out with vague instructions and afterwards to repudiate the result of his labours; if the intentions of the ministry had been clearly put before him now, his resignation might have been offered and accepted, as it eventually was in March 1829. But by that time it was useless, for Wellington's policy had been condemned by the united recommendations of the ambassadors on the spot. If the continental limits for Greece were already 'notorious' in March 1828, by March 1829 they were taken for granted in spite of protocols.

[21] Gentz lamented over the appointment of Stratford—*Aus dem Nachlasse*, 18 July. Ellenborough wrote in his *Diary*, 1 Sept., that "S. Canning has the weakness of those who call themselves *Liberal* in favour of the Greeks".

[22] 10 Feb., 31 Mar., 31 May, in *F.O. Turkey*, 165.

On June 6th Aberdeen consented to renew the Conference in view of the Russian offer of neutrality; this was the offer which Wellington had refused to accept before the change in the ministry. The concession cannot have been due to the advice of Aberdeen, who had been opposed to renewing the Conference on any terms. It was part of the Duke's general retreat, for which he gave the order only after the staff which had recommended it had been dismissed. A conference was in fact held on June 15th, and a protocol was signed by which the Tsar "lays down in the Mediterranean his character of belligerent". The joint instructions to the admirals, suspended since the last conference on March 12th, were at length despatched. At the same time Wellington reluctantly agreed to send an ambassador to Russia, where there had been only a *chargé d'affaires* since the Duke's visit in 1826. Accordingly Lord Heytesbury (Sir William A'Court) was sent to the headquarters of the Russian army with instructions to work for peace, and to agree to a reasonable indemnity, but to annexations—never. Here again Metternich had led the way by sending an ambassador to the front, and Wellington had to follow suit. But Austria was not pleased with the choice of Heytesbury, who was supposed, without much justification, to be, like Stratford Canning, a Russophil and a Liberal; he was in fact an able diplomatist, but his relative politeness to the Tsar, and his lack of sympathy with Metternich, earned him an 'admonitory letter' from London and the loss of the Duke's confidence.[23]

On July 2nd the Conference met again, and drew up instructions for the ambassadors in the Aegean. Four different frontiers were suggested in descending order: Volo-Aspropotamos, Thermopylae-Parnassus, Attica, the Morea at least; but no decided preference was expressed. Euboea, it was suggested, should be excluded from the Greek Islands, being occupied mainly by Turks. In negotiating for the tribute, the indemnity and the method of choosing the governor, the Conference must take into account the financial distress of the country. It will be seen

[23] Instructions to Heytesbury, 13 June, in *F.O. Russia*, 172. Metternich to Gentz, 11 Sept., Dec. 1828, in *Briefe*, III², 328, 336. Ellenborough's *Diary*, index, *s.v.* Heytesbury, especially I, 210, 247; II, 78, 107.

that these instructions went a good deal further than Wellington had wished. In a supplementary instruction of July 4th his influence (and probably the inspiration of Metternich) may be traced in a suggestion that if the Turks prefer, but not otherwise, the ambassadors should consent to unqualified independence, "the Greeks being likely to prefer this, *even within contracted limits*".

Wellington still hoped by means of such bargaining to confine Greece to the Morea, and reconciled himself to the idea of independence, which, in March, Metternich had advised in vain. But even the Morea was not yet clear of Egyptian troops. The French had never ceased to press for their expedition, which was waiting at Toulon, ready to sail. Charles X told Pozzo, and later Granville, that it should go, with or without the English.[24] Wellington had apparently begun to give way; at the end of June Princess Lieven wrote as if his consent were assured. Although he had based his previous refusal on the President's supposed threat of resignation, his real objection lay in suspicion of French motives, soon to be revived by the outbursts of the French press and especially of Chateaubriand in the *Journal des Débats*, which was supposed to take its tone from the Government. He now justified his consent by Capodistrias' official request for troops, but the other reason which he gave must have carried much more weight in his mind—the fact that Metternich had written to urge his consent. The Protocol of July 19th, which authorised the French troops to land in the Morea, covered Wellington's retreat with a vague statement that "recent events had changed the state of things".[25] He hoped also that, with Ibrahim once removed, the Russians would have less excuse for going on with the war: already there was talk of a second campaign. Nicholas was said to be tired of the war: but could he resist his army and the war party among his advisers?

[24] F. de Martens, XV, 69.

[25] Princess Lieven, *Letters*, 30 June. Wellington's memorandum, 13 July; on French press, 18 Aug.—*Despatches*, IV, 526, 630. Protocol in *Parl. Papers*, 1830, XXXII, 241. On the French in the Morea, *Revue des Deux Mondes*, 1 May 1897. Some curious details in *Memoirs of Miles Byrne*, ed. S. Gwynn, Dublin, 1907. Gen. Pellion, who had been an officer in the French army of occupation, described its work in *La Grèce et les Capodistrias pendant l'occupation française de 1828 à 1834* (1855).

CHAPTER VIII

WAR AND DIPLOMACY

I

August—October 1828

IT soon appeared that, as the Tsar had not gone to war for Greece, he was not going to make peace because Greece was safe. At the end of June Lieven wrote to Nesselrode that, although the "extraordinary irritation" of the Duke was beginning to subside, it was "desirable that the Emperor's intentions for the necessary annexation of Anapa and Poti should have no official publicity" until the peace. Heytesbury's report of his first audience with the Tsar was no more encouraging.[1] Nicholas professed great moderation, but he would only make peace on his own terms. "The suspension of hostilities in the Mediterranean was only temporary, should the Turks still obstinately refuse to treat." This was a serious announcement, for the King's Speech had expressed satisfaction at the Russian neutrality at sea, and Wellington had consented to renew the Conferences only on those terms. Heytesbury's warning arrived on September 5th, followed by an official despatch from Nesselrode saying that the Sultan's blind obstinacy might compel Russia to blockade the Dardanelles and force him to peace by famine; on September 18th Admiral Heyden declared a state of blockade.

The Russians had in fact been seriously checked; they had expected to cross the Balkans in three or four weeks from the opening of the campaign, but plague and the unexpected resistance of the Turks before Varna already made success before the autumn very uncertain. Nicholas had entered lightly on the war, assured by his Court and his generals that the army was irresistible. It was difficult for a Tsar to learn the truth about

[1] Lieven to Nesselrode, 30 June, in Nesselrode's *Lettres et Papiers*, VII, 40. Heytesbury to Aberdeen, 11 Aug., in *F.O. Russia*, 173; quoted at some length in Lady F. Balfour's *Life of Aberdeen*, I, c. 6.

corrupt administration, surrounded as he always was by high officials who were either ignorant of it themselves or afraid to confess it, if they were responsible. The strength of the army, as it appeared on paper, was only nominal: the hospitals and supplies were quite unorganised and the plague, once started, raged unchecked. A new levy of two men in 500 was raised in May and another of four in 500 in August, all untrained troops. This unpopular system of levies had not been used for four years and was freely evaded, while the new and even worse method of recruitment by military colonies had not begun to work. The Grand Duke Constantine was bitterly opposed to the war and refused to send any troops from Poland. There were jealousies among the staff of the army, for Diebitch was given an undefined supervision over the nominal Commander-in-Chief Wittgenstein, whose appointment of fellow-Germans to the highest commands was resented. The presence of the Tsar at headquarters did not improve matters.[2]

Nicholas was appalled at the loss of life and was anxious to end the war after some tangible success. The prestige of Russia in the West rested on the quite mistaken belief that in any Eastern war the Turks must at once collapse, and nothing must be allowed to destroy the illusion. The desperate efforts made to obtain a result in this campaign proved that Russia was putting forth her whole strength, and that her failure was not due to the Emperor's 'moderation'. In these straits he could not reconcile himself to remain neutral in the Mediterranean, as he had promised to do. Wellington had not been far wrong in his first impression that it was an impracticable scheme, but he said now that this breach of faith could not be allowed. Ellenborough wrote to him that here was the chance to exclude Russia from the treaty and to settle with France alone. But France was reluctant to separate from Russia, and Wellington himself pointed out that unless the Sultan was ready to treat, England and France could not dictate a settlement of Greece, with Russia

[2] From Disbrowe, 27 Jan., in *F.O. Russia*, 171; from Temple, 6 Apr., *ibid.* 172. Infantry 99,000; cavalry 20,000; reserve 53,000. The actual forces available are put by Moltke at 100,000 in all. Cf. Schiemann, III, 36, 86. On the levies, etc., *ibid.* II, 228, 252.

still at war. The French sent a conciliatory and non-committal note, enclosing a notice to the Porte of the Russian blockade: this was to be sent by way of Russian headquarters, so as to give the Tsar an opportunity of rescinding the orders. At the end of September Aberdeen expressed to Lieven his surprise and regret at the blockade, after a public undertaking to remain neutral: if it were not at once withdrawn, co-operation must again cease. Instructions were sent to Heytesbury to demand exemption for all British shipping which had sailed from England up to that date. This was conceded, but the blockade remained in force and in March 1829 was extended westwards to include the Gulf of Contessa, but was finally withdrawn in June, owing to the protests of England.[3] It is worth noticing that Lord Cochrane thought the blockade useless and not worth quarrelling about. Admiral Collingwood had been of the same opinion, holding that a blockade was useless in summer when corn from Asia and Rumania was plentiful, and impossible to maintain in winter. Indeed it seems to have had little influence on the campaign, but a considerable effect on English trade for that year.[4]

The position of the triple alliance was certainly curious, as ironically described by Metternich: one mediating Power (Russia) at open war with the Porte, with one half of its squadron engaged in a hostile blockade of the Dardanelles and the other half in a 'pacific blockade' of the Greek coast; a second Power (France) engaged in 'amicable hostilities' by land with a nominal vassal of the Sultan, but neutral at sea; the third Power neutral but 'ally and accomplice' of the other two.[5] This tale of anomalies might be multiplied. Before the arrival of the French expeditionary force, Codrington, already under orders to hand over his command on the ground that he had not stringently enforced the blockade, concluded at Alexandria an agreement with

[3] Aberdeen to Lieven, 30 Sept., in P. O. v, 816; cf. Wellington's *Despatches*, v, 88 (draft). Aberdeen to Heytesbury, 2 Oct., P. O. v, 319. Note verbale of Polignac, *ibid.* v, 315. *Parl. Papers*, 1830, XXXII, 590.

[4] Cochrane, quoted in a letter from Malta, 26 Jan. 1829, in *F.O. Greece*, 7. Collingwood, quoted in *Quarterly Review*, Apr. 1828, XXXVII, 386. Cf. Grey to Princess Lieven, in *Correspondence*, 8 Oct. 1828.

[5] Metternich to Ottenfels, 13 Oct., in P. O. v, 323.

Mehemet Ali by which Ibrahim was to withdraw his half-starved and mutinous Arab troops; but in order to satisfy his suzerain the Sultan there was to be a pretence of force by the British fleet and 1200 Turkish and Arab troops were to remain in the fortresses. But when the French arrived, with an army of 14,000 men eager for action, they ignored this agreement and met with no resistance; the Turks surrendered in form after a mock assault on their mud walls, made in order to satisfy the French press.[6]

Again, the Greeks, who had accepted the armistice a year before, were vigorously preparing for a campaign in Northern Greece; while the Turks, who had up to now refused it, could spare no men from the Russian war, and were besides becoming indifferent about Greece. In March they had offered indirectly an armistice, through a letter to the Greek patriarch, which was carried to Greece by three bishops but ignored by Capodistrias. In July the Reis-Effendi wrote directly to the ambassadors, suggesting that, although the Sultan could never formally accept the armistice or the mediation, the former already existed *de facto* and the latter was "implicitly understood": a single meeting would be enough to reach an agreement. He refused to send envoys to the Aegean Conference, but repeatedly invited the ambassadors to return to Constantinople. The ambassadors did not encourage the hint, but Aberdeen wished that it could be construed as an acknowledgment of the treaty for a basis of settlement.[7]

But the French Government again refused to separate from Russia. France could not now shake off the fixed suspicion that Wellington was not seriously determined to execute the treaty, while he in turn was absurdly suspicious of the French proceedings in the Morea. General Maison was disappointed at Codring-

[6] The letter recalling Codrington was dated 5 June. Sir Pulteney Malcolm arrived to replace him, 22 Aug. Convention of Alexandria, 6 Aug., in *Parl. Papers*, 1830, XXXII, 573. See below, p. 143. On the condition of Ibrahim's troops, cf. Prokesch v. Osten, *Aus dem Nachlasse*, 7 Apr. 1828. Finlay, II, 191. Viel-Castel, XVIII, 356ff.

[7] Reis-Effendi, reported in P. O. v, 302. Cf. Gentz to Prokesch v. Osten, 17 Oct., *Aus dem Nachlasse*. Reis-Effendi to Wellington, 6 July; answer, 6 Aug., in *Parl. Papers*, 1830, XXXII, 244. Reis-Effendi to ambassadors, 11 Sept.; answer, 20 Sept., *ibid.* XXXII, 284. Aberdeen, 13 Oct., in Wellington's *Despatches*, v, 132.

ton's agreement with the Pasha, and was at first hardly restrained from attacking Ibrahim, where he lay in camp waiting anxiously for transports to carry him home from the scene of his empty conquests.[8] Ever since Navarin the Pasha, finding himself committed to a losing game, had sought an opportunity to withdraw, without an open breach with the Sultan; Ibrahim too had become restive in his false position and more than once visited the French camp, even dining with the officers. The real intentions of an ambitious Oriental like Mehemet Ali are difficult to discover; it is hard to see why he did not choose the opportunity of the Russian war to attack Syria and break openly with his sovereign. There was less reason then to fear the veto of Europe than when he defied it four years later. Russia could hardly have discouraged a new ally: France was never hostile, and England alone (for Austria would have done little to help) would actively disapprove: even England might have agreed to some conquests in Syria in return for a speedier evacuation of Greece, which would make the French expedition superfluous; Colonel Cradock's mission to the Pasha had failed because he was not authorised to promise anything in return for the evacuation of the Morea.[9] It is possible that a lingering sentiment of loyalty to the Sultan, or at least of sympathy in his struggle against an infidel Power, restrained the Pasha. But more probably his plans were not ripe, and he needed time to repair the losses of his wasted efforts in Greece.

There was still plenty of work for the French troops, in surveying, in reconstructing roads and fortresses, and in organising relief, for which their occupation was gratefully remembered by the Greeks. But General Maison did not forget that he had been sent out to win 'la gloire', and he determined to seek it across the Isthmus by a new siege of Athens; on October 10th he wrote to Mortemart at St Petersburg: "I count on being in Attica towards the end of this month at latest".[10] Stratford

[8] *F.O. Turkey*, 166, from S. Canning at Kalamata, 9 Sept.

[9] See above, p. 86. Sir F. Adam, 23 Feb., in *C.O. Ionian Is.* 48.

[10] Heytesbury to Aberdeen, 15 Nov., in *F.O. Russia*, 173. Maison informed Capodistrias on 5 Oct.: see Capodistrias' answer, 9 Oct., in his *Correspondance*, II, 354.

Canning had already warned Aberdeen of the possibility, and although he was personally convinced that the troops would eventually be necessary, he knew the opinions of his chief; Aberdeen had written to him, with a tinge of regret for his Athenian days: "If after all we are compelled to give up Athens, it will be a cruel sacrifice, but I foresee the possibility of such being the case". And again: "If we succeed in expelling Ibrahim, the limits of Greece will practically be defined by the state of possession. This would not carry us beyond the Isthmus". In September he sent positive instructions not on any account to let the French pass the Isthmus.[11] General Guilleminot, Stratford's colleague previously at Constantinople and now again at the new Conference at Poros, said he had no authority to stop the French troops, and for some days there was considerable excitement. When General Maison was on the point of marching, he was prevented by a veto from the French War Office. When Wellington heard of this episode he was very angry and demanded explanation; the French Government denied any knowledge of it at first, but afterwards explained that Maison must have acted on a private letter from the War Minister, sent, as was alleged, without any authority.[12] Capodistrias was even more disappointed than Maison, and asked instead that the admirals should be allowed to co-operate on the coast with a movement of Demetrius Hypselantes' troops in Eastern Greece. His request was refused; Hypselantes' men were as disorganised as Church's bands in Western Greece, and nearly four more years were to pass before the peaceful evacuation from the Acropolis of the last remaining Turkish troops.

II

November—December 1828

Wellington might well be annoyed, for he was at that moment negotiating once more to confine the new State to the Morea. The anti-Russian party had everywhere taken heart since it

[11] S. Canning to Aberdeen, 2 Sept. (private), in *S.C. Papers*, 20. Aberdeen to S. Canning, 26 July, in Lane-Poole, I, 482; 11 Sept., in *F.O. Turkey*, 164.

[12] S. Canning to Aberdeen, 14, 15, 21 Oct., in *F.O. Turkey*, 167. Wellington's *Despatches*, v, 206ff., 3 to 6 Nov.

had become obvious that one campaign would not bring victory. Aberdeen wrote to Heytesbury that England shared the opinion of Austria about the war; there was only too much ground for suspicion of Russia. Ellenborough, filled with concern for the future safety of India, did not conceal his view that "our policy in Europe and in Asia ought to be the same—to pull down the Russian power". The press was full of indignation about the blockade, and Greece was quite forgotten. Grey wrote to Princess Lieven: "Your paper *The Times* seems latterly to have become very hostile to you", adding elsewhere that *The Times*, being conducted solely with a view to extending its sale, was not a bad barometer of public opinion. Metternich began to hope again that Russia might be excluded from the Greek settlement: "our rôle at Constantinople should now be reduced to that of silence"; in other words, of ceasing to urge concessions upon the Sultan. Aberdeen, however, told Stratford that he must not believe the stories that Turkish obstinacy was being encouraged by Austria: "It is true that Austria had always disapproved of the treaty, but her disapproval has never been a secret. She has regarded this treaty as an evil, but as an evil whose prompt execution would be less disastrous than its indefinite duration". These were just the sentiments of Wellington: yet he had spent his time in delaying the settlement.[13]

The Russian reverses later in the year were reflected in the reviving intransigeance of the Turks. The Reis-Effendi declared that he could not trust the triple alliance, and that the only hope of a stable peace lay in a Congress; indeed general Congresses have always brought reprieve to Turkey. In another outburst he exclaimed:

Jamais, au grand jamais, la Porte ne cédera sur la question grecque, jamais elle n'accédera par un acte formel aux dispositions injustes de nos adversaires, dispositions qui tendent toutes évidemment à l'avantage de la Russie. La révolution grecque est l'ouvrage de cette

[13] Ellenborough's *Diary*, 25 Sept., 10 Oct. Aberdeen to Heytesbury, 19 Sept., in P. O. v, 309, draft in Wellington's *Despatches*, v, 31. Grey to Princess Lieven, 14 Sept., 19 Oct., in *Correspondence*, I. Metternich, 13 Oct., in P. O. v, 323. S. Canning to Aberdeen, 15 Aug., in *F.O. Turkey*, 165. Aberdeen to S. Canning, 20 Sept., *ibid.* 164 (and P. O. v, 311).

Puissance, et son ingérence seule dans les affaires grecques nous est plus odieuse que la mort et la terreur qui l'environne.

In another interview he repeated that the Sultan could never give his sanction to a new order of things, drawing a vivid picture of the way in which Russia would make it a starting-point for new intervention and encroachment; he could not treat for peace without the formal assurances of Austria and even of Prussia that the Russians would not interfere any more in Greek affairs.[14]

There was clearly no chance of a final settlement yet. But Wellington hoped to prejudge in London, as General Maison had tried to forestall on the spot, an issue whose decision had already been entrusted, with the widest discretionary instructions, to the Conference at Poros. The Duke was determined to confine Greece if possible to the Morea and the Islands; the French general was restrained, but on strategical grounds the French Government still favoured the Arta-Volo line. The Duke argued strictly that "the object of the treaty was not to conquer territory from the Porte but to pacify a country in a state of insurrection". But even so, a wider frontier was perhaps the shortest cut to a pacification. Since Ibrahim's departure, Hypselantes and Church had begun to advance north of the Isthmus. Their ill-disciplined bands were not popular among the unfortunate peasantry, but it was no solution to pronounce anathema upon them in London. They could not easily be re-admitted to the Morea, where they would only add to the President's troubles, and they were sufficient to make peace under a Turkish régime impossible. The true policy was clearly to legalise their position and give them a frontier to hold. And if these troops were to be reorganised, they must first be paid: this was the time, if ever, for a loan to tide over the transition. But Wellington was not disposed to make peace by subsidising war, even if a small expense now might achieve a more durable settlement. During these negotiations, his irritation, which had

[14] Reports of M. Huszar, dragoman to the Austrian Internuncio, 4, 7, 8 Nov., in P. O. v, 328–40.

somewhat subsided during the summer, was rapidly reviving. On November 2nd he wrote:

> In respect to Greece, I would confine the limits to the Peloponnese if possible or as near as possible to the Isthmus of Corinth. I think that as Capodistrias says that he cannot go on without foreign assistance, he renders it less expedient to give to Greece an extended frontier. Indeed there never was such a humbug as the Greek affair altogether. However, thank God, it has never cost us a shilling, and never shall.

A Protocol was signed on November 16th placing "the Morea, the islands appertaining, and the Cyclades, under the provisional guarantee of the three Courts until the fate of these countries has been settled by agreement with the Porte, without prejudicing the definitive limits".[15] But the Duke's attempt to "settle the fate of these countries" was doomed from the first. The diverging views of the allies were annexed to the protocol itself; the Russian Court had by now made up its mind to another campaign, and would certainly pay no attention to decisions made in London and derided in Greece. The Conference at Poros was even now preparing a quite different set of proposals: and above all the state of affairs in Continental Greece was entirely ignored.

As soon as the protocol was signed, Wellington wrote to Polignac, insisting that Church and Hypselantes must be recalled from Continental Greece, and that the ambassadors themselves, rather than separate plenipotentiaries, should return to Constantinople. Polignac agreed, without making it a decree of the Conference, to ask Capodistrias to recall his troops. Actually Church had begun in September his advance upon the Gulf of Arta, which was to drive the Turks from Western Greece early in the following year. These troops were only kept together by the pay which the President was able to give them in partial instalments out of the French subsidies.[16] As for the Duke's other point, Polignac preferred to send separate plenipotentiaries, as less likely to give an appearance of dissension with Russia. He thought the Tsar inclined for peace, but not if he was

[15] Memoranda, 2, 10, 16 Nov., in Wellington's *Despatches*, v, 199, 231, 249. Protocol, 16 Nov., in *Parl. Papers*, 1830, XXXII.

[16] See below, pp. 130, 159.

bullied into it. At the end of the year, however, he agreed to send ambassadors, if (to satisfy the Tsar) the Turks would renew their promise of an armistice *de facto* in Greece; and Wellington proposed to use for this purpose a conversation in which the Seraskier had told the English consul at Prevesa that he would do so. The Seraskier (the famous Reshid, soon to be Vizir and to direct the next campaign against Russia) had the best of reasons for promising an armistice, for his Albanians were mutinous, and Church was advancing against him. He hoped no doubt that the armistice would at last be enforced against the Greeks as well. Stratford thought this overture very unsatisfactory, but felt obliged to return an indirect answer: the other two ambassadors ignored it.[17]

Meanwhile the Russians had been informed that France and England proposed to send ambassadors, or at least two special representatives, to Constantinople. "The conduct of the Allies in carrying the treaty into execution has been sufficiently equivocal to entitle the Porte to expect some indulgence." Russia ought to take the opportunity of ending "a war, to say the least, not one of self-defence". The Russian ministers were not pleased at the rumours of this step and they were angered by the "irritating and insulting language" of English and French newspapers: Lieven had refused for some days before November 16th to sign the protocol.[18] Most of all they feared the efforts of Austria to break up the alliance. Metternich exaggerated the ill-success of the Russians in the last campaign, and once more began to hope that the allies might be separated. Taking up the Reis-Effendi's suggestion for a Congress (which probably originated with a hint from Metternich himself, though put into the Turkish minister's mouth), he proposed not only the immediate return of the French and English ambassadors but a general Congress for the settlement of the East, which

[17] Wellington to Polignac, 24 Nov., and reply, 2 Dec., in *Despatches*, v, 281, 301. Aberdeen to Wellington, and reply, 30, 31 Dec., *ibid.* v, 381–4. S. Canning's reports, 15 Dec. 1828, 3 Mar. 1829, in *F.O. Turkey*, 168, 178.

[18] Aberdeen to Heytesbury, 25 Nov.; Heytesbury to Aberdeen, 15 Nov., 14 Dec., in *F.O. Russia*, 173. Aberdeen to S. Canning (private), 18 Nov., in *S.C. Papers*, 22.

should force Russia to make peace. He talked of collecting Austrian troops on the Serbian frontier, but his whole policy since 1821 had been dictated by the desire to avoid mobilisation in the South.[19]

Both France and England rejected the idea either of mediation or of a Congress. Wellington said that though Metternich might talk, Austria did not mean war, for she would have Prussia against her: it was dangerous to attempt a mediation between Russia and Turkey, which might lead to a general war: England must remain with France and avoid Austrian plans. His answer to Metternich (December 26th) was put on rather different grounds. A speedy peace was no doubt essential, but England and France could not mediate until the treaty was fulfilled. "We admit that error and injustice presided at its origin. If it was an evil, it is an evil firmly established on which we must base our policy." If Metternich will only use all his influence to get a settlement of Greece, England will be free of the treaty; France will soon be reconciled to the exclusion of Attica. The failure of Russia must not be exaggerated: the next campaign might succeed, and if the Turks were once expelled, no one would exert himself to bring them back. The last remark is significant, and helps to explain Wellington's change of front after the Treaty of Adrianople next year.[20]

The Russian ministers, whatever Nicholas might feel in private, had no thought of peace: the mere idea was scouted by Pozzo di Borgo in Paris; like his colleague in London, he always pressed a bold and forward policy upon the more timid Nesselrode. In two illuminating despatches about this time, Pozzo attributes the lack of success to the Emperor's moderation in warfare and

[19] *Weisungen nach London*, 241, 14 Sept. 1828. Metternich had some articles by Gentz transmitted to London for publication in the *Courier* and the *Morning Post*: *ibid.*, 242, 18 Dec. 1828; *Berichte aus London*, 243, 7 Jan. 1829. On the general belief about the state of the Austrian army, cf. Esterhazy, *Berichte*, 238, 16 May 1828.

[20] Wellington to Aberdeen, 1, 3 Jan. 1829, in *Despatches*, v, 408, 417. Aberdeen to Heytesbury, 12 Dec., in *F.O. Russia*, 173. Cf. Princess Lieven to Grey, 17 Dec., in *Correspondence*, I, and her *Letters*, 28 Nov. Balfour, *Life of Aberdeen*, I, 231. Aberdeen to Cowley, 26 Dec., in P. O. v, 367 (draft in Wellington's *Despatches*, v, 340).

to Austria's hostile and deceitful policy, as well as to the Sultan's ill-considered obstinacy. A new campaign is necessary—"the Emperor has put the Turkish system to the proof and H.M. has found it to possess a commencement of physical and moral organisation which it hitherto had not"—Mahmud's reforms must not be given time to develop. Moreover, in making peace now, Russia would have to abide by her professions against aggrandisement: after a new and victorious campaign she could raise her demands. "When negotiation takes place we must be in a position to dictate the conditions in a prompt and rapid manner, so that the European Powers shall if possible learn the termination together with the commencement." The aim should be to capture the Danube fortresses, and to keep them and Varna too, but not to threaten Constantinople. "It would be prudent to fortify Sebastopol well against approaches by sea. If ever England should break with us, against this point will her attacks be directed, if she believe it attackable." Pozzo proceeds to sketch the probable attitude of the other Powers during the winter: Metternich is doing his best to thwart Russia by his influence over Wellington, and by a vigorous anti-Russian press campaign—in the *Gazette de France* and *Quotidienne*, and in the English *Courier*. But if Russia pursues her course, Metternich may even go to war if he likes: if Russia only demands at the peace a few modifications immaterial to the Vienna settlement of 1815, Austria would be responsible if a general war should follow. Prussia is favourable, but her friendship must be cultivated assiduously.[21]

France needed the support of Russia: Charles X expressed his friendship for the Tsar and his dislike of Metternich, but also his admiration for Wellington, an admiration shared by Polignac, the French ambassador in London. Polignac came much under Wellington's influence, and did his best to make the French Government conform to the Duke's views. He was soon to prove that he shared the Duke's indifference to unpopularity, but not his gift of usually knowing when to give way. Encouraged by

[21] Pozzo to Nesselrode, 28 Nov., 14 Dec., in *Portfolio*, I, 341, 407; II, 123, 207.

Metternich and by the Duke, he visited Paris about this time, but failed to convert La Ferronays, and returned, reluctantly obliged to follow what Pozzo called "a French policy": so long as La Ferronays was minister, the fidelity of France to Russia was secure. Wellington, therefore, was labouring for the return to power of Villèle or else of Polignac, whom Pozzo described on this occasion as an emissary of the Duke. But La Ferronays refused to have Polignac in his ministry and Polignac was at present too weak to stand alone. When La Ferronays was stricken with paralysis and forced to retire, he was succeeded for the time by Portalis, and there was no marked change of policy. But France could not be counted on to support any and every demand of Russia at the peace.

As to the return of ambassadors to Constantinople, it was clearly deplorable from the Russian point of view. But their efforts for peace would probably fail or else be cut short by the course of the next campaign. Pozzo, at first anxious to protest, was soon inclined not to press the objection, and his advice was followed. On January 2nd, 1829, Heytesbury reported that Russia acquiesced in the sending of ambassadors, on condition that England and France adhered to the terms of the settlement proposed by the Conference of Poros. On the same day, a special French envoy, M. Jaubert, a learned Orientalist, reached Constantinople with instructions to announce the Protocol of November 16th. But, also on the same day, the very different Report from Poros arrived in London.[22]

Metternich's last attempt to break up the alliance and to nullify the treaty had failed. Wellington in a moment of exasperation had begun to listen to his advice; but he was too direct to have any real respect for Metternich's diplomatic methods. He said to Princess Lieven: "I never shared the opinion of his being a great statesman; he is a society hero and nothing more". Metternich, after attempting to deny his plan, was forced to make his best excuses to the Tsar and to watch the

[22] Heytesbury, 2 Jan., in *F.O. Russia*, 179. See below, p. 152. Cf. Russian instruction to Matuscewitz, 3 Jan., annexed to protocol, 22 Mar. 1829, in *Parl. Papers*, and in P. O. VI, 13.

drama being played out.[23] Nothing but the fear of revolution could bring the two Empires together again. It was fortunate for the Greeks that the French Revolution of July 1830 did not come eighteen months earlier.

But although the triple alliance was still in being, it was unable to decide upon a common course. Greece, if not abandoned, was still as far as ever from a settlement. Two things made Wellington's settlement impossible, the course of events in Greece, and the report of the Poros Conference. In the next year the Russian war was to decide the issue.

[23] Princess Lieven to Grey, 29 Jan. 1829, in *Correspondence*, I. Metternich's conversation with Tatishchev, 5 Feb. 1829, in *Portfolio*, II, 69. Ringhoffer, pp. 140–50.

CHAPTER IX

GREECE IN 1828

I

General Church in Western Greece

MEANWHILE, events on the spot had been moving in a direction different from that planned by Wellington. After a year's delay, Church was at last ready to advance; it was surprising that he had been able to keep his clans together so long. Captain Hastings' action in Salona Bay in the autumn of 1827 had opened up communication with Rumelia. Six weeks after the Battle of Navarin, Hastings landed Church with 1000 men in two divisions at Dragomestre in Western Greece.[1] For a week the first division of 500 men lay in a precarious plight. The Turks could easily have destroyed so weak a force, and were prevented by slackness and jealousies rather than by a heroic respect for the armistice which they had hitherto rejected. With the arrival of another 500 men, Church was able to improve and strengthen the camp and to feel more secure. The Turkish forces were formidable, consisting chiefly of Albanian infantry and a strong force of Asiatic cavalry, especially the light mobile Delhidis; they were masters of all Eastern and Western Greece, with headquarters at Larissa and Zeitoun in the East, at Yanina, Arta and Prevesa in the West. But Reshid was short of money: he was at this moment away, and his lieutenant, Omar Vrioni, was intriguing to keep the command; being himself an Albanian, Omar was more popular with the troops. It was not until March 1828 that Reshid returned with his own appointment confirmed.

On December 29th the fort of Vassiladi fell under Hastings' fire, and on New Year's day Church brought 300 men to take

[1] For all these events, see Church Papers, *B.M.*, *Add. MSS.* 36563–5. The reception of the news of Navarin by Church and Cochrane is illustrated, characteristically, by two letters printed below in Appendix III.

part in an attack on Anatolico. There was a misunderstanding between Church and Hastings, and the attempt was given up after failure to take a small island in the lagoon. Church now abandoned the idea of recovering Anatolico and Missolonghi at once, and decided to occupy first if possible the pass of the Makrinoros range, the gateway of Epirus. This would automatically cut off the Turks in Acarnania. But the Greek chiefs of the surrounding hills would not move until a flotilla should first enter and hold the Gulf of Arta. They were not going to commit themselves too soon; indeed most of them kept up negotiations with both sides. Church's men were not well received by the peasants, who thought them merely a band of marauders, and in spite of the general's efforts there was some justification for the idea. They depended entirely for supplies upon the Greek Commission in Corfu organised by Viaro Capodistrias and Gerostathi: the funds of this Commission were drawn largely from the philanthropic subscriptions of Europe for relief of refugees, and were dishonestly applied to this apparently desperate adventure.[2] The supply was irregular, and as the men had no pay, plunder was the alternative. Church himself gave his sanction to "occasional requisitions of cattle when days passed without bread". A discreditable traffic in provisions was carried on by some of the Greek troops with the Turks of Patras.

In such difficulties, the arrival of the President was anxiously awaited. Hitherto the only news was a letter from Ancona, begging Church to prevent the *capitani* from isolated enterprises, and pointing to order and good repute with the Powers as the first essential.[3] Capodistrias had been delayed at Ancona, and did not land in Greece until January 19th. At last, in the middle of February, came a letter with 2000 dollars for Hastings (who had hitherto paid his sailors from his own pocket) and only 14,000 francs for supplies for the army; the troops, having no pay, were jealous of the sailors. Partly perhaps on account of this and of his own difficulties with Hastings, Church told the President that an attack on Missolonghi was impossible, and

[2] Viaro Capodistrias to Church, 1 June 1828, in *C.O. Ionian Is.* 43.
[3] Capodistrias to Church, 31 Dec. 1827, in *Correspondance*, I, 370.

explained his own plan of advance. During March six gunboats were collected, but the Greek admiral, Sactouris, soon departed, having not enough means for a blockade of Prevesa; Lord Cochrane had already left Greece. One of Church's companies was taken away for the President's camp of regulars at Troezen, but he had a small reinforcement in return. In the middle of April Hastings went away to offer his resignation and Church at once decided on a new attack upon Anatolico. The friction between the two was unfortunate, as Hastings alone could support an attack by effective fire from the sea.

The attack on the island fort was this time successful (April 26th) and the town was besieged from the sea side. But now arrived the hated Government commissaries, bringing no pay but practically superseding the general in his command. The half-mutinous troops suffered great hardship before Anatolico, and it was a relief when Hastings, persuaded by the President to remain in Greece, returned and took command of all the boats before the town (May 12th). Veli Bey, who had been reinforced, was now repulsed, and the town was bombarded with rockets. But the commissaries could no longer be put off; for some time Church had resisted the President's new plan of organisation, but at the risk of a mutiny it was carried out. In such confusion it is not surprising that an assault on the town made on May 23rd was not successful. In this attack Captain Hastings was mortally wounded. Under his command the Greeks had gained the best advantage from one at least of the steam vessels ordered for them by the notorious Greek Committee. He was a Philhellene none the less sincere for being entirely unromantic; he professed the greatest contempt for most of the Greek leaders, and relied only on a strict discipline to achieve results. His gunners were the only ones who ever hit anything; the Greek gunners on Cochrane's flagship became so excited when they sighted a Turkish brig that they fired incessantly, taking no aim and all shouting at once. General Church, with his vain but ardent Irish temperament, had not always found it easy to co-operate with Hastings' blunt, sardonic humour; but he felt his loss deeply, and there was now no one capable of carrying out an organised plan of co-operation by sea with his advance.[4]

His plan was to unite after all with D. Hypselantes, now in camp at Megara, and to advance upon Arta together or in separate columns, with the main object of securing the pass of the Makrinoros; he had now 3000 men, and Hypselantes a nominal force of 8000: at the same time the flotilla was to blockade Prevesa, from which Ibrahim was known to be getting provisions. Instead of this, the flotilla was dismissed by the Government Commission. In the middle of July the President visited the camp, landing from the Russian Admiral Heyden's flagship and wearing a Russian uniform; he promised to restore the flotilla and add two steamships, and to make up the army to 6000. With the help of the newly arrived French and Russian subsidies he was able to give the troops six weeks' of the promised three months' pay up to July 18th.[5] But he was disheartened by all that he saw. The armies were drawing rations for a nominal strength up to twice their real numbers. As an official come to restore order, he could not expect anything from Church's guerrilla bands, who were as ready to plunder as to fight, and were held together by personal loyalty alone. The revolutionary time was over, and a disciplined force could alone conquer and hold the new frontier if it was to be extended as the President hoped. He wrote to Nesselrode after his visit to Dragomestre: "J'en ai le cœur serré....General Church n'est pas ici à sa place ...faute de mieux je dois l'y laisser".[6] The promised reinforcement of troops was cancelled; Hypselantes, too, delayed, and when he advanced he was too much occupied in Attica to co-operate with Church. After five weeks' silence the President sent a month's pay only and no ration allowance; there was a

[4] See Hastings' pungent summary of the characters of the Greek leaders, sketched for Lord Cochrane on his appointment as admiral—*Life of Cochrane*, by his son, I, 339 ff. There is a biographical notice of Hastings by Finlay in *Blackwood's*, Oct. 1845, and a pamphlet, *Some English Philhellenes*, I, by Z. D. Ferriman.

[5] The first monthly instalment of 500,000 fr. from France was brought by the new Resident in June. Heyden at the end of May brought a Russian subsidy of 1½ million roubles—Capodistrias, *Correspondance*, II, 180, 128.

[6] Capodistrias, 16 July, in Nesselrode's *Lettres et Papiers*, VII, 61.

mutiny among the men, who were induced to remain only by the personal persuasions of their general. At last the flotilla arrived, consisting of three large gunboats and ten light *misticos*. It was commanded by Passano, a Corsican, who timidly refused to enter the Gulf of Arta by night, but proposed to drag the boats eighteen miles overland and launch them inside the gulf. This fantastic expedient was given up, and on September 19th Church began his advance upon Arta with only 2000 men. The number of the Turkish forces was uncertain, but Reshid was known to be at Yanina, where earlier in the year he had been collecting a force of 15,000 to 20,000 men, and Veli Bey was at Prevesa, whence he had not stirred since the failure of his attacks in May. Church advanced to Actium, and his lieutenant, Dentzel, to Loutraki; on the 23rd Passano with his flotilla appeared before Prevesa, but retired again at once and was only with difficulty persuaded to renew the attempt. At last, on October 3rd, his captains insisted on entering the narrow mouth of the outer gulf, forced all cargo boats to leave Prevesa, and passed in to Loutraki inside the Gulf of Arta. But Passano did not co-operate well with Dentzel; Dentzel, too, had not Church's personal influence over the men, and was obliged to retire to Zaverda. The momentary blockade was abandoned, and the flotilla returned to the Gulf of Corinth. Passano was superseded, and the more enterprising Kriezi (ten years later Prime Minister of Greece) succeeded in making Reshid retire from the coast to which he had advanced from Salona. Reshid abandoned Salona and returned to Arta at the beginning of November; he was soon made Grand Vizir, and the Turks, absorbed in the coming struggle for their existence, made no more serious attempts to reconquer the province. They retired from Karpenisi, and at the end of December the town of Vonitza fell: the castle held out until March 1829.

The blockade of Prevesa from outside was re-established in a fashion by the end of the year: but the incident in October had led to difficulties with the High Commissioner of the Ionian Islands, and with the British consul at Prevesa. Among the boats cut out from their anchorage were twenty-five sail flying the Ionian flag. The status of the Greek forces was very ill-defined; in spite of the nominal armistice which the Treaty of London had set out to impose, no one on the spot regarded it as binding. Even Sir F. Adam, who was supposed to express the official view and was no Philhellene, wrote to Church: "it is neither my wish nor my intention to throw any impediment in the way of the fullest exercise of all your legitimate belligerent rights as a Greek commander". But he pointed out that the intended blockade had never been declared to him, and in any case it never existed effectively. The incident was treated by the Ionian Government as a mere raid for plunder: after some heated correspondence, Church was forced to restore the vessels, and the episode cost the Greeks 1600 dollars in compensation for damage.[7] At the same time Consul Meyer in Prevesa complained of Church's advance; the town was in danger of being sacked by its Albanian garrison, and the consul thought that he would have to withdraw. Reshid's authority was undermined, and it was in these straits that he offered an armistice.

Incidents like these were not likely to appease the British Government's irritation at the continued activity of the Greek forces after the Protocol of November. That unfortunate document was received with indignation in the Levant, and completely ignored by Capodistrias.

II

The President of Greece

The President's first year in office laid the foundation of his unpopularity. The difficulties were appalling. He had to face the half-hearted support of the triple alliance, the suspicion of the English, and before long the discontent of a section among the people. At the time of his election in April 1827 Capodistrias was at St Petersburg; he had much conversation with the Tsar before receiving his final release from the Russian service and accepting the Presidency. It was popularly supposed that promises of Russian support were given on condition that he would

[7] *F.O.* 97/230.

do his best to prevent Greece from becoming an independent State.[8] He spent the rest of the summer in efforts to raise money by subsidy or loan. But he found a cold reception in London, arriving on the day before Canning's funeral. He had originally favoured placing the Ionian Islands under British protection, but his journey to Corfu in 1819, followed by a visit to London to protest against Maitland's régime, had earned for him the active suspicion of Wellington and Bathurst.[9] They now recognised his appointment but would give no advice, and persuaded Russia to withhold any subsidies for the moment. There was no question of raising money in the open market (the old loan was now worth about 15 per cent. of its issue price) and the British Government could not be persuaded to guarantee a new issue. Capodistrias had no better success in Paris. Reaching Ancona in November, he was kept waiting for six weeks before a vessel could be found to take him to Greece; so that when he landed at Aegina on January 19th, 1828, he could show no tangible result to compensate for the long delay of nine months since his election.

The French subsidies began in June 1828, but were suspended at the end of the year for six months: a Russian subsidy came at the end of May and was followed by others at irregular intervals: but Wellington "thanked God we had not spent a shilling". The President had to give up his idea of a force of Swiss or German mercenaries, and owing to the delays of the Conference he could do nothing for the first eight months of his rule, with the Egyptians still in the Morea. The admirals' 'pacific blockade' was not at first very effective, and gave no right of search against the Austrian merchantmen, which regularly supplied Ibrahim

[8] Mendelssohn, who puts the Liberal case against Capodistrias, repeats this allegation, but not positively. Schiemann, II, 193, only says that he was given his orders "in deepest secrecy". See below, p. 196, n. 14.

[9] Cf. a letter from Ugo Foscolo to Lord Holland, 4 Mar. 1824, prefacing an account of the cession of Parga to the Turks—*Prose politiche*, IV, 291 (Firenze, 1850). The writer protests that, although he has been in correspondence with Capodistrias, he has no concern with political intrigue and has done nothing to earn a share of the suspicion in which Capodistrias is held by the British Government. Cf. Webster, *Castlereagh*, p. 207. Two sketches of Capodistrias' character are printed below in Appendix III.

with provisions under the convoy of Austrian men-of-war. After an ineffectual protest the English Government, without claiming a right to prevent this traffic, asked Metternich to co-operate if he was sincere in wishing to hasten a settlement. It was difficult to prevent a similar traffic carried on from the Ionian Islands by small fast boats over the short distance to the mainland; but Sir F. Adam more than once wrote home asking for a more stringent blockade.[10]

The suspicions of Wellington were due partly to the peculiar position of the Ionian Islands and partly to the Russian connections of the new President. English rule in the nominal 'Septinsular Republic' had a very uneasy hold, and although it brought many material benefits to the islands it created interests opposed to the future course of our Balkan policy. Capodistrias himself had supported the arrangement at the Congress of Vienna, insisting only on the formal independence of the islands; Ugo Foscolo, himself a native of Zante, would have preferred to entrust them outright to England, and so to bring the administration under the control of the British Parliament. But by this anomalous settlement, the discontented had no means of appeal: while plotting against the protecting Government, they could still affirm their loyalty to a shadowy Republic. As soon as the President arrived in Greece, he sent for his brother Viaro, a lawyer in Corfu, and asked him to bring Ionians with him. Reports came to England that the President was biassed in favour of Russia, that his division of the Morea under Corfiots and Russian Greeks would fill the Assembly (by corrupt elections) with Russian partisans. In October the High Commissioner wrote: "All manner of speculations are afloat among our imaginative Ionians as to their future destiny", and in November he visited Aegina and found "twenty-two Corfiots at one importation...all very free in abuse of the Ionian Government". The new British Resident in Greece, Edward Dawkins, was full of the same complaints about the President's "distrust of native Greeks,...every office of trust held by

[10] Dudley to Cowley, 11 Apr. 1828, in *F.O. Austria*, 203. Adam, 11, 23 Feb., in *C.O. Ionian Is.* 48.

Ionians exclusively devoted to himself". There was no doubt some truth in all this, but the writers' fears magnified their suspicions: and Dawkins already showed something like a personal animus against the President, who declared that he had only three Ionians in high office. In fact the list sent by Dawkins himself shows only two Ionians, the President's brother and Metaxas, in the Panhellenium, and three Ionian judges.[11]

It was after all natural that if a new State was to be formed, Russian and Ionian Greeks, like other Greeks of the dispersion, should seek their fortunes there. The Ionians, however mixed in blood, were of the same religion and language as the Greeks of the Morea: once the new State was firmly established, there was sure to be an agitation for union which might well cost more to control than the doubtful strategic value of the islands could justify. The islands were ceded to Greece in 1864, at a time when the use of steam in the navy was making Malta a more effective base than before for the Eastern Mediterranean, and when Egypt had become more important than the Dardanelles. But for the present there was little fear of a sudden demand by the islanders to share the bankruptcy of the infant State. Ionian traders had grown rich in supplying provisions to the Egyptian army; they now looked with a jealous eye on the future trade of Patras in currants, which they feared would undersell the Ionian crop. Ionian landowners were not anxious to bear the chief burden of the heavy taxes which Capodistrias was obliged to impose. After a year, Adam thought the disaffection not very serious.[12]

On the whole the President, in a difficult position, must be

[11] Capodistrias to Viaro C., 5 Feb. 1828, in *Correspondance*, I, 392. There were thirteen divisions (including, with Samos and Candia, six groups of islands), for each of which an Extraordinary Commissioner was appointed. Trikoupes justifies the change on the ground that the old ἐπαρχίαι were too numerous, and that a return to the Byzantine arrangement had been already recommended at the Assembly of Troezen in 1827. Ἱστορία, IV, 257 ff. Adam, 5 Oct., 8 Nov. 1828, in *C.O. Ionian Is.* 51. Dawkins, 30 Dec. 1828, in *F.O. Greece*, 2. Dawkins took the cue from his instructions (22 Sept.), which required him to note specially any bias in the President's conduct. He reached Aegina at the end of November. A French *chargé*, Juchereau de Saint Denys, had arrived in June, and a Russian, Bulgari, in September.

[12] 22 July 1829, in *C.O. Ionian Is.* 54.

acquitted of any extreme subservience to Russia in the early days of his rule. His methods were not those of an English constitutional government, but neither were his people English citizens. The English and French Residents are rather to blame for their unconcealed hostility, from the very first, to the President whom they were supposed to support. The Russian war naturally made the Greeks look once more to the Orthodox Empire for salvation. The President was justified in using the war as an opportunity to improve his frontier. Hostile critics attributed to him the opposite motive, that of using the agitation on the frontier as an opportunity to help the Russians, and they supported their argument by alleging his neglect of Church during the following winter when the Russian campaign was over. But the evidence hardly seems to justify the assumption. In a proclamation he claimed that Russia's war was a new proof of her interest, but added that Greece was under the aegis of *three* Powers. If the Western Powers suspected the President's motives, the remedy lay with them—to declare at once the independence of Greece and proceed to choose a sovereign to whom no one could object. It seemed as if neither the President nor the Russian Court, to whom such sinister motives were imputed, had at first any objection to this course.

The President was not only faced with official suspicion, but he soon fell foul of the English Philhellenes. As soon as he arrived, Lord Cochrane sailed away and returned only for three months at the end of the year: Capodistrias did not much want him back and made no difficulties about his final resignation in November 1828. Hastings was ignored and left without supplies: he made up his mind to leave but was persuaded by the President to remain with promises of better support. But there was not money to satisfy all: when the President sent Hastings 2000 dollars in February, Church's troops began to complain. Something has been said of the difficulties between Church and the President, for which it is hard to blame either, for their tempers were incompatible. Church complained of neglect from the beginning, the President demanded discipline and organisation first. The general offered to resign in May, and the President would have accepted had there been anyone to replace him. Before long Church began to share the general distrust of Capodistrias. When the Conference at Poros began, the President tried to limit the advance of the Greek forces, and it was tactless of him to appear in the Russian flagship when he visited Western Greece. The advance in the autumn of 1828 began in a bad atmosphere: Church replied indignantly to a letter in which he was reproached for abusing the President as a Russian and was told that he should either resign or support the Government. With the success of his advance, he began to forget his grievances; but in February 1829 insult was added to injury by the appointment of Agostino, the President's feeble brother, as 'Lieutenant-Plenipotentiary' for Western Greece—that Count Agostino "whom His Excellency's fiat made of an agriculturist a general, but whose sole claims to that distinction were a pair of epaulettes and four aides-de-camp".[13] Church finally resigned in August 1829: unfortunately, like some other Philhellenes, he did not leave Greece but stayed to become increasingly hostile to the Government. The President's great object was to stand well with the Powers, and to make the revolution respectable. He refused to recognise any claims for service previous to his own arrival: no doubt some of the clamorous veterans deserved little and expected more than was to be had; but the President, instead of attempting to gild the pill, hardly disguised his contempt for their demands. In a country where decorations, brilliant uniforms and festivities counted for much, the President, immersed in business all the day, lived in the simplest fashion and held no receptions. During his retirement at Geneva since 1822, he had used his influence and his fortune on behalf of the Greeks; in coming to Greece he made a sacrifice of any new prospects in the Russian service and of the cultivated society of which he was fond. He was under no illusions as to the task he undertook, saying to Esterhazy: "I know what I shall be exposed to, and that I shall not be safe from

[13] Capodistrias to Church, 29 Aug., in *Correspondance*, II, 301. Church to Capodistrias, 15 Sept., in *B.M., Add. MSS.* 36559, f. 123. On Count Agostino, see a letter from Argos, dated 10 Aug. 1829 (cutting from the *Morning Herald*), in *B.M., Add. MSS.* 36544, f. 353.

dagger or poison". Even the seat of government at Nauplia was hardly safe from armed factions. It is ungenerous to ascribe to mere love of power his anxiety to serve according to his lights the country of his birth.[14]

It was not long before he began to be unpopular not only among the chieftains but among other classes. The people hailed his arrival with delight, in spite of some murmurs at the long delay in coming. But an incident at Poros, which he visited at the end of January, was afterwards recalled as the first sign of the *τύραννος*. Pig-keeping was the chief occupation of the people, who allowed their herds to wander at large about the narrow dirty alleys, or in and out of the wretched cabins which made up the 'town': the President, in the interests of sanitation, at once ordered every pig to be shut up.[15] Equally unpopular were the measures taken when plague broke out at Hydra and Spezzia in May: the President isolated the islands by means of sanitary police, and took the opportunity of sending his brother Viaro, the attorney, and Kolettes, once Court physician to Ali of Yanina, with full powers to govern the independent islanders. In this way his most well-intentioned acts were turned to his own undoing. He already had cause to reproach the rich Hydriots for not contributing more generously to the National Bank, which was really a device to raise money by a forced loan. It is only fair to say that many of them had spent freely in support of the war during the past seven years.

A National Assembly was due under the terms of the Constitution of Troezen (May 1827); but the President's action, on the very day of his arrival in Greece, in postponing the meeting until April, was wise and necessary, and was generally acquiesced in at the time: only when his unpopularity had grown from other causes was it condemned as the sinister beginning of

[14] See a letter, justifying his régime, in his *Correspondance*, II, 454–66, 15 Dec. 1828; cf. Michaud, *Correspondance d'Orient*, I, 84ff. (June 1830). Capodistrias' conversation with Esterhazy, 18 Sept. 1827, in *Austrian Extracts*.

[15] *Wanderings in Greece*, p. 31, by G. Cochrane, a relation of the admiral, with whose staff he went to Greece. The picturesque side of the revolution is well described. Cochrane's progress was more like an adventurous yachting trip than a naval expedition.

a tyrant's career. Elections would have been impossible while the Egyptian army was still in occupation, and until the frontier was settled there would be many doubtful deputies; the legislative body had shown itself incapable and corrupt; the peasants cared nothing for elections, if they could be freed from the ravages of both armies and allowed to sow their fields in peace. When April came, the Assembly was again indefinitely postponed. But in his first acts of government the President did nothing to conciliate the men actually or nominally in power during the revolution. His aim was to begin anew with a clean sheet, and to remake the institutions of Greece after a pattern laid up in the bureaucratic heaven. On his way to Greece he wrote to his learned friend Mustoxidi, a Greek of Venice, begging him to ransack the Venetian archives for precedents from medieval Greece, and to send him codes of banking, law and justice. He did not believe that there was anything in the modern Greece on which to build. "Il faut éteindre les brandons de la révolution"—that was his cry, and there was much truth in it. But the revolution had not quite obliterated such institutions as the Greeks possessed under the Turkish rule: the primates, however ignorant and oppressive, were still by custom and consent the centre of local affairs. The President tried to sweep them away at a blow, with the result that he made enemies of them all. He appointed new governors for each district, avoiding local men. The administration of justice was at first entrusted to the governor himself, or to demogeronts of the old type but chosen by the President.[16]

After Ibrahim's departure the President proposed a new organisation; there was to be a Ministry of Justice and a Court of Appeal, a High Court civil and criminal, and a judge in each district, with two assessors appointed by the litigants in civil cases but by the governor in all criminal cases. These judges were to be nominated by the President from lists prepared by the local governors, and must not be natives of the district. This in effect gave him complete control over criminal justice; it

[16] Constitution of Troezen printed in *S.P.* 15, 1069. Capodistrias to Panhellenium, in *Correspondance*, 9 Feb., I, 400; 12 and 14 Apr., II, 6, 11.

contravened one of the laws of the Constitution of Troezen, and earned for him the opposition of his Panhellenium (Senate) and the hostility of the demogeronts, who had been used to settle local disputes in the times of Turkish rule. His mistake seems to have been in attempting to introduce a centralised government before he had money to pay for his new army of officials. He counted on continued subsidies until a loan should be negotiated.

He thus made enemies of the local leaders of the revolution, when he had yet no means of binding to himself the professional classes. Greece, then as always, swarmed with a disproportionate number of lawyers, doctors, and professional politicians, who formed a kind of intellectual proletariat, perhaps the lineal descendants of the sophists of old. All these flocked round the President in the hope of places in the new Government,[17] and their presence was resented by the less talented men who had won the war. Capodistrias' rule by means of governors with dictatorial powers was equally offensive to both parties—the rulers by right of custom or force, and the would-be rulers for whom offices could not be manufactured fast enough: neither class was inspired by a real hatred of *τυραννίς*. The most powerful chiefs, such as Kolokotrones, had to be placated by tax-farming contracts, generous to themselves but highly oppressive to the peasantry.

The spirit of Capodistrias' rule, as interpreted and approved by Russia, was summed up in a letter of Count Bulgari to Nesselrode at the end of the year, a letter supposed to have been drafted by the President or to express views given by him in conversation. It rejects the idea of a federal government for Greece, which would "hand over the provinces to the primates' tyranny": or of constitutional government, for which the Greeks were unfit. The Powers had a right, it was claimed, to decide the proper form of government, for they interfered in Greece only to stop bloodshed and

> to destroy the Greek revolution by the establishment of a government compatible with the magnanimous views..., to strike at the heart of

[17] Capodistrias to Panhellenium, 13 June, in *Correspondance*, II, 171.

the demagogues of all countries in proving to them that there is no revolution which is not necessarily put an end to by the union of the Allied Sovereigns.

Language like this was grotesquely out of place: it confounded a national with a social revolution. The primates here denounced as demagogues were afterwards the first to sign addresses to Prince Leopold, in spite of the President's attempt to suppress them.[18]

All these things combined to make the President an unpopular man by the end of 1828.

[18] Bulgari to Nesselrode, 14 Dec. 1828—attached to protocol, 22 Mar. 1829, in *Parl. Papers*, 1830, XXXII; and *Portfolio*, V, 566. Bulgari was a Corfiot who owed his advancement in the Russian service to the President; he came in September 1828 as the representative of Russia.

CHAPTER X

THE CONFERENCE OF POROS

I

September—December 1828

MEANWHILE the Conference at Poros had begun its labours.[1] Stratford Canning, on his way out, visited his old friend Church[2] at Dragomestre in Western Greece; so that he had some opportunity of judging the condition of the Greek forces, 'whiskered ragamuffins' as he called them. He reached Kalamata, in the Messenian Gulf, at the beginning of September 1828, a few days after General Maison had anchored there with the French expeditionary force. On September 5th a conference was held with Ibrahim, whose troops had been in camp around Navarin since March. It had been feared in May that he would seize the harvest for his half-starved troops, but his only movement during the summer had been a march begun early in August, apparently towards Patras—a district in which a number of the peasants had submitted by negotiation to the Turkish garrison during the past year. But he soon returned to Modon, and was now awaiting the transports which were to carry him away in accordance with Codrington's Convention signed at Alexandria on August 6th. General Maison was itching to attack the Egyptians; he felt that he had been forestalled, for he had not been a party to the Convention, which was not made in the name of the alliance. Stratford was fortunately able to prevent a breach of faith. The case of the Turkish fortresses was rather different; Patras and Castel Tornese in Achaia, Modon and Coron in Messenia, had

[1] S. Canning's despatches during the Conference, in *F.O. Turkey*, 166–8. Aberdeen to S. Canning, *ibid.* 164. Final report also printed in *Parl. Papers*, 1830, xxxii, 637, and *S.P.* 17, 405.

[2] Stratford Canning and Church began a lifelong friendship at Constantinople in 1811, when Stratford was a young *chargé d'affaires* of twenty-four, and Church (two years older) was on leave from his command over a Greek militia regiment in the Ionian Islands.

remained in Turkish hands throughout the revolution, Navarin since Ibrahim's arrival in 1825. The Pasha had stipulated that 1200 Egyptians should be allowed to remain with the Turkish garrisons; but he had no authority to make terms on behalf of those garrisons, and it is doubtful whether Codrington had any right to make such a promise. He certainly had no specific authority to do so, and the garrisons must have been removed in the end. General Maison therefore felt justified in disregarding this part of the Convention. The Turks complained, excusably, of bad faith; but the event was fortunate, both for the allies in removing yet another possible cause of contention and for the Turks in deciding by a summary method what their rigid law would have made it difficult to concede in negotiation. All the garrisons surrendered on a show of assault, except that of Castel Tornese ('Castle of the Morea'), which held out during eleven days' preparation for a siege and a few hours' bombardment.

Stratford's first interview with the President was on board ship, at anchor off Kalamata, on September 11th. Capodistrias enquired anxiously about the boundaries and said that he "would be no party to a narrow and precarious arrangement". He also privately mentioned that he hoped for some German prince as eventual ruler of Greece.[3] Stratford guessed, wrongly, that the House of Weimar was intended, but in any case he was obliged to be non-committal. Reaching Poros, a small island close to Hydra, he found his colleagues already assembled. General Guilleminot was a 'classical' Philhellene, who delighted in identifying the names of places and in reconstructing the ancient provinces of Greece; as a Liberal and a Bonapartist, he was elated at the arrival of French troops to share in the glory of saving Greece, and ardently advocated the widest possible frontier. Ribeaupierre, the Russian, generally supported him in conference, though not so enthusiastically. Stratford himself, though hampered by the feeling that he had not the full confidence of his Government, was personally in agreement in most cases with the other two, and was not sorry to acquiesce in their conclusions. Had Wellington chosen an envoy who would really

[3] S. Canning to Aberdeen (private), 11 Sept., in *S.C. Papers*, 20.

represent his views, the Conference must have broken up over the report, for the French and Russians were not in the least inclined to give way. As it was, Stratford became involved in a good deal of friction with his chief and was afterwards made the scapegoat for the result.

The most pressing question was that of the boundaries. On September 22nd Capodistrias submitted a memorandum on the subject, making a formal bid for a line from Delvino to Salonica, and putting that from Prevesa to Zeitoun as the lowest limit. But there was really little discussion about the continental limits; the line from Arta in the West to Volo or at least to Zeitoun was already taken for granted by everyone on the spot: the advance of the Greek troops in the West was beginning, and before long the Turks themselves began to be indifferent. There was some doubt about the inclusion of Acarnania, but Guilleminot on military grounds would not hear of anything less. General Maison's attempt to invade Attica caused a momentary excitement, and Stratford himself wished that he could have allowed it. Before the report was signed, Church's advance enabled the Greeks to claim in some sort *de facto* possession of Acarnania. When Admiral de Rigny and General Maison tried to force the Greek flotilla to raise the blockade of Lepanto, they were censured by the ambassadors. All were agreed that the only defensible military frontier was from Arta to Volo or Zeitoun; Wellington did not deny it, but said that it was not our business to give a defensible frontier to Greece—an essential condition of any pacification.[4] Negropont (Euboea) was adjudged to Greece on the same grounds, but also in order to give it "the place which nature and the wants of Greece assigned to it"; Wellington equally condemned this "revolutionary sentiment". Although the island had taken little part in the revolt and the Turkish proprietors were in peaceful occupation, their number was only 4500, as compared with about 25,000 Greeks.

On the same principle the ambassadors reported that they

[4] See, in *Quarterly Review*, Oct. 1830, an article written by Dean Phillpotts in defence of Wellington's policy, under the Duke's superintendence; his letter to Wellington, and the reply, 12 and 15 Aug., in *Despatches*, VII, 155, 170. See below, p. 202, n. 1.

"considered it a sacred duty...to devise some principle which may require them to include Samos in Greece". (These phrases in the report suggest French drafting.) Samos had been practically autonomous before the revolution, collecting its own tribute and handing it to a Turkish governor, who resided in the island with a small garrison: there was no Turkish population. There was now an assembly of deputies and a Greek governor, 'Lycurgus' Logotheti, who had helped to defend the island from the Turkish fleet in the early days of the revolt; many of the people, especially the clergy, seem to have been ready to return under Turkish suzerainty, on condition that the governor should not be a Turk and that the tribute should be merely sent to Constantinople: they would thus be free of Greek tax-collectors and probably safer in a strategic sense as part of the Turkish Empire. Their position made them dependent upon Asia Minor, and likely to be the first victims of any new dispute with Turkey. But the Greek officials sent to Samos roused some national feeling, and the island was not reconciled even after the settlement of 1832, which forbade the return of a Turkish garrison, and placed the island under the rule of a prince appointed by the Porte, generally a Fanariot Greek and often in fact a non-resident.[5]

Candia (Crete) was a still more controversial point. Elsewhere, although Stratford knew that his Government was against any extension beyond the Morea, he had no absolutely positive orders; his own opinion supported the official view of his colleagues, and their joint instructions left them considerable discretion. But Candia had not been mentioned in the protocols of the allies since September 1827, when the island had been included in the blockade, not as part of the revolted territory, but as a base used by Mehemet Ali for supplies to the Morea. As soon as Ibrahim had been removed to Alexandria, there was no further excuse for the blockade, although the Russians did not wish to abandon it. Soon after the Treaty of July 1827, Baron Rheineck, a German Philhellene, had landed in a corner

[5] There is a short but convincing sketch of opinion in Samos in Michaud's *Correspondance d'Orient*, III, 446 ff., written immediately after a visit to the island, 30 Dec. 1830.

of the island with 2000 Greeks, and a cruel but desultory warfare had been going on ever since, in which the natives were to be found on both sides. There were three classes among the Greek-speaking inhabitants, who slightly outnumbered the Turks: the *capitani*, whose trade was fighting, were ready to negotiate with either party: the native Sphakiots, the tillers of the soil, took no part unless they could thereby secure the safety of their harvest and of their olive trees: besides these the island was infested with "lawless and desperate characters" like the famous pirates of Grabusa—the romance of brigandage has always been marred in Greece by disgusting cruelty.[6] The movement for joining Candia to Greece had not then taken on any solid form. Foreign troops would have been necessary in the first place to conquer the island. It would have been a burden upon the new State, which must have manned a considerable fleet to put down piracy, and maintained a large force to check brigandage. Any outrage upon European traders would be visited upon the Greek Government and lead to complications with the Powers.

The President would have been wiser not to agitate for a large overseas province so soon; and he was exposed, somewhat unjustly, to the charge of using Candia merely as a diversion in aid of Russia. It is known that he was already thinking of a German prince, and had sounded Leopold in London. It is possible that Leopold, who afterwards showed great anxiety about Candia, had made its inclusion a kind of condition of acceptance. Stratford was equally anxious for it: before meeting the President, he recommended, against the British admiral's advice, that the blockade should be continued for the present. When the Conference opened, he found the Russian ambassador for inclusion, but the French opposed. All agreed that in any case the Powers should insist (for what that was worth) upon mild treatment and local liberties for the Cretans. Admiral Malcolm, Codrington's successor, wrote to say that he thought a blockade impossible after October, and useless if the island were not to be a part of Greece. At this moment the President

[6] Dawkins to Aberdeen, 1830, summarised in *F.O. Greece*, 26 (*Abstract of proceedings since Feb. 1830*, f. 34).

produced a report from Baron Rheineck of a recent massacre of Greeks; there is no reason to doubt the truth of such a report, unfortunately all too probable, but it was only an incident in the bloody warfare which was renewed by the Baron's ill-considered expedition, begun after the Greeks had accepted the armistice provided by the treaty. It is hard to see how in winter a few ships-of-war could prevent massacres inland, and the mere stopping of supplies from Egypt would be likely to make matters worse instead of better. Still, the Conference at once ordered the admirals to continue the blockade, and Malcolm wrote that, as they desired it, he would do so as best he might. The ambassadors regarded the blockade as a political move towards the inclusion of the island in Greece.[7]

Meanwhile Aberdeen, as soon as he heard of Stratford's ideas, wrote privately and officially to warn him about Candia. If his warning was timely, his reasons were disputable. He spoke of the Government's

> determination not to see an island, of such paramount importance and commanding the whole of the Levant, in hands hostile to Great Britain. That such will be the case with the Greek State I have little doubt. Even if not under the control of Russia, the sight of the superior wealth, happiness and prosperity of our Ionian Islands will for years produce hatred and jealousy among Continental Greeks.

He wrote to Wellington: "I am very anxious about this question of Candia, as it seems to me more important than all the rest of Greece put together": and sent another strong despatch to Stratford.[8] But it was his own policy which was likely to throw Greece under Russian control and to earn the hostility of the new State. It needed more imagination then than later to conceive that "there is no barrier like the breast of freemen", for the spirit of national freedom was not everywhere vocal, and in the Levant was more vocal than reliable. It was not the policy of including Crete, but the occasion that was probably unwise.

[7] S. Canning to Aberdeen, 1 Sept. (from Navarin), and 27 Sept. Malcolm to S. Canning, 25, 30 Sept., 5, 9 Oct., in *S.C. Papers*, 21.

[8] Aberdeen to S. Canning (privately), 20 Sept., 2, 28 Oct., 18 Nov., in *S.C. Papers*, 22; (officially), same dates, in *F.O. Turkey*, 164; to Wellington, 23 Oct., in Wellington's *Despatches*, v, 165.

The island was sold by the Sultan to Mehemet Ali in 1830, but returned under Turkish rule ten years later on the defeat of the Pasha. The most extreme Russophobes had to admit before many years that Greece had not fallen under Russian domination. These separate warnings were followed by a definite joint instruction of the London Conference to raise the blockade. Even now, on his own authority, Stratford suspended the order, on the ground that when it was drawn up the news of the massacre had not reached London, and that Guilleminot had come round to the view of the other two.

The final report of the ambassadors was signed on December 12th, before any new orders from London could reach them.[9] It recommended the inclusion of Samos and Negropont, that of Candia less confidently: and of Continental Greece from the Gulf of Arta to the Gulf of Volo, leaving the northern shore of each gulf to the Turks. This gave a defensible frontier, but included districts which had never been in revolt, and ran counter to the ambassadors' instructions which had not mentioned Acarnania among the alternatives proposed.

The question of the status of Greece was bound up with that of the frontier. The ambassadors had more definite instructions on this head, with freedom to determine only the form of nomination of the governor, and the amount of tribute and compensation. But Wellington had thrown out the suggestion that if the Turks preferred it, absolute independence might be granted *in exchange for contracted limits*. This form of bargaining was not only unworthy but quite unsuitable: independence would be if anything an argument for larger limits; if Greece was not to follow Turkey in peace and war, she must have a defensible frontier. The only justification for confining Greece to the Morea would be if it was to remain an autonomous Turkish province.

[9] Aberdeen's last rebuke about Candia, dated 18 Nov., did not reach Poros until 15 Dec., three days after the final report had been signed. Hearing that despatches had come, Stratford seems to have taken care to sail out of the harbour before having them delivered, so that he was finally separated from his colleagues and no question could be raised—*S.C. Papers*, 22. The incident is an example of Stratford's manner of dealing with unwelcome orders from home.

As Aberdeen himself wrote: "The Morea alone gives, not a military frontier between independent States, but prevents daily contact of hostile populations in two provinces of the Turkish Empire".[10] The ambassadors, therefore, in accordance with their recommendation about the frontiers, went as far in the direction of independence as their instructions allowed. They recommended a hereditary prince, giving the Sultan no right of nomination, but only of investiture. Stratford thought that the President was at this time really tired of his task, and there is no trace yet of the selfish intrigue of which he was accused in 1830. He spoke to Stratford again of a German prince, and, after the report was signed, disclosed his meaning. "The person whom he designs for his German prince is no other than Prince Leopold, and he has assured me in confidence that the Prince is willing and that he had sounded H.R.H. when in England." Capodistrias probably hoped that the hostility of the English Government would be appeased by the prospect of a dynastic tie with Greece. His proposal shows how unjust was the prevalent abuse of him as a mere tool of Russia: the appointment of Leopold could not conceivably serve peculiar Russian interests.[11]

On the question of tribute and indemnity, the Conference took a correspondingly generous line; it was hampered by the lack of information, which came at best from a very partial source. The President made great delays: he seems to have suspected his own commissioners, who had been sent to collect statistics, of poisoning the minds of the demogeronts against his rule.[12] The Conference decided that the tribute was to be based only on the taxes paid exclusively by Christians, that is, on the *haratch* or poll-tax, and on the house-tax, besides one-eighth of the old tithe assessment: it was calculated that seven-eighths of the tithe regularly disappeared before it reached the Sultan, a reckoning which would seem fantastic if its probability were not other-

[10] Aberdeen to S. Canning, 2 Oct., 18 Nov.

[11] S. Canning to Aberdeen (private), 26 Nov., 15 Dec., in *S.C. Papers*, 20. The Russian Cabinet itself proposed Leopold in Jan. 1829—Wellington's *Despatches*, VI, 425.

[12] *Correspondance*, 14 Nov., II, 415; the statistics are printed in an Appendix to vol. IV.

wise attested. The total annual tribute was fixed at a million and a half piastres (about £60,000), but a proportion only was to be paid for some years.[13] As the value of the piastre had almost halved itself since 1820, the whole amount was a mere fraction of the taxes paid under Turkish rule. The question of compensation bristled with difficulties. Before the revolution, two-thirds of the Morea belonged to Turkish proprietors, whose lands had since been proclaimed national property, and had been pledged as security for the first Greek loan in Europe. The Conference recommended compensation only to those individual proprietors who could produce their titles before a special mixed commission within two years. This was an important qualification, as many of the Turks had been murdered or driven forth in the first orgies of the revolution and they or their heirs had no titles to produce; no compensation was allowed for public lands, military fiefs (*timars*) held direct of the Sultan, or ecclesiastical lands (*vacoufs*) belonging to the mosques (except those leased to individual Turks).

Stratford continued to press the need of subsidies and of a loan for Greece, but Wellington was determined not to spend a shilling. Aberdeen insisted that the treaty was not philanthropic: the Government would not support a new loan, "though the desire of gain may possibly lead men into still more desperate undertakings". In October the several thousand refugees who had been supported by the British Government in the Ionian island of Kalamos were turned out into the Morea, only just free of the Egyptians. Stratford signed the report with little hope of its acceptance; he urged Aberdeen to make at any rate a *speedy* settlement: if the boundaries must be contracted, a negotiation should be begun at once, with or without Russia: better still, the new frontier should be occupied by the French troops, and the Sultan forced to acquiesce. The future government too must not be left long in doubt; Capodistrias' expressed intention to retire "would greatly facilitate a final adjustment. He can never be acceptable to the Turks, and he

[13] See above, p. 103. The tithe alone was estimated in 1823 at 2,764,300 piastres—P. J. Green, *Sketches of the War in Greece* (1827).

has by no means succeeded in conciliating the affection or the confidence of the Greeks, notwithstanding his high reputation and services".[14]

The President concurred in the report, which he was permitted to read only on the advice of Ribeaupierre. The Russian ambassador, who was throughout anxious to make the recommendations as binding as possible, knew that the terms would thus become common knowledge, and that it would be more than ever difficult for Wellington to avoid their conclusions.

II

January—March 1829

In spite of the November Protocol limiting Greece to the Morea, the Greeks who knew anything of European complications had some reason to be satisfied with the results of the Conference. Any settlement must have seemed niggardly to those whose expectations were unlimited, even extending to large conquests to be undertaken for them by the rest of Europe. On the other hand, the report of the ambassadors was denounced by the friends of Turkey as a partisan and sophistical document, hurriedly composed on highly suspect information and dictated by Philhellenic sentiment. It is perfectly true that two at least of the ambassadors were prejudiced in favour of a large measure of Greek independence, and paid more attention to the interests of the Greeks than to those of the Turks. But that was to them the *raison d'être* of the alliance, in spite of Wellington's contrary interpretation: a strict 'pacification' could have been secured by aiding the Turks to crush the revolt, as Metternich had openly or covertly attempted to do. No territorial settlement after a revolution can be based strictly on legal right; once the fact of the revolution was acknowledged, there was everything to be said for setting it on a firm basis by a settlement as bold and generous as could be obtained by negotiation. Generosity was not to be expected of the Turks, and the allies were thereby forced into the position of partial arbitrators. Short of sacrificing

[14] S. Canning to Aberdeen, 14 Dec.

the essential results of the revolution, the Conference did everything reasonable to satisfy Turkish claims. They went too far, however, for one at least of the allied Governments.

The Report reached London at the New Year. Nesselrode, foreseeing that the coming campaign would be a critical time for Anglo-Russian relations, sent an able diplomat, Matuscewitz, to London. The Lievens were by now on thoroughly bad terms with Wellington, who disliked the Princess's spirit of intrigue; but the new envoy was more open and conciliatory in his manner. His immediate task was to get the Poros report accepted; on no other condition would Russia agree to the return of ambassadors to Constantinople.[15] The British ministry, absorbed in the Catholic question, had little time to attend to Greece. But at the end of the month they still hoped that the policy of the November Protocol might be carried out, although they were not prepared to break with Russia over it. The sudden illness of La Ferronays made them hope for a French foreign minister less friendly to Russia. Polignac hurried to Paris, but returned disappointed at the end of February. Portalis, temporarily filling the Foreign Minister's place, declared in the French Chamber "qu'on ne s'est point engagé à laisser l'Attique en dehors de la Grèce".[16]

The French envoy, Jaubert, sent to announce the November Protocol, reached Constantinople also at the New Year. The Turks begged for the ambassadors' return, but showed as usual no sign of concession: they would "deviate a little from the strict line of justice" but would never forego their fortresses, their right to nominate a governor and so forth. It was perfectly clear that, unless England honestly supported the Poros settlement, the Russian campaign alone could decide the issue. Wellington was not blind to the chances: he did not believe, as Metternich affected to do, that the Russians would necessarily fail again. General Diebitch, in spite of enemies, was made commander-in-chief with an authority more real than he had

[15] Instruction to Matuscewitz, 3 Jan. 1829, annexed to Protocol, 22 Mar., in *Parl. Papers*, 1830, XXXII. See above, p. 125.

[16] Viel-Castel, XVIII, 454 ff., 497 ff.

enjoyed the year before. The army was rested and refitted, and the campaign began early with an important success, the capture of Sizepolis from the sea side (February 15th). But the Duke could not bring himself to recant in time.[17]

When the London Conference met again in March, he agreed to the Poros report as the *basis of negotiation* only. Its conclusions were taken over in the Protocol of March 22nd with a few qualifications—Samos and Candia to be excluded, and the Greeks to have no voice in the election of a prince; above all the Greek troops must be forced to retire from Acarnania. It might seem surprising that, having consented to the Arta-Volo frontier, the protocol should insist pedantically on this retirement. But the last clauses made it quite plain that the consent of Wellington at least was not serious. The two ambassadors were to treat in the name of Russia too, but each reserving the right to weigh the objections of the Porte and if necessary to substitute other proposals. The inconsistent views of the allies were elaborated in memoranda attached to the protocol. France argued for the full acceptance of the report and for regarding the treaty as something more than an instrument for pacifying an insurrection. Polignac seems to have been rebuked by his Government for signing the protocol as it stood. Russia would consent to the ambassadors' return only if the allies *first definitely* decided the terms. The British memorandum was in a clean contrary sense: it was unlikely that the extended frontier would be accepted by the Porte or conquered by the Greeks: the idea of a hereditary prince was a new demand, for which the Porte might be compensated by being asked to cede less territory: still, the British Government would consent to use the terms not as an ultimatum but as a basis of negotiation. The Duke's explanation to Metternich was still clearer: "...it is to be presumed that the objections which the Porte will be able to establish against a further extension of Greece, will accordingly be admitted by England". France might be content if the Porte would at once admit the autonomy of the Morea and Cyclades, or in the last resort, of

[17] Metternich to Esterhazy (Apr.), in Wellington's *Despatches*, v, 602. Heytesbury to Aberdeen, 20 Feb., 7 Mar., in *F.O. Russia*, 179.

Attica as well. Finally, "the co-operation of the Cabinet of Vienna should be eminently useful in the negotiations at Constantinople". In other words, the Poros report was to be abandoned at the first objection.[18]

On February 21st Stratford wrote from Naples that he could not undertake the work unless under definite orders to secure the limits recommended, with complete exclusion of Turks up to those limits, and a guarantee by the alliance. His conditional resignation was accepted,[19] and Aberdeen's brother was appointed to take his place. Sir Robert Gordon was described by Matuscewitz as an honourable but mediocre man, a supporter of Turkey on principle, and a great admirer of Metternich: by Esterhazy as a man well-disposed but obstinate, who must be managed, not driven. He was instructed to treat the Porte as our friend: "It is not possible that we should be insensible to the arguments by which a counter-proposition may be successfully urged".[20] Stratford was deeply disappointed at the result, but he was perfectly right to resign; he wrote to Dawkins: "As matters now stand the fate of Greece will turn almost exclusively on the fortunes of the Russian campaign".[21]

[18] Aberdeen to Cowley, 22 Mar., in P. O. VI, 41. Gentz to Metternich, 11 Apr., in *Briefe*, III², 336. Esterhazy to Metternich, in *Berichte*, 243, 15, 25 Mar.

[19] Aberdeen to S. Canning (private), 27 Mar., in Lane-Poole, I, 480. Official acceptance, 10 Apr., in *F.O. Turkey*, 178.

[20] Matuscewitz (who also spoke of Wellington as "grand capitaine malgré l'opinion d'autres, et premier ministre malgré la sienne... *la nécessité seule le meut*"), quoted in F. de Martens, XI, 395. Esterhazy, *Berichte*, 243, 31 Mar. 1829. Aberdeen to Gordon, 9 Apr., in *F.O. Turkey*, 179.

[21] S. Canning to Dawkins, 13 Apr., in *S.C. Papers*, 22. Stratford's services were rewarded, later in the year, by a G.C.B., and he devoted his energies to Parliament, to which he had been 'elected', as member for Old Sarum, in 1828.

CHAPTER XI

THE PEACE OF ADRIANOPLE

I

April—July 1829

IN 1829, as in the year before, the coach of the triple alliance jolted on its way over pot-holes which all but rattled it to pieces. Russia was dissatisfied with the Protocol of March 22nd, but would not openly protest for fear of a real break with England. Everything depended on the campaign, and it was vital for the Tsar to keep the alliance at least nominally in being: he had more to lose than England had by such a break, except for one thing—a separation from Russia would at this time mean for England a separation from France as well. For this even the Duke was not prepared: he had to agree with Peel's view that, if it were not for France, it would be best to withdraw altogether from the treaty; but that the French occupation of the Morea, the joint negotiation begun at Constantinople, and even our obligations to the Greeks forbade it.[1] This, rather than any love of blind reaction in France, was the reason of his unhappy anxiety to see Polignac at the head of the French ministry. His irritation was reinflamed by a number of fresh and provoking incidents.

The blockade of Candia by the British squadron, probably never very effective during the winter, was formally raised in January.[2] Capodistrias, who had not given up his claim, at once (January 21st) protested to Malcolm and Heyden on the ground that they had promised to prevent the Egyptians from sending their reinforcements to the island. He told Rheineck too not to expect any from Greece either, but to organise his own forces

[1] Heytesbury to Aberdeen, 27 Apr., in *F.O. Russia*, 179. Peel to Wellington, 24 Apr., in Wellington's *Despatches*, v, 598. Ellenborough's *Diary*, 29 Apr. 1829.

[2] S. Canning to Malcolm, 6 Jan. See, for the following incidents, *Parl. Papers*, 1830, XXXII, 283 ff.

and wait; and he appointed an Englishman, Captain Hane, as Chief Magistrate of the island.[3] The two admirals were no longer acting in co-operation, but Heyden told Malcolm (January 27th) that in consequence of the President's letter he would send a squadron to cruise between Budrun and Candia (the port): he was ready to withdraw it, when and if Malcolm should undertake the service instead. The English admiral had no authority to act on so vague a rumour: Heyden's suggestion that the Morea was threatened was absurd, and his appeal to treaty obligations had no weight; Mehemet had no desire to burn his fingers again in Greece. It was no business of the allies to prevent the movement of troops between Egypt and an island blockaded only while it was a base for Ibrahim's troops in the Morea. But since Russia had repudiated her neutrality in the Mediterranean, Heyden was justified in blockading the island, so far as it was a measure of war against the Sultan and his nominal vassal. On February 2nd the President wrote again, talking of a threatened Egyptian expedition to Candia: Heyden promptly pursued and captured a brig and a corvette (which did not return his fire), and warned Malcolm of "warlike preparations at Alexandria". He wrote to Mehemet Ali complaining of his hostile conduct and threatening to capture more ships and to detain them 'in deposit'. At the same time he suggested in a letter to Lieven (February 25th) that a joint Convention should be arranged with Mehemet "to define his position or limit his action". This was as much as to ask the allies to help in the Russian war, on the pretext of a measure arising out of the Treaty of London. It was against this inconsistency that Wellington chiefly protested, although he did not in any case admit Heyden's right to blockade the island as a separate measure of war. He really feared that Russia, if victorious, would dictate terms including Candia in Greece despite all protocols. He called a conference, at which France gave him cautious support and Lieven defended the admiral's action.[4] Nesselrode added his own assurances, and

[3] Capodistrias to Rheineck, 24 Jan., in *Correspondance* II, 539; to the 'Conseil de Candie', 28 Feb., *ibid.* III, 51.

[4] Conference, 21 Apr. The protocol was not signed until 11 May.

although the blockade continued, no more ships were captured. During the spring, Wellington also successfully protested against the blockade of the Dardanelles being extended westward to include the Gulf of Contessa.

Not only the Russian fleet, but the French troops, were a thorn in the flesh to the Duke. His reluctant consent to the expedition had been won only by a promise that it should return as soon as Ibrahim had gone, or in the following spring at latest. Common sense and all the reports from Greece agreed that the French troops could not leave so hastily; since General Maison's flutter in the autumn, they had been devoted to pioneer work instead of to glory: but Wellington's career, spent in fighting the French, had bred in him an absurdly exaggerated suspicion. At the beginning of 1829 he had so far impressed his view upon the French that their subsidies to Greece were suspended and the troops were expected to leave in March; the French Government offered in their place to allow Colonel Fabvier to return and organise a regular force, within the Morea, of two or three thousand men drawn from Rumelia. Fabvier was not popular: he was suspected of having surrendered the Acropolis short of extremity in 1827, and his expedition to Chios early in 1828 had been a costly failure.[5] The President refused the offer, and prophesied disaster if the French troops were to leave so soon. He was genuinely alarmed at the prospect of an army of turbulent Rumeliots being admitted to the Morea, where they would be regarded as foreigners and enemies: he was advised even by the English Resident to garrison the Isthmus against a possible incursion of these bands: moreover he had no intention of giving up his Continental advance. The French troops accordingly remained: but, in the face of continued protests and threats from England, one division returned in June, and most of the rest embarked in December, leaving only a single brigade of less than 2000 men under General Schneider. This force remained at

[5] Fabvier, like the English Philhellenes, quarrelled with the President and resigned in June 1828, but returned in December and joined the opposition party until he was recalled to France with Gen. Maison in June 1829. He was succeeded in command of the regular troops by the Bavarian Col. Heideck, afterwards one of the regents for Otto.

Navarin and Modon on the Messenian coast, and did not finally return to France until August 1833.[6]

The proceedings of the Greek fleet and of the Greek troops were equally unwelcome to Wellington's views.[7] Their combined action was quickly driving the Turks out of Western Greece. A Greek blockade of the coast north of the Isthmus from Volo to Missolonghi was formally declared in March, but it was only effective before Missolonghi and Anatolico. At the end of April Aberdeen threatened to ignore it if it were not raised at once. Though this was a decision of the British Government independently, it was represented by Sir F. Adam, owing to an error of the Colonial Office, as a decision of the Conference. On May 12th Captain Spencer was sent from Corfu to order the Greek admiral, in the name of the allies, to raise the blockade. He found Miaoules in front of Anatolico, which was daily expected to capitulate; he was bound to insist against Miaoules' refusal, but he tactfully delayed taking any forcible steps until the town surrendered on May 17th. His presence fortunately prevented a breach of the capitulation on the part of some insubordinate Greeks, who perhaps remembered the scenes at the capture of the place by the Turks three years before. The French Government's protest against this attempt to enforce the armistice made another of the petty sources of irritation between the allies.

At the same time the British Resident, as instructed, demanded that the President should cause the Greek troops to retire (May 18th). Dawkins cannot have pressed the demand with much conviction, for he had already come round to the view that the limits recommended at Poros should be adopted after all. The Turks were in great straits, and the Greeks confident of holding the Arta-Volo line. The President, sure of the support of Russia and probably of France, refused (May 23rd) to admit as sufficient the armistice *de facto* offered by the Reis-

[6] Cf. Dawkins to Aberdeen, 10, 17 Jan. 1829, in *F.O. Greece*, 4. Capodistrias to La Ferronays, 15 Jan., in *Correspondance*, II, 512. *S.P.* 17, 1295. See above pp. 112. 117, and below, pp. 200–1.

[7] For the following incidents, see *Parl. Papers*, 1830, XXXII, 573. *F.O. Greece*, 4. Wellington's *Despatches*, 27 June, V, 622.

Effendi in September 1828, and put forward the technical point that the Protocol of November 16th had never been communicated officially to the Greek Government. Western Greece was already liberated, and he knew that if he could only hold it until Russia should make peace, all would be well. When the two ambassadors on their way to Constantinople wrote again (June 9th) insisting upon the retirement, he avoided a definite answer by forwarding to them his correspondence with Dawkins (June 27th). In London, Lieven refused to *force* the Greeks to withdraw, only consenting to '*require* it' (*réclamer*), a non-committal promise. At the same time the gulf between the policy of England and her allies was emphasised by the renewal of the suspended French subsidies and by the arrival of a new Russian subsidy of one million roubles.[8] The Government of the Ionian Islands, though not expecting any active insurrection in the islands, was still uneasy at the unrest in Albania which was diligently fomented by Greek agents.[9]

Thus the Russians would not give up the blockade of Candia; the French would not withdraw their troops from Greece; the Greek fleet and the Greek troops both refused to give up the campaign beyond the Isthmus. Although the President had in the autumn ordered Church not to advance a step beyond the Makrinoros, he was thought to aim at including eventually both the town of Arta and even Prevesa. It was important, in order to prevent collisions, that the Gulf of Arta should belong exclusively to one party, in Sir F. Adam's view to the Turks; for if the Greeks were once admitted beyond the passes as far as the northern shore of the gulf, the movement would spread northwards into Albania and Epirus, leaving no hope of peace or

[8] Capodistrias, *Correspondance*, 13 Apr., 5 June, III, 105, 160.

[9] The following is a pleasing specimen of rumour or propaganda. "Friend Antony,...I now write to acquaint you that the Governor [it is said] has with Russia and France renewed [*sic* ? renounced] the Protocol of 20 March and they wish Greece free to Epirus. Russia has withdrawn her minister from England for having signed the Protocol. Wellington has committed suicide. The Emperor of Austria has abdicated his throne in favour of his son Ferdinand"—Miaoules (the admiral's son) to a friend in Albania, 18 June. Translation in *C.O. Ionian Is.* 54. *Ibid.* 55, 59–60, for more intercepted letters.

safety for Ionian trading vessels. For the same reason, both shores of the Gulf of Corinth should be wholly in Greek hands. As long as the Greeks held the country up to the mouth of the Aspropotamos, it would be an advantage to leave Acarnania to the Turks. This fear for the safety of British rule in the islands was the secret of Wellington's anxiety about the Greek limits. At one moment Aberdeen even suggested unpractically: "In the event of our being finally compelled to go beyond the Morea, what do you think of making the Northern State under a separate government?"[10] This device would no doubt have been frustrated, just as it was by the Rumanians and by the Bulgarians later in the century. The Duke, who seldom wasted time over the absurd, took no notice of the hint.

II

July—September 1829

The Tsar was much exasperated by the "injurious suspicion and extreme irritation" of the Duke, who came near to threatening war. Lieven was authorised to complain to George IV about the conduct of the ministers, but refrained; for with the progress of the war he could afford to ignore the Duke's discomfiture.[11]

The campaign had begun badly, with plague raging among the armies. But the Turkish resistance was not equal to that of the year before. On June 18th Silistria fell: Diebitch made a feint against Shumla, then suddenly marched with 40,000 men and crossed the Balkan passes on July 21st. The 'Russo-maniacs' were in a state of panic. In one breath they announced the contemptible weakness of Russia, in the next they drew lurid pictures of the Russians holding the Dardanelles and beginning a career of conquest in the Mediterranean. Actually the Russian policy was less ambitious. The phase of conquest was over for a time, and the new policy of keeping Turkey as a feeble and dependent neighbour had already been sketched; a special committee sitting in St Petersburg reported in June to the Tsar to

[10] Aberdeen to Wellington, 19 July, in Wellington's *Despatches*, VI, 29.
[11] F. de Martens, XI, 398.

that effect. When Lieven, elated by the sensational victory, urged Nesselrode to have done with Turkey once for all and to dictate a national peace after a national war, the minister rebuked his enthusiasm.[12] The commander of the Russian army was less easily restrained. A few days before the fall of Silistria, Diebitch had made an offer to treat, but did not interrupt the campaign. The Vizir referred his proposals to the Sultan, who resisted obstinately until he was forced by the success of the Russian advance to ask for a truce (August 6th). Diebitch replied that he had delayed too long; but representatives might meet, without an armistice. He issued a proclamation calling on the Bulgarians to continue offering prayers for the Sultan, their lawful sovereign, but in spite of this distributed arms among them.

A real proof of the Tsar's anxiety for peace rather than conquest *à outrance* was the mission of the Prussian General Müffling to Constantinople, which was arranged during the visit of the Tsar to Berlin in June and became known about the middle of July. Offers made by Prussia to act as the only possible mediator had been refused in the previous autumn, for the Tsar and the army were determined on a second campaign. But St Petersburg was now full of pessimism, and Nicholas wanted to make sure of peace in good time. The Russians denied that this meant a regular mediation by Prussia, or that General Müffling had been told definitely the terms he was to offer. But there is no doubt that the Tsar outlined the terms to the King of Prussia, so that Müffling might be able to induce the Sultan to treat; and that he was anxious not to force the issue to a possible collapse at Constantinople.[13] The course recommended by policy was now enforced by necessity. Diebitch began his march with

[12] F. de Martens, XI, 411. S. Goriainow, *Le Bosphore et les Dardanelles*, pp. 25 ff.

[13] Nesselrode to Lieven, 27 July, in *F.O. Russia*, 183. Bernstorff, 5 July, in P. O. VI, 79. On the origin of Müffling's mission, see Ringhoffer, pp. 160 ff. Bernstorff's Instruction to Müffling, in Schiemann, II, 465. Müffling was not to admit to the other ambassadors that he came as a mediator, and was not given specific terms for direct communication to the Turks, but if they should ask for terms he was to transmit the request to Russian headquarters. Cf. Tsar's admission to Maj. Reitzenstein, *ibid.* 492. Müffling, *Aus Meinem Leben* (1851), describes this mission (in § 4, of which an English translation was published in 1855).

only 40,000 men: in ten days 10,000 were sick or unable to march, and not more than 12,000 men reached Adrianople. Although there was something like panic in Constantinople, and the Sultan could not reckon on the loyalty of the populace, Diebitch was threatened by a considerable force in and around the capital, and by an army said to number from fifty to sixty thousand men marching up in his rear under the Grand Vizir and the Pasha of Scodra (Scutari).[14] He must come to terms quickly before the Turks could recover from the surprise of his lightning advance.

Meanwhile the English and French ambassadors, reaching Constantinople on June 18th, had been pressing vainly for a settlement of the Greek question. They began with little hope of even limited success. Austria offered to support the independence of the Morea, but not the protocol of March 22nd. At a conference held on July 9th this protocol was presented; it was answered three weeks later by a haughty refusal. The only move of the Turks was to issue a firman offering pardon to the *rayahs* of the Morea and a chief of *codja bashis* (primates) to reside with the governor and intercede for them as before: all Mussulman property must be restored and the fortresses given up. But the Russian army was now in Rumelia: there was discontent and panic in the capital, and men bewailed the loss of the Janissaries, the traditional if tyrannous protectors of the Sultan in the past. The Reis-Effendi at last, on August 15th, put his name to an agreement wrung from him in three long conferences during the preceding ten days. By this agreement the Porte consented to the Treaty of London as applied to the Morea and Cyclades only, with certain other stipulations.[15]

[14] Mustafa, Pasha of Scutari, was waiting to back the winner. He offered, should Turkey collapse, to leave Widdin and Orsova to the Serbians and to pay tribute to Russia as a vassal ruler of Albania. Letter of Milosh Obrenovitch to Diebitch, 20 Aug., in Schiemann, II, 338, 360 ff. After peace had been signed, the disappointed Pasha threatened to attack Adrianople in earnest; but Diebitch sent a force to stop him, and through Gordon and Royer at Constantinople easily awoke the Sultan's fears of his ambition. Mustafa was forced to deny any hostile intention and gained nothing by his duplicity. Schiemann, II, 372 ff. Müffling puts the numbers of his army at 25,000–30,000.

[15] I.e. (i) tribute to full former amount, (ii) restoration of war-material in fortresses, (iii) Greeks to have only a police force, (iv) no emigration from Turkey into Greece—P. O. VI, 91.

It was not satisfactory, and it was certain that Russia would supersede it at the peace. General Müffling had arrived on August 4th, but would not publicly reveal his terms. They were supposed to include adherence to the Convention of Akkermann, free navigation of the Bosphorus, an indemnity which was understood to be nominal, and the cession of Anapa and Poti on the Black Sea. As a result of his interview (August 6th) the Reis-Effendi drew up a minute, offering to fulfil the first two conditions; he would not say anything about an indemnity, and stipulated that there should be no cession of territory. Above all, he would not yet consent to send plenipotentiaries to treat. Müffling sent this offer to Diebitch, recommending him to forego indemnities; but, as he expected, Diebitch, who reached Adrianople on the 20th, refused to do so.[16] In this deadlock the ambassadors at last (August 24th) persuaded the Turks to send two plenipotentiaries to Adrianople under the escort of Major v. Küster, a Prussian officer on Müffling's staff, who had long been *chargé d'affaires* at St Petersburg. The English ambassador refused to support the demand for an indemnity without knowing the amount, and the question was left formally undecided. But the Sultan was now so certain of peace that he set Russian prisoners at liberty and withdrew some of his troops to the Asiatic shore. There was now less fear of the Russian army than of a rising among the populace or the troops themselves against the Sultan whose reforms seemed to have brought disaster. The British fleet, which had been cruising off Tenedos and Vourla since the middle of June, anchored in Besika Bay at the end of August and found the Russian Mediterranean squadron already there. Guilleminot, who feared that if either tried to pass the Dardanelles there would be a collision, kept the French fleet out of the way at Smyrna. Besides the English and Russian ships, about equal in numbers, there were only a couple of French and three Austrians watching each other and the event. Ellenborough would have liked, now and even a year earlier, to "pass the English and French fleets through the Dardanelles",

[16] Müffling to Diebitch, 17 Aug., in P. O. vi, 94. Diebitch to Müffling, 23 Aug., *ibid.* vi, 96.

but neither the Duke nor Polignac was prepared for such risks.[17]

On August 29th Diebitch ordered a suspension of hostilities and began the negotiations. There was again a deadlock over the indemnity, and a message was sent to the capital for a decision: on September 9th the Porte gave way. Müffling had already left Constantinople, his mission being ended with the actual meeting of the plenipotentiaries. It was understood that the Turks would probably be able to reduce the indemnity by a special mission of appeal to St Petersburg. On the same day Gordon and Guilleminot succeeded in making the Sultan promise to subscribe without reservation to any decisions of the Conference under the Treaty of London, thus in the end forestalling a settlement by Russia alone; but it was only a technical victory of diplomacy, for nothing but the presence of the Russian army could have brought the Sultan to yield. Having won his point, Gordon offered on his own responsibility to bring the British and French fleets into the Sea of Marmora (although the French were still at Smyrna), "for the preservation of tranquillity" only. The offer was not accepted, but Gordon seems to have thought that the news of it influenced the Russians to come to terms at once (September 14th).

None can say what might have happened if peace had not been signed. Gordon afterwards declared that "all hopes of defending Constantinople were abandoned by the Turks". General Müffling also thought that Diebitch could easily have taken the city, but he knew that this was not the Tsar's own intention, and believed that it would not much benefit the Russians, who would enter a city deprived of supplies and would be forced to pursue the campaign into Asia. The ambassadors did not know, what the Turks now suspected, the dangerous plight of the remnant of the Russian army. If the Sultan had possessed the confidence of the people he might have stood firm and

[17] Ellenborough's *Diary*, 11 Nov. 1828, and 12, 13 Aug. 1829. Admiral Malcolm at Vourla received orders from Gordon on 25 Aug. to bring part of the fleet, and on 28th to bring the whole fleet to the mouth of the Dardanelles: he arrived there on 31st—*Admirals' Journals*, 168.

successfully challenged the Russian general's campaign of bluff.[18] But in that case it would have been hard to hold him to the promise made to the two ambassadors in a moment of panic. Diebitch at least took no notice of it when peace was signed, but insisted on a separate article in the treaty, binding Turkey not only to the Treaty of London but to the March Protocol.[19] His object was not so much that the Greeks should gain a better settlement as that Russia should add something to what was already secured by the alliance. The Turks, indeed, tried to shuffle out of the additional promise, and delayed over some of the other preliminary conditions. The alarms were not quite over, for Diebitch mistrusted the Turks' good faith and threatened four times to march on Constantinople. The fleets remained near the Dardanelles until the beginning of October.

Throughout the crisis, Wellington in London, like Gordon at Constantinople, had done his best to forestall the Russian settlement. His behaviour was typical of his methods of conducting government; growing irritation, angry threats, resistance to the last, and then a sudden volte-face to meet the inevitable. He was ready to treat as a final and sufficient settlement any result which might be obtained by the ambassadors before the issue of the campaign, so that his hands might be free to threaten the Russian advance. Heytesbury at St Petersburg was convinced that the Emperor really desired peace, but this complacency was not shared at home. "I don't", wrote Wellington, "believe one word of the desire for peace of a young Emperor at the head of a million of men [!], who has never drawn his sword." Why, it was asked, has he not revealed his terms? 'Moderation' in his eyes might seem extravagance to England.[20] In the Prin-

[18] Gordon to Aberdeen, 16 Sept., in *F.O. Turkey*, 181. Müffling, *Aus Meinem Leben*, p. 63; and Müffling to Wellington, 30 Sept., in Wellington's *Despatches*, VI, 188. Cf. Lane-Poole, *Life of Gen. Chesney*, pp. 171 ff. Sir A. Slade thought that the Sultan could have resisted. He says that Gordon was misled by our consul at Adrianople, who did his best but had never seen an army before, much less tried to estimate numbers—*Records of Travels* (2nd ed., 1854), pp. 190 ff.; cf. *Turkey, Greece, Malta* (1840), p. 393.

[19] Text of Peace of Adrianople, 14 Sept. 1829, in *S.P.* 16, 647.

[20] Heytesbury to Aberdeen, 22 July, and Aberdeen to Heytesbury, 6 Aug., in *F.O. Russia*, 180, 178. Wellington to Aberdeen, 21 Aug. 1829, in *Despatches*, VI, 98.

cipalities, the reorganisation of the government on European models, with a new Constitution drawn up for them by the Russians, seemed to portend annexation.[21]

The news of the crossing of the Balkan Mountains brought matters to a head early in August. On the 10th Wellington wrote: "Matters are in such a state that we cannot delay any longer to speak out". On the 18th the Conference considered a suggestion of the ambassadors that the allies should cut the knot by recognising at once the independence of the Morea and the Islands, simply notifying the Porte of the fact. Aberdeen was anxious to discuss the idea, but the others would only promise to refer the matter home. Lieven knew that the issue would be decided before he would have to give an answer. Polignac, who with Wellington's approval was now at the head of the French ministry, disappointed the Duke by supporting Russia as much as his predecessor had done.[22] Wellington was at the end of his patience; he threatened to ignore the Lievens and told Aberdeen to "do all your business through Heytesbury". On August 25th he wrote in despair:

> We can talk of nothing excepting in the tone and quality of a power that is degraded. What I see is that Russia will dictate to the Porte the Protocol of March last. She there has us bound....If our Protocol of the other day (August 18th) reaches her in time, she will probably stipulate for an independent Greece *with* the limits of March last.[23]

The next day came the news that the Porte would be ready to yield on conditions. Wellington clutched at this straw and called another conference; Aberdeen wanted still to adopt the

[21] This Constitution was a real benefit to the Principalities. Schiemann, II, 392 ff., points out that this, the one substantial reform carried out by Nicholas during his reign, was outside his own dominions; cf. I. L. Evans, *The Agrarian Revolution in Rumania*, p. 29.

[22] Wellington seems to have been quite blind to the folly, from his point of view, of installing a man like Polignac at the French ministry. Pozzo di Borgo saw well enough that a revolution was the probable result, and Aberdeen was not comfortable about it. On Wellington and Polignac, cf. *Memoirs of Stockmar*, I, 128 ff.; A. Sorel, *Essais d'Histoire*. Esterhazy, too, foresaw that Polignac the minister would not be the same as Polignac the ambassador—*Berichte*, 244, 12 Aug. 1829.

[23] Wellington's *Despatches*, VI, 107.

ambassadors' idea, but Wellington said the settlement must now be *negotiated.* The Conference which met on August 29th refused to take any notice of this partial adherence to the treaty.[24] On September 4th there was an angry interview at the Foreign Office about the Greek troops beyond the Isthmus, Lieven refusing to force them to withdraw. Wellington complained that the Lievens were intriguing against him, and in fact his doings in conference were recounted with zest by Princess Lieven in her letters to Grey.

The news of the occupation of Adrianople at last convinced the Duke that further resistance would be futile. He put no faith in assurances of moderation, so long as the Russians still refused to disclose their terms of peace. He jumped to the conclusion that Constantinople must fall, and prepared for a total change of policy: "We must reconstruct a Greek Empire and give it to Prince Frederick of Orange, or Charles of Prussia".[25] Grey had come to the same conclusion about the fall of the city: but having been no alarmist hitherto, he was content with less heroic remedies now, thinking that it would be best to restore the Turks for the moment until a plan should be made for dividing their dominions. Princess Lieven continued to assure him that in any event Russia would demand "not an inch of territory", and Grey admitted that there was now little cause for England to distrust Russia; there was more fear of a new Holy Alliance to maintain the Bourbon dynasty in France.[26] The rest of September

[24] Wellington was acting only on a report from Gordon, dated 7 Aug., foreshadowing success: the Reis-Effendi signed nothing until 15 Aug., and had the danger passed meanwhile he would certainly have evaded doing so. Even when the news of the signature reached London (5 Sept.) the Conference again refused to act, on the ground that adherence was not complete. Wellington protested in vain. See Protocols of Conferences, 12, 19 Sept.

[25] Wellington to Aberdeen, 11 Sept., in *Despatches*, vi, 152. Lord Stanmore ascribes the new policy to Aberdeen "with little support except from Peel and to some extent Goulburn. The Duke still clung to his Turkish sympathies". But it is clear from this correspondence that the Duke pushed the idea himself for a moment at least. Cf. Metternich's alarm, in *Weisungen nach London*, 247, 28 Oct., 24 Nov., 16 Dec. 1829, and Esterhazy's report that the Duke was quite 'dérouté', and liable to sudden 'embêtements'—*Berichte*, 244–5, 31 Aug., 20 Sept.

[26] Princess Lieven and Grey, 14, 16, 20 Sept., in *Correspondence*, i.

was spent in anxiously awaiting the terms of peace; on the 29th it was announced that Diebitch would include acceptance of the March Protocol among them; on October 7th the full text reached London. Wellington was still in desperate uncertainty.

"It would be absurd", he had written, "to think of bolstering up the Turkish Power. It is gone, in fact; and the tranquillity of the world, or, what is the same thing, the confidence of the world in the permanence of tranquillity, along with it. I am not quite certain that what will exist will not be worse than the immediate annihilation of the Turkish Power. It does not appear to me to be possible to make out of the Greek affair any substitute for the Turkish Power: or anything of which use could be made hereafter in case of its entire annihilation and extinction. All I wish is to get out of the Greek affair without loss of honour and without inconvenient risk to the safety of the Ionian Islands."[27]

But, although the Duke had not much faith in Greece as the future heir of Turkey, he did not at once abandon his new idea, and he was even disappointed at the compromise by which it seemed to him that the Porte was reduced to a mere state of dependency, a state to which immediate dissolution would have been preferable. He was not quite convinced by Metternich's promptings to look for salvation in a Concert to guarantee Turkey, if only as a means of being in at the death when the time should come. He refused to guarantee a loan to Turkey which was being considered by the House of Rothschild, and seemed to agree with the head of the firm in London that it would be useless to pick a quarrel with Russia.[28] But in the end a despatch was sent to St Petersburg attacking every article in the treaty without exception, in a tone of impotent remonstrance which could have no effect but to embitter the relations between England and Russia without hope of altering what was done. The only important concessions obtained were a reduction

[27] To Aberdeen, 4 Oct., in Wellington's *Despatches*, VI, 192.

[28] Political reasons led the firm to refuse this loan, just as they had refused a loan to Russia in Mar. 1828. Nathan to Solomon Rothschild, 12 Oct. 1829, in Corti, *The Rise of the House of Rothschild*, p. 409. Ellenborough's *Diary*, 11 Oct. 1829.

of the indemnity and a speedier evacuation of the Principalities, both of which Nesselrode had already promised to make; Diebitch had in fact gone beyond his instructions. England's protest against a *fait accompli* could only, as Nesselrode said, begin a paper war of recrimination. Apart from the indemnity, Grey thought the terms reasonable compared to the Russian situation now, though not moderate compared to the original purpose of the war.[29]

The treaty did in fact increase the Russian influence navally in the Black Sea, politically in the Principalities, and commercially in Turkey generally. Wellington objected especially to Article VII, which gave Russian shipping absolute immunity from Turkish authorities in Turkish waters. But Turkish officials were notoriously vexatious; though Russian shipping gained an exclusive advantage, Russia might claim that she was after all more nearly concerned than any other Power. All countries which had not yet obtained the right by special treaty benefited by the opening of the Straits to commerce in the Black Sea in time of peace.[30] Wellington's suspicious attitude went here beyond a sense of proportion.

The moral influence which Russia gained by having had an army within striking distance of Constantinople was less easily measured, but even less a matter for solemn diplomatic protest. The gains in Asiatic Turkey were not of immediate significance. Ellenborough was already talking of "fighting Russia on the Indus", but the Duke was less nervous about the "schemes of ambition in Asia, which Russia may reasonably entertain". Nesselrode shortly expressed what the Russians considered they

[29] Aberdeen to Heytesbury, 31 Oct., in *F.O. Russia*, 178 (printed for Parliament in 1854, in *Parl. Papers*, 1854, LXXII, 1). Nesselrode's reply, Jan. 1830, in *F.O. Russia*, 189. Heytesbury to Aberdeen, 30 Sept., in *F.O. Russia*, 181. Cf. Princess Lieven to Grey, 22 Oct., in *Correspondence*, I. Convention, 25 Apr. 1830, in P. O. VI, 187. St Petersburg was disappointed at the moderate results of the war, ascribed to the Tsar's so-called 'Grossmutpolitik'—Schiemann, II, 379. Grey to Princess Lieven, 7, 17 Oct., in *Correspondence*, I.

[30] England had obtained access to Crimean ports by treaty in 1799, followed by France (1802), Sweden (1805), Prussia (1806) and Sardinia (1823)—Schiemann, I, 260. But the remaining restrictions were due to Russia rather than to Turkey.

had gained: "réduite à n'exister plus que sous la protection de la Russie, cette monarchie convenait bien plus à nos intérêts politiques et commerciales que toute combinaison nouvelle". To Metternich he wrote: "les ministres anglais...ont voulu museler le Cabinet russe qui les a mis dedans, tout ce qu'ils ont voulu empêcher est arrivé, et ce qu'ils ont voulu amener a manqué".[31]

As for Article X, which concerned the Treaty of London, Wellington was so uneasy about it that he managed to obtain from the Conference a declaration that the inclusion of the March Protocol in the Treaty of Adrianople should not prejudge their own decision. The Russians had secured their own points, but the sequel showed that they would not insist on a part of the settlement which did not concern their own interests. Wellington was able for the moment to protect British interests in the Ionian Islands by the exclusion of Acarnania from Greece. But Aberdeen still played with the idea of a new Greek Empire. A long despatch was sent to Constantinople in which the 'ancient ally' was spoken of in terms unheard since the death of Canning. Aberdeen must have fancied himself almost back in his Athenian days. The British Government allowed itself to "suspect...that independent of all foreign or hostile impulse the clumsy fabric of barbarous power will speedily crumble into pieces". A change of policy was therefore necessary. We had "hitherto endeavoured to contract within the narrowest limits the extent of territory to be exacted from the Porte". But if the Empire must fall, we could not restore it:

> We cannot be blind to the detestable character of Turkish tyranny. Every day renders more certain the impossibility of any European sympathy with a system founded upon ignorance and ferocity.... The composition of the Greek State becomes a matter of infinitely greater importance than if the Turkish power had been preserved essentially unimpaired.

[31] Ellenborough's *Diary*, 3 Sept. Wellington's *Despatches*, VI, 217, 10 Oct. 1829. Nesselrode to Grand Duke Constantine, 24 Feb. 1830, in *Recueil* (1854), p. 60. Nesselrode to Metternich, quoted in Mendelssohn, *Geschichte*, II, 527.

It was desirable to find "an arrangement which at the period of its dissolution should offer in the Greek State a substitute.... An extension of frontier might not be adverse to the general interests of Europe". The new State might be given "some degree of consistency under a moderate and prudent Prince".[32]

While Aberdeen was penning a despatch so congenial to his real sympathies, the Turkish ministers were drinking the King's health in bumpers of champagne at an entertainment given by Aberdeen's own brother in the British embassy; the Reis-Effendi even danced a polonaise with one of the 'Frankish' ladies. Rejoicing in these evidences of Turkish regeneration, Sir Robert Gordon was bewildered and a little irritated when he learnt the sudden change in the sentiments of his Government. Only the day before, he had written home to say that he did not believe in the imminent collapse of the Empire. The Peace of Adrianople need make no difference in the policy of upholding Turkey: on the contrary the Empire was entering on a new lease of life, determined in future to pay a wiser attention to foreign Powers. As the months went on and the Peace of Adrianople seemed to bring no startling consequences, Wellington began to recover his normal balance and told Gordon that he was to continue to assure the Turks of our friendship; the despatch of November 10th did not mean that we ceased to support them, only that we had to contemplate the possibility of collapse.[33]

Metternich was equally alarmed and needed reassuring. For a moment he believed that Turkey in Europe could not survive much longer: "le mal est fait, les pertes sont irréparables". His agent, Prokesch v. Osten, now at Smyrna, had already begun to argue, with a quick change of front, that

> if the Greeks attain the natural frontiers which history and nature would give them, European sentimentality is satisfied; and Mavrocordato's idea, that the interests of the new State necessarily align

[32] Aberdeen to Gordon, 10 Nov., in *F.O. Turkey*, 179. This despatch was marked by the King: "Excellent, nothing can be better! G.R."

[33] Gordon to Aberdeen, 11 Nov., 15 Dec. 1829, in *F.O. Turkey*, 181; and 7 Jan. 1830, *ibid.* 189. Aberdeen to Gordon, 26 Feb. 1830, *ibid.* 188.

it with those of the Powers which form the dam against Russia, seems to me not without truth and a basis for diplomatic action.

It is true that if you want to establish a race of pirates, a centre of disorder and intrigues, and so lay a train to be fired by Russians and Liberals, then you should make the Isthmus the limits of a tributary Greece. If you want the people to settle down, to learn to know their own good and love peace, and to make ties of relationship with other States, then you should do nothing by halves. The Porte hardly counts any longer.[34]

Metternich was hardly ready to assent to this doctrine, but made no more difficulties about Greece. In the larger question of the whole future of Turkey, he was probably less shocked by the contemplation of possibilities than by Wellington's proposal for meeting them. A decent partition was what he hoped one day to see, but not now; in the crisis of September an "idle and malevolent" rumour at the embassies, that Austria was preparing a plan of dismemberment, was officially traced to a *Mémoire* by a German "political speculator", and it seems to have been without foundation.[35] Meanwhile Austria was arranging a loan to lighten the burden of the Turkish indemnity.

The French Government was less cautious. One of the first acts of Polignac as minister was to disappoint the hopes of Wellington by drawing closer the Russian alliance; he produced a grandiose plan of exchange of territory, which reached St Petersburg too late for any discussion before peace was signed. Russia was to be satisfied with the Principalities and an extension of frontier in Asia, Austria with Serbia and Bosnia. France would take Belgium, Dutch Brabant, Luxemburg and German Alsace; to Prussia would fall Saxony and the rest of Holland, whose dethroned kings would be consoled, one with Rhenish

[34] Metternich to Esterhazy, 6 Sept., P. O. VI, 180; and 28 Oct., in Mendelssohn, *Geschichte*, II, 525. Prokesch v. Osten to Gentz, 18 Aug., 3 Sept., in *Aus dem Nachlasse*. Gentz to P. O., ? Oct., in *Zur Geschichte*, p. 196. Aberdeen to Cowley, 14 Nov. 1829, in *F.O. Austria*, 211.

[35] Seymour to Aberdeen, 1, 23, 28 Sept., 6 Nov., in *F.O. Prussia*, 159. Aberdeen to Stuart, 17 Nov., in *F.O. France*, 390. Stuart to Aberdeen, 23 Nov., *ibid.* 397. Cf. Sorel, *Essais d'histoire*: "L'alliance russe et la restauration", pp. 108 ff. Metternich described it as one of the wild rumours spread by French embassies. Nothing in the Austrian archives gives any support to the rumour.

Prussia and the other with a kingdom formed out of the remainder of Turkey in Europe. The Dutch colonies were to be England's share.[36] It is worth noting that nothing was said of Egypt, where the French already built their hopes on the friendly Arabian power of Mehemet Ali, and even hoped for his assistance in the projected conquest of Algiers.[37] The main feature of Polignac's scheme, the reconstruction of a Greek Empire, coincides so far with Wellington's suggestion. However wildly impracticable, it was from one point of view a sound move, indicating the line which the Western Powers would take up towards a partition by the Eastern monarchies. It is hardly fair to criticise it from our later knowledge of nationalist movements: even travellers who knew the East hardly noticed the Bulgarians as having an identity of their own.

For the time at least all such projects faded into the background: all that remained was that Wellington, like Metternich in March 1828, was at last reconciled to making Greece a small but fully independent State. His conversion had been as usual tardy but sudden.

[36] Polignac to Mortemart, 4 July; Mortemart to Polignac, 22 Dec. 1829, in Schiemann, II, 379 (text in App., pp. 511 ff.). Cf. Sorel, *Essais d'histoire*, criticising this "monument de déraison chimérique". F. A. Simpson, *Rise of Louis Napoleon*, pp. 54–5, n.

English travellers, like the rest, amused themselves with schemes of partition. In April 1826 Sir Hudson Lowe, the 'gaoler of Napoleon', then on his way to an appointment in Ceylon, sent a report on the military position of the Dardanelles, and added his ideas of the future. Greece to have all up to the Balkan Mountains including Constantinople; Russia, Moldavia; Austria, Wallachia and Bosnia; France, Syria; to England would fall Egypt and a protecting control over the Dardanelles. Lord Bathurst wrote in the margin: "military interesting, political part, stuff"—*S.C. Papers*, 14. Parts of this letter are printed in the Appendix to an anonymous pamphlet (clearly by Sir H. Lowe), entitled *Observations upon the affairs of Russia, Greece and Turkey*, and dated May 1829. The pamphlet reiterates the idea of a timely partition in concert with Russia, leaving England free to resist the Russian advance in Asia, the only real danger.

[37] E. le Marchand, *Europe et la conquête d'Alger* (1913), cc. 6–7. Cf. Metternich, *Weisungen nach London*, 247 (1 Sept. 1829) and 251 (4 Jan. 1830), enclosing (? intercepted) copies of Guilleminot's despatches. The plan to enlist the aid of Mehemet Ali is described as a favourite scheme of the French ex-consul in Egypt, the Bonapartist Drovetti. On Wellington's objections to the conquest of Algiers, see his *Despatches*, VI, 576, and vol. VII *passim*; Ellenborough's *Diary*, 10 Jan. 1830, and onwards.

CHAPTER XII

PRINCE LEOPOLD

I

The Prince and the Conference

WHILE the ultimate fate of Turkey was being canvassed in a variety of schemes of fanciful partition, the concrete work of an immediate settlement for Greece went on. Austria henceforward made no more difficulties; she favoured both the independent status and the Arta-Volo boundary. Austrian merchants were crying out for a proper representative and consuls in Greece.[1] A consul was sent in May 1831; three years later Prokesch v. Osten was appointed minister, and spent fourteen years at Athens, collecting materials for his monumental history of the revolt. The Russians accepted without great difficulty the idea of giving the Greeks an independent prince and a smaller territory, though preferring their alternative (foreshadowed in the protocol of March 22nd, 1829, and embodied in the Peace of Adrianople) of a tributary State with wider limits. Lord Grey, disgusted with the endless haggling, was, through Adair in Paris, actually the author of the compromise frontier, from the mouth of the Aspropotamos to the Gulf of Zeitoun. These were the limits of the blockade ordered by the ambassadors in September 1827 (but contracted on the eastern side from Volo to Zeitoun). The intervening points were not definitely fixed, but were to include the summit of Mt Oeta and the ridge of Mt Oxias, which proved, owing to defective maps, impossible to reconcile on the spot.[2] Wellington, in spite of Aberdeen's new theory of strengthening Greece, agreed only with great reluctance to include Euboea. After the first moment of panic, his idea was to

[1] Prokesch v. Osten to Gentz, 20 Jan., 8 July; Gentz to Prokesch v. Osten, 16 Feb., 18 June 1830, in *Aus dem Nachlasse*.

[2] For Grey's part, see Trevelyan's *Lord Grey*, p. 229, and *Correspondence* with Princess Lieven, 14 Sept., 2 Oct. 1829. See above, pp. 83, 144.

make a Greek State, small while Turkey lasted, but independent and therefore a possible nucleus of something much bigger. This method of settling boundaries on *a priori* grounds, without reference to conditions on the spot, was characteristic of the time.

Aberdeen was for avoiding any more negotiation with the Porte and for simply announcing the decision of the Conference. Wellington fought against what seemed a high-handed line towards our 'ancient ally', and Sir R. Gordon, a consistent supporter of the Turks, objected to recommending independence otherwise than as a friend of the Porte. The promise extracted from the Sultan, on September 9th, 1829, to abide by whatever decisions the Conference should adopt, had its uses after all. Without referring to Article X of the Peace, the Conference was able, abandoning the question of the alternative, to found the grant of independence upon the Porte's desire to narrow the limits, and upon "the force of events". The force of events was always leading the Duke to sudden reversals of policy.[3]

The choice of a prince was a more difficult matter. A province more or less to Greece was not of so much interest to Europe as the dynastic ties of the new State. Fortunately for Greece, the mutual jealousies of the Powers made it certain that the candidate chosen must be a neutral one. There was still in Germany a reserve of competent minor royalties unimportant enough to be inoffensive. Nevertheless many names were brought up and rejected. The first British candidate was Prince Philip of Hesse, an Austrian general with little to recommend him save a willingness to become Orthodox in religion. The French objected, suspecting Metternich in the background, and brought forward a Catholic, Prince Charles of Bavaria, but he refused at once. Aberdeen insisted on Philip, refusing to "have the Emperor [of

[3] Aberdeen to Wellington, 31 Dec. 1829, 2 Jan. 1830; Wellington to Aberdeen, 1, 18 Jan. 1830, in *Despatches*, VI, 356, 372 and 362, 422. There appears to be no English record of the conferences leading to the protocols of 3 Feb. 1830, except the accounts sent by Princess Lieven to Grey in their *Correspondence*, vol. I, Oct.–Dec., and the letters of Aberdeen and Wellington in *Despatches*, vol. VI. Isambert, pp. 387 ff., has used the French archives. On the claims of Bavaria, see below, pp. 205 ff.

Russia] as umpire between us and France": in this deadlock the Conference adjourned for more than a fortnight. Early in November two new names were discussed, Prince Maximilian of Este, and Prince Frederick of Orange. France again objected, to the first as an Austrian, to the second as a Protestant, and proposed another Catholic, Prince John of Saxony. Apart from the diplomatists' concern for political interests, there was good reason against the choice of a Catholic, for the Powers were choosing a ruler for devout and even fanatical members of the Orthodox Church, who regarded Catholics as little better than Turks. The offer was made to Prince Frederick, who refused after some delay.

Prince Leopold had already been mentioned, but since he was connected with the English royal family, as widower of Princess Charlotte and uncle of Victoria, Aberdeen was shy of bringing him forward. Had the Duke of Clarence died before George IV, Leopold might perhaps have become Regent for his niece Victoria during her minority, or at least would have had great influence with his sister, the Duchess of Kent, who after George IV's death was in fact designated for the regency. On November 13th Aberdeen told Stuart in Paris that "if Russia and France propose Leopold, we have no objection". About November 20th Charles X gave up the Saxon prince and promised his support for Leopold. Leopold arrived in England on the 24th, but Prince Frederick remained the British candidate until his refusal was known. Wellington thought Leopold the "least desirable of our candidates", but that his nomination was "at least respectable". The prince was friendly with some of the leading Whigs, and therefore at any other time distasteful to the Tories; but the Duke was at this moment trying vainly to strengthen his Cabinet by getting Grey to join it, and the choice of Leopold might help to conciliate him. Moreover Leopold in Greece might be less inconvenient than at home. But Grey would not leave his retirement to join a sinking ship under such a captain as the Duke. The feebleness of both the French and English Governments was reflected in their foreign policy, and was the chief reason why Russia had been able to attain her objects unchecked. It must not be forgotten that, even among those who least desired it, a change of ministry was thought to be inevitable soon in England, and a violent catastrophe was openly prophesied in France. Tsar Nicholas told Heytesbury that "when he read of the triumphant progress of Lafayette [in America] he felt as if a bucket of water had been thrown upon his head".[4]

The idea of Prince Leopold was not new in Greece; his name had been mentioned by those Greeks who made overtures to Canning in September 1825, but Canning had said that, as a member of the royal family, Leopold would not in any case be admissible. Ever since the first successes of the revolution there had been obscure attempts in different quarters to get the reversion of a Greek crown; deputations of two or three, claiming to represent the Greek people, had offered to put themselves under the protection of England, France and Russia in turn,[5] and Philhellenes of each country encouraged the notion of Leopold, the Duke of Nemours, or Capodistrias as ruler. Capodistrias, having been elected President, soon saw that the Western Powers would never allow him to be *sole* ruler of Greece. During his visit to London in the summer of 1827 he approached Leopold and certainly proposed his name to Stratford Canning during the Conference of Poros.[6] Leopold was a strong candidate, and likely to be an acceptable one in Greece as well as among the Powers. He was not a Roman Catholic, and if the difficulty of his connection with the royal family could be got over, his candidature would be welcomed in England. And England under Wellington was of the allies the least friendly to the Greek prospects and, therefore, the most to be propitiated. Capodistrias hoped by this means to gain more territory for Greece. A connection between the Greek and the English Courts might overcome Wellington's objection to the inclusion of Samos and Candia. So far it seems clear that the President was sincere, but a change soon became apparent.

[4] *F.O. Russia*, 181, 14 Oct. 1829.

[5] I.e. England, 1 Aug. 1825; France, Oct. 1825; Russia, Dec. 1826. See above, pp. 44–6.

[6] See above, pp. 143, 149.

After the protocol of March 1829, which made the appointment of a hereditary prince certain, Leopold sent Charles Stockmar, brother of the more famous Dr Stockmar, with a letter to Capodistrias asking about the terms on which a sovereign (unnamed) could accept the throne. Stockmar travelled by way of Naples, where he probably discussed the affair with Stratford Canning (now on his way home), and reached Greece in May. As a result of conversations, Capodistrias gave Stockmar a written answer that he could not lay the name of any sovereign before the Assembly without a promise of Samos and Candia.[7] Leopold was thus early impressed with the notion that Candia was an essential part of the new kingdom. The President also stipulated that the sovereign must embrace the Orthodox religion and must conclude *with the nation* "les bases de l'administration". The first decree of the National Assembly at Argos gave the President authority to negotiate with the Powers, but any settlement was to be invalid until ratified by the Assembly (Article III); special attention was drawn to this article in the closing proclamation. The deputies from Candia were admitted to the Assembly. The decision to make Greece an independent kingdom seems to have confirmed the change in the President's views. He knew that he would have less influence over a sovereign than over a vassal prince, and might even be ousted altogether.[8] In spite or perhaps because of his unpopularity he was less and less inclined to abandon his post to another. As opposition hardened, his determination took on a fatalistic colour. He had worked unceasingly and earned much hatred in the interests, as he believed, of Greece; it was his right and duty

[7] *Memoirs of Stockmar*, I, 80 ff., where these letters are printed. See above, p. 146.

[8] The elections for this Assembly at Argos were mostly 'arranged'. The deputies for Corinth were told "qu'ils n'ont pas le droit de donner une opinion contraire à celle du Président". Dawkins to Aberdeen, 18 July 1829, in *F.O. Greece*, 5. Similar incidents are described at Kalavryta, Missolonghi and Nauplia; at Modon the Commissioner threatened to imprison the elected deputy if he would not resign. Cf. Trikoupes, IV, 356. The French Admiral de Rigny thought that the President aimed at retaining his position in a vassal State, and feared to lose it by independence. Gordon to Aberdeen, 30 Oct. 1829, in *F.O. Turkey*, 181.

to carry through the task. He hated England, and the English Government was the most determined not to see him stay as ruler. Whatever his real motives, he began to work against the success of Leopold's candidature.

Early in December the Conference again adjourned, and Leopold had some conversation with Wellington about the conditions of acceptance, but apparently little was said about the boundaries. The difficulty of his family connections was overcome by showing that he was not in any case in the English line of succession, and by making his annuity independent of Parliament; French anxiety for the Catholics in Greece was met by special stipulations in their favour. The Cabinet consented on January 11th to a draft protocol. The only remaining difficulty was the violent opposition of George IV, who favoured yet another German prince, the son of the Duke of Mecklenburg-Strelitz. The King nearly caused a scandal by making overtures to this prince, without Wellington's knowledge and through that bugbear of all ministers, the Duke of Cumberland, who was brother-in-law to the prince's father.

George IV hated that another member of his family should be called King, and it had to be impressed upon him that Leopold was only to be 'Sovereign' of Greece; then he offered to consent if Leopold would give up his annuity, though his wealth was one of his best recommendations in Greece, which could not afford a large allowance to the Court. But Wellington had a way of carrying through his policy with a high hand, and he was not sorry to assert once for all his own influence over that of Cumberland. He went down to Windsor on January 14th and even, it is said, threatened to resign. At last the King ungraciously consented, and there seemed to be no more obstacles.[9]

On February 3rd three protocols were signed, deciding to offer the crown to Leopold as ruler of an independent kingdom, guaranteed by the three Powers, but with the Aspropotamos-Zeitoun boundary and only diplomatic safeguards for Candia

[9] Wellington's *Despatches*, VI, 358 ff., 426. The Duke once told Lord Clarendon that "he had had to do with many Sovereigns and always found he could bring them to reason"—Maxwell's *Clarendon*, I, 179.

and Samos. There was to be a general amnesty and a right of emigration to both parties; in fact large numbers of Greeks were driven by poverty and misery to emigrate into Turkish territory.[10] But since Leopold had not even formally accepted, the Conference might have omitted from the protocol an unctuous sentence in which the "Courts sincerely congratulate themselves at the close of a long and arduous negotiation". This tone of absolute finality was meant to discourage the Greek irredentists, who considered what had been done to be a mere beginning.

At the end of January, before the protocols were signed, Leopold had suddenly demanded the inclusion of Candia: he had kept back this claim hitherto, and Aberdeen insisted that his acceptance must be unconditional. The question of boundaries had in fact been shirked between Leopold and the Conference. But he continued to press his new objections and conditions, which show how sketchy must have been the preliminary conversations. As in the demand for Candia, so in stipulating that he should be allowed to withdraw if the Greeks objected to him, he followed the lines of Capodistrias' conversations with Charles Stockmar. This very natural request was ignored by the Conference, but Leopold kept resignation in view if he should not prove acceptable in Greece.[11] At the same time the subject was raised in Parliament by a motion of Lord Holland attacking the whole of Wellington's Eastern policy, which consisted, he said, towards the Turks—of hollow friendship, and towards the Russians—of impotent ill-will. "Quid stulti proprium est? non posse et velle nocere." But his resolution, demanding for Greece "sufficient territory for national defence" and "a government with full powers to adapt its laws and institutions to the wants and wishes of the people", had to be withdrawn. Wellington at first curtly refused to give any financial support, but on February 20th the Conference agreed to guarantee a loan for raising troops only; meanwhile the remaining French brigade was not to be withdrawn for another year. On the 24th Leopold accepted the

[10] For these protocols, and Leopold's acceptance and resignation, see *S.P.* 17, 452–528, or *Parl. Papers*, 1830, XXXII and 1831–2, XLVIII.

[11] Leopold to Capodistrias, 20 Feb.

sovereignty; at last there seemed some hope of a new era in Greece. But the details of the loan had yet to be negotiated, and the allies reckoned without the Greeks and their existing ruler.

The revived negotiations had brought again to the surface all the simmering irritation between the English Government and the Russian. The Duke sent by the common post a letter to Heytesbury, full of complaints and accusations against the intriguing spirit of the Lievens; on his side Lieven wrote: "Quel purgatoire, bon Dieu, que celui qu'il m'a fallu traverser...toutes les passions réveillées". During March and April the discussions about the loan went on, and more than once nearly ended in a rupture.[12] No man in his senses would have undertaken the government of Greece without money for other purposes besides the upkeep of troops; the fact that the loan was afterwards squandered by the Bavarian regents does not prove its unwisdom. Seeing the other allies against them, the British Government at last, on May 1st, consented to guarantee their share of the full loan demanded, 60,000,000 francs. The last difficulties seemed to be overcome: but Leopold, hearing rumours of trouble, was growing more anxious about his reception in Greece. He had written to the President: "I have heard tell that men have expressed repugnance here and there to have me for Sovereign. I beg of you to let me know the truth, nothing in the world would induce me to impose myself on Greece".[13] Waiting for letters from the President, he still raised minor points of difficulty before the Conference.

On May 15th he received the news which finally turned the scale, and on that day he wrote to prepare the Conference for his resignation, in view of the "dangers and odium of forcing the Greeks to accept an arrangement to which the Senate [Panhellenium] has declared that it will not be a contracting party". The Conference argued that the Senate had no authority to offer its own remarks upon the subject, and that in any case it had

[12] Lieven, in F. de Martens, XI, 425. Leopold to Stein, 10 Apr., in Pertz, *Stein*, VI, 866, quoted in Stockmar's *Memoirs*, I, 105.

[13] Leopold to Capodistrias, 22 Apr., in *Correspondance*, IV, 45. The friction was the worse because Leopold was negotiating in person: but on 2 May he refused to communicate any more with the Conference except in writing.

now acquiesced, according to a letter from the President addressed, on April 16th, to the Conference. But Leopold replied that the President's letter to him was far from containing a full and entire adhesion, and on May 21st he formally resigned. Wellington, Ellenborough and others, seeing the close relations of Leopold with the Whigs during the whole affair, suspected a different motive: early in April the King had grown suddenly weaker, and the Whigs might again hope to see Leopold as Regent. There would be more probability in this theory if the sick man had been not George IV but the Duke of Clarence, who was the real obstacle to a regency. George IV might die any day, but the Duke of Clarence was only sixty-five and showed no signs of dying; Victoria was already eleven years old. It is unlikely that Leopold, having once accepted, was influenced decisively by such considerations. It is clear, however, that he was encouraged by the Whig leaders in his demands for a more generous settlement and for taking the opinion of the Greek Assembly.[14] The Whigs were unwise in continuing the agitation for a better frontier at the risk of delaying what Greece most needed, a definite settlement. Wellington's Government could not last for ever, and their chance might come to make a change; but Greece was not a decisive line of attack, and the great aim for the moment should have been to make Leopold's acceptance safe. But early in May Leopold had agreed, though reluctantly, to the conditions imposed; there is little reason to doubt that his own explanation was the true one, and that it was not so much Whig influence as the news from Greece which led him to resign.[15]

II

The Prince and the President

If this be so, Capodistrias bears a heavy responsibility for the discouraging tone of his letters; if he deliberately exaggerated

[14] The *Westminster Review* published a translation, from a French pamphlet, of a protest 'from Cephalonia' against his candidature and the boundaries imposed—XII, 522 (Apr. 1830).

[15] Dr E. C. Corti, in his *Leopold I* (Vienna, 1922), pp. 39–43, gives more weight to Leopold's English ambitions. French (enlarged) edition (Brussels, 1927), pp. 61–6.

or even manufactured difficulties, the charge is graver still. It has been seen that during the summer of 1829 his tone, at first favourable, began to change. After Leopold's candidature was taken up by the Conference, he still professed his readiness to "serve this country whatever the position and title which is to be assigned to me in the new order of things", but only provided that a worthy settlement should be made. He forced into prominence the questions of Candia and of the Continental frontiers, knowing well that the unpopularity of accepting the settlement of the Conference would thus fall upon Leopold's head. Early in December 1829 he talked of retiring, but a fortnight later he wrote:

> People alarm the country by new rumours. There is talk of a Protocol, of the Prince who is to come, etc.... At Poros last year I showed my readiness to further any settlement, but did not expect that the Protocol of March 22nd would announce an arrangement not ready for execution and made a ground of intrigue.[16]

He complained bitterly of the hostility both of the English Resident and of the Philhellenes. Official England objected to his supposed subservience to Russia, and above all to his alleged designs on the Ionian Islands, but had no more sympathy with constitutional opposition in Greece than in the Islands themselves. Unofficial Englishmen in Greece, represented by men like Finlay, were ready enough to let the Ionian Islands go to Greece, but were outraged by the President's arbitrary proceedings. The Philhellenes for the most part professed advanced democratic principles: the islands were governed by military administrators, with a rough justice but little imagination. The Ionian Government and the Resident in Greece feared the President as a Russian who was opposed to British interests: the Philhellenes attacked him as a ruler without political principles and as a diplomatist without experience of administration. However natural, the hostility of both sections had unfortunate results.

[16] Capodistrias to Eynard, 20 Nov., 10 Dec.; to General Maison, 24 Dec. 1829—in *Correspondance*, III, 402, 421, 428.

Capodistrias freely accused England of bribing the chieftains of the Morea against him, though a commission of his own appointing failed to trace any evidence for this. But Sir F. Adam made no secret of his dislike; when Griva, one of the most factious *capitani*, wrote to ask him whether a revolt against the President would have English support, he was not exactly given encouragement, but he was politely answered and not emphatically condemned.[17] To give any countenance to the lawless brigandage of the *capitani* was to undo the one solid benefit of the President's régime; whoever was to be sovereign in the end, the President must have authority meanwhile. The liberal Philhellenes, too, forgot that only his 'tyranny' could have brought some semblance of peace to the countryside. The old leaders of the revolution, who now posed as the constitutional opposition, had shown themselves incapable of preserving order. No one could deny that the peasantry were absolutely devoted to the President, whom they believed to be personally responsible for the battle of Navarin, the expulsion of the Egyptians, and the return to comparative peace. The monks of the famous Arcadian monastery of Megaspelaion were violently against a change.[18]

Such was the President's side of the case. But knowing as he did that, right or wrong, England would not tolerate him as the ruler of Greece, he should have kept to his originally sincere resolution and prepared men's minds for the coming change, so winning an honourable name for unselfish patriotism. Instead, no one was allowed to speak of the March Protocol or of a possible change of government; two peasants were imprisoned for mentioning that a prince was coming. Viaro Capodistrias was said to be preparing addresses, and even a new *Hetaireia*, against the appointment of a foreign sovereign, while his brother, Agostino,

[17] Dawkins, 9 Jan., 20 Mar. 1830, in *F.O. Greece*, 10. Adam to Griva, Jan. 1830, in *C.O. Ionian Is.* 59.

[18] Report by Capt. Trant of a journey in the Morea, 16 Feb. 1830, in *C.O. Ionian Is.* 59. There is in the Church Papers (*B.M.*, *Add. MSS.* 36566, f. 175) a long letter from the monks to Church, recounting their services to the Greek cause throughout the war—150 fathers in arms, 10,000 refugees given shelter, contributions of money and plate, and even two loads of valuable books sent to make cartridge-papers at the siege of Tripolitza in 1821.

publicly announced that the limits were to be enlarged, and were to include the Ionian Islands. In Thessaly all the Greeks believed that the frontier was to extend to Salonica; disappointed, they traced the report to the monks, who excused themselves by saying that they, and presumably the President too, had been deceived.[19] As the protocols of February 3rd, 1830, became known, Capodistrias, seeing perhaps that there was no immediate chance of a larger territory, turned more to the constitutional point, that the Greeks must have a voice in the settlement: "I shall be the first to receive the prince in legal form, that is to say when I have taken the opinion and votes of the nation". Again, in language new to him, he wrote: "This country, uncivilised as it still remains, is yet not without its public opinion".[20] He began to talk of summoning a National Assembly and of framing a constitution, of which no more was heard when once Leopold had resigned; he announced the protocols to his local governors in a tone of great dissatisfaction. It was a dangerous game to play.

In his letter of April 6th to Leopold he spoke gloomily of the "immense task", "serious crisis about boundaries", and of the privations which the new sovereign would be expected to endure if he hoped to win the affection of the people. He declared again that in order to satisfy the Greeks, Leopold must embrace the Orthodox religion and grant a constitution. He added in a postscript that the Senate had repudiated the settlement. A fortnight later, on April 22nd, he wrote that the Senate had now acquiesced, but enclosed their *Mémoire* protesting against the boundaries and the restitution of property to the Turks, and rejoicing that Leopold was unwilling to accept without the assent of the Greek nation. This implied a new National Assembly and further delay. These were the letters which led immediately to the prince's resignation. Capodistrias was right to warn Leopold of the difficulties which he must expect, but he managed

[19] Dawkins to Aberdeen, 24 Nov., 25 Dec. 1829, *F.O. Greece*, 6. Cf. reports of Consul Crowe at Patras, 14, 27 Mar. 1830, *ibid.* 17. Urquhart, *Spirit of the East*, I, 289.

[20] To Kolokotrones, 8 Feb., in *Correspondance*, III, 456; to Eynard, 4 Mar., *ibid.* III, 490.

to create the false impression that there was among the Greeks generally a feeling of violent hostility to any foreign prince.

The *Mémoire* in question was presented ready made to the Senate: it was signed by only thirteen out of twenty-seven members of a body practically nominated by the President himself, and by four of these after much opposition. It was printed at once and rapidly distributed, while Leopold's acceptance was never printed at all. When the resignation became known the Senate showed its real views in a declaration signed by its President, Sissinis, that it had no right to express an opinion on the protocols.[21] Meanwhile a movement for signing addresses of welcome to Leopold was suppressed by the President, who spoke of its organisers as "une poignée de misérables, meneurs d'intrigues" and so forth. These men were in fact the leaders of the opposition to the President, and though some were inspired more by hatred of him than by love of a foreign prince, they included most of the well-known figures of the revolution, who had resigned or been driven from office under the President's régime.[22] The wiser heads recognised that, if the Greeks were to have independence, they had disqualified themselves for any but a foreign ruler. The bitter jealousies aroused under the rule of an Ionian Greek had already been seen, and no one of the leaders of the revolution had enough prestige to be singled out. Unfortunately the opposition contained more ignorant self-seekers than enlightened patriots, and these men brought discredit on the whole movement. The President at least chose to regard these addresses of welcome as a mere manœuvre directed against himself; he was all the more annoyed because they were encouraged by the French and English Residents, who had been drawn, like most of the Philhellenes, into ill-concealed opposition to his government. Dawkins was anxious to send the addresses

[21] Dawkins to Aberdeen, 30 June, in *F.O. Greece*, 11.

[22] Miaoules, Konduriottes and Mavrocordato all refused office after the Assembly of 1829. Trikoupes had resigned in Feb. 1829, refusing to publish an electoral decree without submitting it to the Panhellenium. This decree provided for presiding officers, nominated by the Government, to conduct the elections. Trikoupes came back, however, as foreign minister—Trikoupes, IV, 340 ff.

straight to the Conference in spite of the President; but he could only do so as one of the alliance, and the Russian Resident refused. The three Residents were supposed to act in perfect accord: but the Russian soon became identified with the President's party, while the French and English Residents were in touch with different sections of the opposition. Matters were not improved when, after the July revolution in Paris, the Russian Resident refused for some weeks to recognise the tricolour flag hoisted by the Frenchman. Meanwhile Capodistrias sent a circular condemning the addresses as being unofficial and therefore illegal: he did not tell Leopold, until he knew of the prince's resignation, that revised official addresses had been prepared.

It is impossible to believe that the President's conduct was quite straightforward. He was no doubt really anxious about the frontier, and possibly hoped that if Leopold were sufficiently alarmed, the Conference, tired of the whole affair, would secure his acceptance by including Acarnania and Candia after all. But this explanation does not account for his conduct in Greece: such diplomatic subtlety might seem to him an admirable way of bluffing the Conference, but there was no need to deceive the Greeks as well. The judgment of Finlay must stand, that in this crisis he sacrificed his country to ambition.

Leopold has generally been condemned, either for accepting in the first place or for faintheartedly retreating before mere discouragement. He afterwards lamented that he had been "entreated and stormed out of my views in January" about the frontier.[23] But he could not have hoped to win concessions on that point from Wellington, and had rightly decided not to leave Greece in chaos for the sake of Acarnania, which must fall in some day—perhaps under the next Whig Government. Indeed, the promptness with which Palmerston, on coming into office, arranged to alter the frontier may indicate a previous pledge to do so. Having once accepted, Leopold needed a very grave reason to justify a retreat; whether the news from Greece was reason enough is a question on which it is difficult to pass

[23] To Stein, 10 June, in Pertz' *Stein*, VI, 870, quoted in Stockmar's *Memoirs*, I, 108.

judgment. His own excuse was his original objection to the terms of settlement, followed by the Senate's address and the President's letters, besides letters from General Church and others in Greece. Church was in despair at the coming abandonment of his own conquests in Western Greece, and unfairly laid the whole blame on the President.[24] A younger and less calculating man than Leopold would have accepted in spite of all; but what Greece lost, Belgium gained.

[24] A pamphlet by Church, *Observations on the Greek frontier*, was printed anonymously in England during the summer of 1830.

CHAPTER XIII

GREECE, 1830–2

I

1830

IF Capodistrias intended to get rid of Prince Leopold, it was at the price of still greater unpopularity. He had chosen his path and did nothing to conciliate his enemies, for whom he had an exaggerated contempt. Their motives were often doubtful and their demands impossible, but they were the Greeks whom he had to govern. He had not the means of setting up an acknowledged despotism, which would have required a foreign force to support it; his Government and his institutions were provisional, and meanwhile he overrated what one man can do in a position of virtuous isolation. No man, however justly conscious of superior wisdom, could afford to rule in Greece without the confidence of the traditional if often tyrannical leaders of the people.

In May 1830 a revolt in Maina began the personal feud which ended in the President's assassination. The old chief Petrobey, good-natured and self-indulgent, had been given a place in the Senate, but his incessant demands for money for his family could not be met out of an empty treasury.[1] The Mainots were at once the fiercest and the most honourable clansmen in Greece. They lived under a strict rule of patriarchal custom, and punished immorality or breach of faith by a code of personal vengeance. Bound to each other by all the ties of clan and custom, they thought nothing of plundering and torturing the strangers who passed their coasts; but a guest once admitted to their hospitality found safety and generous entertainment. Of taxes they knew little, for they had never admitted the Turks to collect from them the *haratch*, although since the revolt of 1770 they

[1] E.g. Capodistrias to Kolokotrones, 22 Feb. 1829, in *Correspondance*, III, 40.

had been forced to pay an annual tribute, and to allow the Capitan Pasha a right of confirming the nomination of their own chieftains. They naturally resented bitterly the invasion of their domain by the officials of a central government. The President would have done well to leave them for a time to themselves, only exacting a lump sum for taxation through their chiefs, and suppressing piracy by watching their coasts. The revolt was easily crushed and the unpopular commissioner recalled, but its leader was lured to imprisonment at Nauplia by a false promise of security. The Mavromichalis family were henceforth bitter enemies of the President.

The people of Hydra and Spezzia, led by George Konduriottes, the richest man in Greece, also put forward extravagant claims for compensation for their losses in the war.[2] The Government had commandeered without payment a field belonging to Konduriottes, in order to make experiments in potato-growing. The potato and a land problem were thus introduced together into Greece by an Irishman named Stevenson. Apart from such trivial grievances, the islanders, who enjoyed practical independence and great prosperity before the war, came out of it with their commerce badly hit and their liberties curtailed. But after the Peace of Adrianople trade began to revive, and they might have forgotten their grievances if they had not been irritated by the interference of an extraordinary commissioner, who was a lawyer from Corfu and a brother of the President.[3] Just as in the case of the Mainots, the President could more

[2] E.g. Capodistrias to Primates of Hydra, 23 Feb. 1829, in *Correspondance*, III, 45. The President's fiscal arrangements were fiercely attacked: but at least the situation improved under his régime. The relation of revenue to expenditure (in units of 100,000 drachmae) was roughly this:

1828	25: 76	1831	49: 88	1835	107:168
1829	48:117	1833	70:136	1836	123:168
1830	33: 68	1834	94:201	1837	257:319

S.P. 23, 960; and 26, 69.

During 1832 no accounts were kept. Under the extravagant Bavarian regency there was not so much improvement as the settlement should have brought. The Powers' Loan was soon spent in making up deficits.

[3] Many Greeks returned to the old habit of sailing under the Russian flag until the Turks were induced to recognise that of Greece. On Viaro Capodistrias' proceedings, see Trikoupes, IV, 292.

easily have resisted the Hydriots' fantastic demands upon the treasury if he had interfered less with their other affairs.

The primates were equally sore at being unceremoniously displaced by officials of the central government. The *capitani* were ranged on different sides as convenience dictated.[4] All these different elements became the strange allies of the 'constitutional' opposition headed by Fanariot and European Greeks. This party, led by Mavrocordato, was growing stronger every day. The President's opportunist appeal against Leopold and the Conference to constitutional rights and to public opinion now recoiled upon himself. He had talked glibly in February of a constitution and of a new Assembly, which he was now above all things anxious to postpone. He hoped to appease discontent by a policy of land-settlement attractive enough to the disbanded soldiers but not satisfying to the politicians of the early governments of the revolution.[5] Unfortunately, absorbed in the diplomatic prospects and yet holding the whole administration in his hands, he never pursued with energy this and other beneficial schemes.

The French revolution of July fanned the flame. The tricolour brought memories of Napoleon's emissaries, who had persuaded the despotic Ali of Yanina to pose as the friend of liberty and equality; it soon became the symbol of opposition to the President. He was already disliked by the English and detested them in return: he now began to lose the support of the French as well. The doings in Paris were good news to most of the French army, which had not forgotten the Napoleonic tradition of France as the awakener of the East. General Maison, first commander of the expedition, was so active a Liberal that Charles X had hesitated to appoint him.[6] In the early years of the revolution, before Ibrahim's army came, there had been various efforts to start an unofficial press. Byron had laughed at the London Committee and the "typographical Colonel Stanhope" over

[4] See Appendix IV (*b*).

[5] *Correspondance*, IV, 132, 20 Sept. 1830.

[6] Viel-Castel, XVIII, 386. Pellion, *La Grèce et les Capodistrias*, c. 6 onwards, describes the French difficulties with the President. His bias is strongly anti-Russian.

their academic zeal for the liberty of the press. Greece had now its official gazette; but a literary paper, Ἠώς, started in March 1830, was suppressed after eight numbers for its covert attacks on the President. Until the appearance of the *Apollo* at Hydra a year later the opposition was kept alive mainly in the *Courier de Smyrne*, to whose attacks the President was extremely sensitive.

It was easy to pour scorn on these protagonists of Western Liberalism and to say that Greece, a half-Eastern country just emerging from a chaotic revolution, needed not liberal institutions but peace and order, by whatever means enforced. Some of the opposition were selfish seekers after power; but others really felt that the whole future of Greek institutions was at stake. Greece might be half-Eastern still, but the whole meaning of the revolution, in the eyes of European Greeks, was that her future lay with Europe and not with Asia. The Greeks after all belonged to Europe, though Easternised by centuries of Turkish rule: Fallmerayer's wholesale rejection of their claims to racial continuity is not now endorsed.[7] It would have been different, they argued, if the President had shown himself a friend of good government, reluctantly compelled to use dictatorial methods. It was inevitable, they admitted, that if Greece was to be turned towards the West, the process must be begun by painful means; but they feared that under Capodistrias a Russian system of administration was to be the rule and not the temporary expedient. The men who had managed their own affairs and those of their easy-going masters the Turks were not likely to be grateful for a dictatorship whose agents were personal followers of the President, purposely set in authority over districts to which they were strangers. Moreover it was not, like the Bavarian régime which succeeded it, an organised bureaucracy with a proper division of labour. A system abhorred by every Englishman living on the spot (and not all Philhellenes were 'cranks') probably had practical as well as theoretical dis-

[7] Fallmerayer shocked the Philhellenes by publishing in 1830 his contention that, long before the admitted Albanian invasion of the Morea in the 14th century, a 6th century Slav invasion had completely obliterated the old Greek race. See below in the bibliography.

advantages. But unfortunately the opposition had nothing to offer in exchange, except a puppet government at the mercy of the chieftains. From Leopold's resignation until the tragic ending, this struggle was the absorbing interest in Greece.[8]

For one thing at least Greece was afterwards grateful to Capodistrias, that he kept on postponing the exchange of territory until the turn of fortune came. In spite of the protocols of February 1830, he still had no intention of giving up Acarnania if delay could prevent it. Wellington's Government was losing strength every day, and France and Russia were on the President's side. The July revolution in France, if it prolonged the uncertainty and disorganisation in Greece, at the same time delayed the enforcement of the boundaries of February 3rd, 1830. But there was continual trouble with the troops beyond the Isthmus. In Western Greece the incapable Agostino Capodistrias had been put in command over the head of Church, who finally resigned in August 1829. By this foolish appointment the President lost a man with an extraordinary personal influence over the Rumeliot troops, and drove him into open opposition. In Eastern Greece Hypselantes could not keep his ill-paid men from mutiny every two or three months. After long inactivity he advanced, and forced to a surrender the handful of Turkish troops remaining at Thebes. There was now only a small garrison of Albanians still holding the Acropolis of Athens. The President's plea, in reply to the summons of the Powers, that he could not withdraw the irregular troops from Continental Greece because he dared not, was less ludicrous than it appeared to Wellington. Disbanded on the spot, they would have taken to brigandage: inside the Morea they would have demoralised the small and painfully constructed regular force, and paralysed the authority which the civil government was beginning to

[8] Finlay, II, c. 2. Cf. H. H. Parish, *Diplomatic History of the Monarchy of Greece*, reprinted from *Portfolio*, III. Pellion, *La Grèce et les Capodistrias.* Mendelssohn, *Graf Kapodistrias.* For the President's side, see *Renseignements sur la Grèce...par un Grec*...(1833); *Mémoires* by A. Papadapoulovrétos (1837); *Capodistrias—Zur Vorbereitung*...(1842); and for a modern defence of his policy, 'Ι. Καποδίστριας, by 'Α. Μ. 'Ιδρώμενος (1900). See bibliography below.

acquire. They remained, therefore, in a more or less disorganised state; the most troublesome *capitani* were separated from the men by the device of inviting them to join a corps of officers at Argos, where they were maintained on double pay and rations with nothing to do.

II

January—October 1831

The year 1831 opened badly. The choice of a sovereign was already expected to fall upon Prince Otto of Bavaria.[9] But the Greek opposition took no comfort at the prospect of a boy king with the hated Capodistrias as regent during a long minority, and the rumour only redoubled the zeal of the President's enemies. The prospectus of the *Apollo* newspaper so much alarmed the President that, on January 13th, the proof-sheets of the first number were seized and suppressed. The editor, Polyzoides, was a Greek of European education, who had formerly edited the Government gazette when Mavrocordato and Konduriottes were in power; he appealed unsuccessfully to the Senate, and thereupon removed his press by night from Nauplia and took refuge in Hydra.

The Mavromichalis family was also on the move. Katzakos escaped from Argos; Constantine was allowed to leave Nauplia in order to go home and pacify his relations: he reached Maina and promptly began a revolt. At the same moment old Petrobey Mavromichalis, who had been kept under the surveillance of the police in Nauplia since the Mainot troubles in the year before, escaped on the Philhellene General Gordon's yacht, which flew the Ionian flag. There was no distinct charge against him and nominally no restraint on his liberty, but Capodistrias at once demanded his surrender on the ground that he was deserting his duties as a senator. Dawkins was inclined to refuse an order for his extradition, but the question did not arise after all; Petrobey was forced by weather to land at Katakolo, where he was at once arrested, brought back to Nauplia, and shut up without

[9] Dawkins, 21 Nov. 1830, in *F.O. Greece*, 14.

trial in the Palamidi fort.[10] Constantine and his brother George were also secured and kept under guard. In May a rising at Thebes, led by an adventurer named Karatasso, was easily put down,[11] but the President made a most unpopular choice of a man for the task, his own brother Agostino.

At the end of March the first number of the *Apollo* appeared at Hydra, and was published twice a week until the President's assassination. The islanders demanded fifteen million francs as indemnity for their sacrifices in the war, a sum amounting to a quarter of the whole loan offered to Greece by the allied Powers. It was impossible to satisfy their claims, but the President did nothing to conciliate them.

The disaffection was spreading all over the Archipelago, one important centre being the island of Syra, which was then the 'clearing-house' of the Aegean; in 1831 the value of trade passing through Syra was nearly four times that of the imports and exports of Continental Greece.[12] All the islands had practically ceased to acknowledge the President's authority. He became violent as his fears increased. No one doubted his personal courage—twice he refused a bodyguard of French troops, and his house was never guarded—but he had no prescription except force for discontent. He admitted and excused the use of torture on some peasants by the old brigand Kolokotrones in his capacity of chief tax-farmer.[13] A press law aimed at the *Apollo* was passed in May and the President determined to enforce it by refusing ships' papers to the Hydriots and then blockading the island. But for this purpose he needed the support of the allied fleets, a support which none but the Russians were prepared to give. He refused to meet the Hydriot leaders and was very angry with the English Resident for admitting them to an interview. Dawkins had been instructed to support the Government, but to encourage a change of system: both he and the French Resident agreed to urge the Hydriots to give up the press, and

10 Dawkins, 12 Feb., 13 Mar. 1831, in *F.O. Greece*, 20. Cf. Capodistrias to Dawkins, 5 Feb., *Correspondance*, IV, 200.

11 See Appendix IV (*b*).

12 Dawkins, 14 Apr. 1832, in *F.O. Greece*, 29.

13 Dawkins, 19 July 1831, in *F.O. Greece*, 22.

both were willing to stop Hydriot ships found sailing without papers; but they would not agree to a blockade, which in the temper of the islanders would have meant open civil war.[14]

The President, believing that the Residents were concerned in the "general plot to overthrow the Government", wrote a letter direct to Palmerston, complaining that "the information which Your Excellency has received on the position of this Government is devoid of any truth".[15] On July 19th Rizo, the minister for foreign affairs and shipping, resigned over the question of blockading Hydra: he was succeeded by Glarakis, a man "without strength or morality". The Russian Resident had not the same scruples as the other two: but the actual issue was forced on by the Hydriots themselves. On the night of the 26th the fort and arsenal at Poros, together with the frigate *Hellas* and the steamboat *Karteria* lying in the harbour, were seized by Miaoules and fifty men: these two vessels made up the President's whole navy.

When the news reached Nauplia, the Russian admiral, Ricord, at once sailed to the spot, and a force of Greek regulars was sent under the command of a Cretan, Kallergi, to encamp opposite Poros. The Residents could not refuse to condemn publicly this outrage committed by the Hydriot party: but the French and English naval captains refused to promise "moral *and material* support" to Ricord, who was anxious to begin a bombardment. They returned to Nauplia in order not to be impotent spectators of the issue. They were convinced that Miaoules would quietly surrender the fleet, if summoned *peacefully* to do so by the united authority of the allies. Both entrances to the harbour of Poros were blocked by the Russian admiral: on August 8th a boat attempting to sail in with provisions was turned back, and some firing followed: Kallergi attacked the town of Poros[16] but had to

[14] Capodistrias to Dawkins, 2 July, in *Correspondance*, IV, 290. If we may believe Dawkins, the President told him that he had "promised the Emperor never to grant a Constitution to Greece"—Dawkins, 19 Apr., in *F.O. Greece*, 21. Palmerston to Dawkins, 8 June, in *F.O. Greece*, 19. See above, pp. 132–3.

[15] Capodistrias to Palmerston, 21 July, in *Correspondance*, IV, 308.

[16] Dawkins asserted that this was done by special order of the President, because a courier was sent to Kallergi the night before. But the President's letter of 7 Aug., as printed by A. Papadapoulovrétos, refutes this. (The book in question is, however, a panegyric on the President.)

retire. Three days later Miaoules was again summoned to surrender: the fort containing the arsenal was then bombarded and Kallergi's troops occupied the heights above the town. On the 13th Miaoules actually carried out his threat of blowing up the *Hellas* if the blockade were not raised. Kallergi's troops thereupon entered and sacked the town of Poros. The French and English captains arrived, just too late, with a letter offering amnesty if the Hydriots would promise to "desist from any further attempt against the actual order of things". But they were fortunately able to dissuade Ricord from sailing straight to Hydra, as the President desired,[17] and bombarding it into submission. Each party blamed the other for this useless sacrifice of the only modern ship in the Greek navy.

The Hydriots acted foolishly and desperately under a good deal of provocation; Admiral Ricord, on his side, did not disguise his anxiety to chastise them. The London Conference, which had just resumed its sittings when the news came, was only prevented by the opposition of Russia from censuring him, and the Residents were simply told to continue supporting the Provisional Government.[18] This incident destroyed the last appearances of unanimity among the Residents, as well as the last chances of reconciliation between the President and the opposition. The elections for the new Assembly, which he had been obliged to summon, returned a great many opposition candidates in spite of intimidation: but in many cases the Government simply nominated new deputies.[19]

On October 9th the President was assassinated by George

[17] Capodistrias to Ricord, 18, 30 Aug., in Mendelssohn, *Geschichte*, II, App., pp. 550ff.

[18] Compare postscript (29 Sept.) to Protocol of 26 Sept. in draft (*F.O.* 97/233) and in its final form (*F.O.* 97/231). The Protocols of the London Conference from 22 May 1830 to 25 July 1832 are printed in *Parl. Papers*, 1831–2, XXVIII.

[19] See particulars of eighty-five fraudulently elected deputies, sent by Dawkins to Stratford Canning and described as an exaggerated but mainly true statement. S. Canning to Palmerston, 13 Jan. 1832, in *F.O. Turkey*, 209. Cf. an account from Consul Crowe of an 'election' held near Patras. Some Athenians actually asked that the Turkish evacuation should not take place so long as Capodistrias was President. Dawkins to Backhouse (private), 18 Sept., in *F.O. Greece*, 23.

and Constantine Mavromichalis, and Greece relapsed once more into a state bordering on anarchy. The tragedy of Capodistrias' rule in Greece was not mainly of his own making; in so far as it was aggravated by him, it was not by lack of goodwill but by deficiencies of character. He was not formed to rule over a turbulent people just emerging from a revolution. Nesselrode, who nicknamed him "le huitième sage", once wrote comparing him with Pozzo di Borgo:

> Je conviens à toi que Capo d'Istria a l'âme plus pure, les sentiments plus nobles, plus désintéressés, avec moins de passions et de vanité, mais il est loin d'avoir les moyens...et surtout *cet esprit pratique* indispensable pour bien conduire les affaires de ce bas monde....Il a l'air de travailler pour un monde composé d'êtres aussi parfaits que lui....Je voudrais avoir Pozzo pour ministre et Capo d'Istria pour ami.

But in spite of the abuse which was showered upon him by his enemies at home and abroad, he was never unpopular with the mass of the people, and the Greeks have recently taken a less disparaging view of his services.[20]

III

After the President's death the Senate was the only authority in Greece until the Conference in London should make up its mind. Capodistrias had arranged by a decree of the National Assembly of 1829 to leave, in case of his death, instructions for a regency and an outline of policy: but, as no such instructions were found, the Senate appointed as President Agostino Capodistrias, a name ill-calculated to reconcile parties. The two other members of the 'Commission of Government', the old *klepht* Kolokotrones and Kolettes leader of the Rumeliot troops, were only named by right of force; they were taken to represent the 'Russian' and the 'French' parties. Two leaders of the old opposition, the primate Zaimes and Spiridion Trikoupes, sup-

[20] Nesselrode to his wife, in *Lettres et Papiers*, VI, 115; for the whole passage, see below, Appendix III (3). Even Trikoupes, although of the constitutional party, defended the President in his *History* (1853–7) against the charge of Russian bias, and praised his personal qualities.

ported the new Government as the only refuge from further anarchy; but A. Capodistrias refused to receive the deputies from Hydra into the new Assembly, unless all political refugees were first banished from the island. The French and English Residents, who tried to mediate between the parties, advised the Hydriots to reject these terms, which meant in effect handing over all the opposition leaders to the tender mercies of the Government. The Assembly opened at Argos on December 19th with every prospect of a faction fight. A. Capodistrias had on his side Kolokotrones and his armed personal followers, and also the nominated deputies of the Morea: Kolettes had the Rumeliot deputies and the Rumeliot troops. Fighting began on the 21st: Kolettes, who had meanwhile been 'outlawed' by Agostino, asked the Residents to intervene, but the Russian refused to move until Stratford Canning, who had just arrived on the way to Constantinople, persuaded him to join in urging conciliatory measures on the Government. When the Rumeliots had exhausted their ammunition, they marched away to Corinth and started a new Assembly of about eighty members of their own; this made, with the deputies at Hydra, three rival claimants to authority. The Mainots, sufficient unto themselves, kept aloof from the whole proceeding.

Stratford was impressed with the urgency of finding a settlement, and meanwhile of persuading Agostino to conciliate the different factions by an amnesty. He wrote a long minute to the Conference to this effect, and privately begged Palmerston to hasten the affair. But Agostino was himself the mere tool of a faction: he had none of his brother's ability and was blindly devoted to Russia. He gave offence to all except his own partisans by announcing in his opening speech that "the rights which Russia has earned to the respect and gratitude of Greece have been strangely neglected....The Emperor is still solicitous for your welfare". The Russian Cabinet wanted to see the Hydriots not reconciled but chastised. A letter from Nesselrode to Agostino got into public circulation, and gave rise to new fears of forcible interference by Russia. It disclaimed any "patronage exclusif", but warned the Greeks "qu'aucune combinaison relative à leur pays ne saurait être accomplie et consolidée sans l'assentiment de la Russie, et que l'Empereur n'accordera jamais cet assentiment à un ordre de choses qui menacerait de faire de cette contrée un théâtre de troubles, d'essais révolutionnaires, et de crimes". Finally Nesselrode asked Agostino to correspond with him regularly.[21] But it was clear even to Admiral Ricord that Agostino could not take the high line of a powerful Government. The Rumeliot troops, who had seized Salona and threatened to invade the Morea in force, were masters of the situation.[22] The French forces occupied Kalamata and Nisi in Messenia and were anxious to advance to Argos in support of Kolettes against the existing Government.

At the end of February came a new protocol from London ordering the Residents to show unanimity in supporting the Provisional Government set up in legal fashion by the National Assembly. The French Resident disliked applying this to Agostino's Government; he was overruled, but he and Dawkins succeeded in getting a declaration of amnesty to go with their announcement of the protocol. Both sections of the opposition protested against the recognition of Agostino's Government; the arrival a few days later of two more protocols, reversing the previous instructions and advising a reconciliation, encouraged them not to give way.[23] At last, on April 6th, Kolettes, with two or three thousand men, occupied Corinth and advanced on Argos next day, where he stayed in the house of the French Resident. Yet another protocol confirming Stratford's advice arrived in time to legalise this revolution.[24] Agostino Capodistrias fled, and on April 19th a new Government of the opposition chiefs was proclaimed. The public chest was found to contain a sum of

[21] The Russian Resident would not either acknowledge or deny the authenticity of this letter: enclosure in Dawkins to Palmerston, 14 Feb. 1832—*F.O. Greece*, 28.

[22] Cf. Proclamation of Kolettes, 12 Feb., in P. O. VI, 289. Dawkins, 17 Feb., in *F.O. Greece*, 29.

[23] Protocol, 7 Jan. (not sent until 2 Feb.), arrived 8 Mar. 1832. The amnesty was to all who should lay down arms in ten days—P. O. VI, 293–5. Protocols, 13 and 14 Feb., based on S. Canning's *Mémoire* of 28 Dec. 1831.

[24] Protocol, 7 Mar., "the provisional government does not correspond to the nation's wishes".

£4. 15*s*. 7*d*. and unpaid bills amounting to £16,666. Such was the confusion of the following year that no public balance-sheet was produced. The constitutional opposition was now on its trial: not a fair trial perhaps, considering the bankrupt inheritance on which it entered, but the people knew only that Greece was once more at the mercy of the military chiefs. Kolokotrones may have been oppressive as an official tax-farmer, but now, excluded from the Government, he was still more intolerable as unofficial dictator. A French force landed at Nauplia in May, and soon other detachments occupied Argos and Tripolitza; but they were too few to control the country, and had lost their popularity owing to persistent but unfounded rumours that they harboured designs of conquest. The nation was all the more ready to welcome the announcement (July 29th) of the choice of a king, with or without a constitution.

CHAPTER XIV

A SETTLEMENT AT LAST

I

The Crown

In London the Conference had barely time to recover from its wrath at Prince Leopold's desertion, before the death of George IV and the events in France threw Greece and its perplexities into the shade. The Whigs attempted to make a full-dress attack on the Government's conduct, but as Grey despondently wrote, "The whole business is buried in such a mass of papers, creates so little interest and is so little generally understood that though many objections may be made to the conduct of our Government, I do not think they will make much impression".[1] In July 1830 the French again proposed to extend the frontier in return for limiting the Greek right of immigration from Turkey, but Wellington refused to hear of it.[2] He had by now quite forgotten his scheme of erecting a Greek Empire, and relapsed into his old opinion: "I think we have seen enough of the objects of Russia in it to be very certain that the establish-

[1] Grey to Princess Lieven, 11 June 1830, in *Correspondence*, II. Wellington's policy had been attacked in an article in the *Foreign Quarterly Review* (Nov. 1829) which showed so much inside information that Pozzo di Borgo was suspected of having furnished some of the details—Princess Lieven, in *Correspondence*, I, 397; Wellington's *Despatches*, VI, 327, 390. The article praised Capodistrias. Wellington replied by commissioning his friend Dean Phillpotts to defend his policy in the *Quarterly Review* (Oct. 1830). The Dean was at great pains to prove from classical literature that the Acarnanians had never invaded Aetolia across the Aspropotamos: therefore the river would be a respectable frontier between Turks and Greeks. Whatever the value of this argument, it is plain that the Duke, intent upon curtailing the frontier in return for independence, knew nothing and cared less about such considerations. Indeed the Prime Minister could not be expected to know: but he had before him the conclusions of the Conference of Poros, which he set aside—*Despatches*, VII, 75, 78, 86.

[2] Aberdeen to Wellington, 17 July 1830, in *Despatches*, VII, 125. Dean Phillpotts heard of the proposal and was quite prepared, if it were accepted, to change his argument accordingly—*Despatches*, VII, 155, 170.

ment of the Greek Power can never be otherwise than disadvantageous to this Country".[3]

But the end was near at hand. The elections consequent on the King's death went badly for the ministry, and the country only waited for the meeting of Parliament to see the Whigs come in. While the Tories were prophesying red revolution, an outside observer—no lover of democracy—was less disturbed. Princess Lieven wrote to prepare the Russian ministry for the change: there was "no need to take alarm at the word 'Whig'; there are no greater aristocrats". Esterhazy on the other hand shared the panic of the ultra-Tories; later he compared the week May 8th–15th, 1832, to the events of 1789, and thought it hardly strange that Charles X should leave his asylum in England in fear of the new spirit. On November 16th, 1830, Wellington resigned and the new Cabinet was formed. Princess Lieven was active as ever, and wrote, perhaps with less than the usual absurd exaggeration of her own influence: "It is somewhat curious that *twice already* I have prevented Lord Lansdowne having the Foreign Office.... Palmerston is preferable to him and we, Russia, will certainly have good cause to think well of him". Sketching the new ministry, she described him as "perfect in every way".[4] She soon had cause to change her mind; but for the time there was every reason to be satisfied. His record in foreign policy hitherto was certainly not one to please the enemies or to alarm the friends of Russia.

Palmerston had not been six weeks in office before he took the first steps towards carrying out the views which he had pressed in opposition. He instructed the English Resident in Greece to delay the evacuation "on any fair pretence", in view of a probable improvement of the frontier.[5] The President had

[3] Wellington to Aberdeen, 31 Aug., in *Despatches*, VII, 217.

[4] Princess Lieven, *Letters*, 20 Nov., and *Diary*, ed. Temperley, pp. 163 ff. Esterhazy was soon complaining of Palmerston's *insouciance* but admitted him to be, alone among the Whig ministers, "practical and well-informed on foreign affairs"—*Berichte*, 253, 4, 27 June 1831.

[5] Palmerston to Dawkins, 28 Dec. 1830, in *F.O. Greece*, 9 (received 24 Jan.). In January 1831 he told Esterhazy of his intention and apparently hoped at first to include Crete as well. Austrian 'Précis historique' in Mendelssohn, *Geschichte*, II, 319 and App. p. 537. As early as 23 Nov. 1830 Esterhazy reported that a change of frontier was likely—*Berichte*, 250.

demanded the help of the allied fleets and forces in the unpopular task of evacuating the ceded province: to his great disappointment he had been taken at his word, for the London Conference had offered all the assistance necessary, and directed the boundary commissioners to start at once. The Turkish commissioners left Constantinople in July 1830; the English representative, Colonel Baker, started from London soon afterwards; but the French and Russians took no steps to hasten the day. The French were not anxious that their troops, which two years earlier had nearly marched to attack the Turks beyond the Isthmus, should now enter Acarnania, not to conquer, but to watch over the surrender of the province. In August Capodistrias promised to give orders for the evacuation as soon as all the boundary commissioners should arrive. Three months later the French representative was still missing. The surrender of Acarnania in exchange for Euboea and of Vonitza for Athens, provisionally fixed for December 1st and January 1st respectively, was postponed for three weeks and again for another month, the French and Russian Residents still professing to have no instructions.[6]

Rumours of the coming change had in fact preceded Palmerston's despatch, and it was not difficult to seize upon a minor difficulty, raised by the Turks, as an excuse for referring back to Constantinople. The proclamations for the exchange were stopped just in time; Acarnania and Aetolia had been saved to Greece by the persistence of the President, the connivance of France and Russia and the timely accession to office of the Whigs. For the time the province remained in great disorder, the refuge of every robber who escaped across the frontier from the justice of the neighbouring Pasha. Nominally, the evacuation was only delayed, for the new frontier had to be obtained by negotiation and it was not actually traced until the end of 1832. The Tsar was not very anxious to re-open the frontier question, but consented to the principle.[7]

[6] Protocol of Conference, 1 July 1830: cf. drafts in *F.O.* 97/233. Dawkins to Aberdeen, 19 Nov., 12 Dec. 1830, 7 Jan. 1831, in *F.O. Greece*, 14, 20.

[7] Dawkins to Palmerston, 9 Feb. 1831, in *F.O. Greece*, 20. See the account

Occupied with the affairs of Belgium, the three Powers did not renew the Conference about Greece until September 1831. The delay, however disastrous, was perhaps the unavoidable legacy of past mistakes. After the promises of finality made in the protocols of February 1830, it needed little to excite the most stubborn resistance of the Turks to any further concessions. If the three Powers had simply announced their decision, they would have had to enforce it without ceremony, involving them perhaps in a display of force most inconvenient in the midst of other troubles. A negotiation might equally end in abrupt failure, if the Porte were not convinced of agreement among the allies.

A prince was still to seek: it was not easy to have two crowns on the market at once. There were two candidates left in the field after Leopold's resignation—Prince Frederick of Orange, or a Bavarian prince. The English Court favoured the former as a Protestant, but he was unlikely to accept, having once before refused. The Bavarian King had a claim upon the gratitude of the Greeks for the help and relief which he had lavished upon them in the spirit of an enthusiastic classical archaeologist.[8] He carried his zeal to the point of building a church at Munich and celebrating services there in the Orthodox rite. Professor Thiersch of Munich, an active Philhellene and a somewhat intriguing spirit, seems to have been the first to make the direct suggestion of a Bavarian candidate for the throne.[9] The French Government favoured the idea, and King Ludwig himself promoted it by indirect means. After the Peace of Adrianople, a certain Count Rumigny reported the approach of a Greek deputation to thank the King for his services to Greece, and on this foundation an active campaign was set on foot in favour of

of an agreement reached, 11 Aug. 1831, for the surrender of robbers to the Turkish authorities, in *F.O.* 195/87 (Archives of Legations). Heytesbury to Palmerston, 19, 31 Jan. 1831, in *F.O. Russia*, 191.

[8] See K. Heigel's *Ludwig I*, pp. 149 ff.

[9] Thiersch to Ludwig I, dated from Bad Kreuth, 8 Sept. 1829, in *Hausarchiv*, Munich. Thiersch to Eynard, 10 Nov. 1829, printed in Löwe's *Leben Thiersch's*, I, 332: a copy was sent to the Tsar, 3 Dec., "with the assurance, perhaps superfluous, that my Sovereign has no knowledge of it"—*Hausarchiv*.

a Bavarian prince.[10] But since the King's brother Charles refused, and the choice of one of his own sons involved a minority in Greece, with Capodistrias probably as Regent, the English Government would not listen to the proposal. King Ludwig was bitterly disappointed, kept his ministers busy until the choice of Leopold was beyond a doubt, and revived the claims of Otto directly after Leopold's refusal, even throwing out the suggestion that he, Ludwig, should act as Regent himself. Russia was more favourable this time, and in July 1830 Nesselrode seems to have made some promises at Karlsbad; but the European crisis led to a long delay, and when the conferences were at last renewed in September 1831, the Bavarians had to complain of the 'unaccountable hostility' of Russia.[11] The resulting protocol gave no decision about the crown, and the Bavarian King was left once more in suspense. But two days before the murder of the President, Professor Thiersch landed in Greece to canvass the claim of Otto, and during the winter there was no other name remaining in the field.

Prince Otto was only seventeen years old. It was unfortunate that no prince who had reached years of discretion would accept so uneasy a crown. But apart from this there was now not much to be said against the choice. The offer was not formally made by the Conference until February 1832, and a long negotiation preceded the Convention of May 7th.[12] The King refused to bind his son's conscience as to a change of religion, and despite Russian protests, Otto remained in fact a Roman Catholic; owing to this difficulty he never went through a coronation ceremony. The King also refused to renounce his son's right of succession to the Bavarian throne, but at last agreed to a formula

[10] The whole correspondence is in Munich, *Staatsarchiv, Greece*, 1. See especially Ludwig I to Pfeffel (in Paris), 16 Oct. 1829, Armansperg to Ludwig I, 10, 19 Nov., and the King's notes endorsed on these reports.

[11] Armansperg to Ludwig I, 17 June 1830; Gise to Armansperg, 10 June 1830; Lerchenfeld to Armansperg, 22 Jan. 1831 (from St Petersburg); Cetto to Armansperg, 30 Sept. 1831 (from London), in *Staatsarchiv, Greece*, 1.

[12] Convention, 7 May 1832, in *S.P.* 19, 1246, so dated, though actually signed four days later: the Whigs had meanwhile resigned and returned in the final crisis of the Reform Bill. Ratifications were exchanged on 1 July—*Staatsarchiv, Greece*, 2.

forbidding union of the two crowns. The Bavarian treasury refused to spend money on foreign purposes, and the King had to forestall the three Powers' loan out of his own purse. He insisted, after the experience of the last years, "que l'Assemblée nationale remît au Prince la charge de pourvoir aux institutions politiques que les besoins du pays et son état de civilisation rendraient expédientes"—in other words, there was to be no premature talk of a constitution. The Conference went further and laid it down that there was no need to get the votes of the Assembly to ratify the choice of Otto.[13] It recommended instead that "a unanimously elected deputation" should be charged with offering him addresses. In spite of the artifices to which it had to resort, few would now dispute that the Conference acted wisely. The Bavarian 'tyranny', after the interlude of an extravagant and incompetent regency, was both more benevolent and more scientific than that of Capodistrias.[14] It made the mistakes and incurred the unpopularity which any foreign rule was bound to do. But it put down the armed bands and made justice a reality. Above all, it was not open to the suspicion of sinister subservience to one of the three guaranteeing Powers. National jealousies lay at the bottom of much of the hatred of

[13] The words "Il serait absolument superflu de les recueillir" were erased from the draft, and replaced by the words "son suffrage est donc déjà donné". These points, as well as the Bavarian demand for a grant of lands to the King, were omitted from the Parliamentary Papers—*F.O.* 97/233. The actual Convention avoided all mention of a definite constitution, merely providing that Greece was to be "un état monarchique indépendant", and that during Otto's minority, "ses droits de souveraineté seront exercés dans toute leur plénitude par une régence". But the general impression was that a constitution had been promised: Professor Thiersch in canvassing for Otto had certainly led the Greeks to expect it. Dawkins to Palmerston, 21, 25 Mar., 18 June, in *F.O. Greece*, 29, 30. Cf. Finlay, II, 300–1. Thiersch's activities much embarrassed the Bavarian Court; it was publicly denied that he had any mission from the King, and he was privately recalled. Gise to Ludwig I, 2, 10, 13 Aug. 1832, and to Erskine, 29 Sept. 1832, in *Staatsarchiv, Greece*, 2. In spite of the Residents' efforts to stop it, the National Assembly met and ratified the choice of Otto, 8 Aug. 1832—*S.P.* 19, 1251.

[14] Cf. Finlay, II, 337–8. A volume of statistics (*Greece as a Kingdom*, ed. F. Strong, 1842) shows the minute thoroughness of German administration, which catalogued every man and animal in the country under appropriate headings. The census of occupations showed a lamentably large percentage of 'brigands'.

Capodistrias: from these the Bavarian régime was comparatively free; at least, having no close connection with any great Power, it escaped their worst consequences. Ten years later a constitution was obtained by a peaceful revolution, and even the *Portfolio* had to admit that the frenzied prophecies of a Greece fallen under Russian domination had not been fulfilled. The European Greeks, who had fought against a Russian dictatorship, submitted with a fairly good grace to the constraint of a paternal administration, although King Otto became personally unpopular.[15] Only those (and they were many) who had begun the revolution without thinking or imagining where it must lead, remained permanently discontented or even irreconcilable.

II

The Frontier

The mischief of all this delay was not only in the uncertainty for Greece but in the prolongation of foreign interference. Until the fate of Greece was finally settled, the allies or their representatives in Greece could not avoid becoming involved in the internal affairs of the new State. The officious anxiety of the Russian Resident to take decisive action was bad enough, but the constitutional sympathies of the other Residents brought them into a partisan position which did equally little good, however well meant. The strife among the 'Franks' in Greece seemed to plain people the strife of factions, not of principles; it was a painful lesson in the danger of meddling even with the best intentions.

It has been seen that the protocol of September 26th, 1831, gave no decision about the Crown. But concerning the frontier it pointed out that the limits laid down on February 3rd, 1830, had been drawn on a wrong map: that to patch over the mistake would not be satisfactory: and that a new negotiation was there-

[15] In the archives at Munich there are some curious reports of the King's physicians and of the regents, on the difficult moods and cloudy spirit of the young prince just before he came of age, Feb. 1834–May 1835. The last of these minutes actually gave the opinion that he was unfit to reign—*Staatsarchiv, Greece*, 6.

fore to be set on foot for the full Arta-Volo line. The Turks were to be offered in exchange either increased compensation or new concessions in the assessment of *vacoufs* (ecclesiastical lands). But if the Turks should refuse absolutely, a new compromise frontier was to be suggested.[16] France and England were to begin the negotiation, but Russia was to join in later.

The illness of Sir Robert Gordon conveniently excused him from undertaking a business little to his taste: he left Constantinople in August 1831 on leave of absence, and Stratford Canning was fitly chosen to obtain the frontier for which he had resigned his post two and a half years before. He felt very doubtful of the success of the negotiation: he had little to offer to the Sultan in return for a new sacrifice of territory, a sacrifice unwelcome to any ruler and forbidden by Mohammedan law. He could only represent that the greater part of the territory was actually in Greek hands and that its restoration would merely be a burden on the Empire. But before he reached Constantinople, a new weapon presented itself.

The Pasha of Egypt had not given up his designs upon Syria.[17] Since Navarin his loyalty to the Sultan had been sorely strained; in 1828 he had the mortification of seeing his old enemy Chosrew recalled and made Seraskier: in 1829 his offer to release Turkish troops for the defence of Constantinople by sending an army into Asia Minor was rejected by the justly suspicious Sultan: in the next year he asked in vain to be allowed to pay, in return for Southern Syria, a large share of the indemnity to Russia. At last, in 1831, his perennial quarrel with Abdullah, Pasha of Acre, culminated in an open breach; his chief complaint was that Abdullah hindered the passage of Egyptian manufactures on the caravan route to Bagdad. In November he invaded Syria and took no notice of the Sultan's firman (December 2nd) order-

[16] Mouth of R. Spercheius, Mt Veluchi, Mt Agrapha, Arta. In a separate instruction (12 Nov.) Stratford was told that *negotiation only* was contemplated. If he could obtain no result in a reasonable time, he was to come home.

[17] See Ernst Molden, *Metternich's Orientpolitik*; Prokesch v. Osten, *Mehemet Ali*; Schiemann, III, 208ff.; *C.H.F.P.* II, c. 4; J. R. Hall, *England and the Orleans Monarchy*, cc. 5, 7, 8; F. S. Rodkey, *The Turco-Egyptian Question*, 1832–1841, Univ. of Illinois Studies, XI, 3 (1923).

ing both Pashas to lay their grievances before him. The Sultan was determined to crush Mehemet once for all, and although Europe had as yet taken little notice of these events, the ambassadors at the Porte encouraged him to resist. Stratford in particular was quick to see the use which might be made of the Sultan's danger, in order to ensure the success of his own negotiation.[18] He reached Constantinople at the end of January 1832 and found the Turks ready for discussion. David Urquhart, now a member of Stratford's staff, had been sent from Nauplia through Albania to visit the new Grand Vizir Reshid, without whose support the negotiation must fail; he secured at least the neutrality of the old soldier, who had nothing but contempt for the Greeks, but was tired of the whole business.[19] The negotiation went on with the usual long delays; it was a delicate business, for apart from the ostensible conferences Stratford was communicating secretly with the Sultan through a Greek favourite of the Palace, Vogorides, and by his means was able to work upon Mahmud's fears. Ibrahim began his attack on Acre with 88,000 soldiers and a navy employing nearly 40,000 men; the resources of Egypt were drained to supply this enterprise of ambition. All that the Sultan could do was to place a ban upon Mehemet and his son (April 23rd, 1832), and to send to sea the Turkish fleet, whose admiral was ignorant of the fact that some of his guns could never have fired a shot, being made without touch-holes. On May 27th Acre fell; Mehemet replied to outlawry by "branding the Sultan as an Infidel", and did not conceal his intention of marching upon the capital. Ibrahim announced, in a letter to Hussein Pasha, that he was coming to Constantinople "to lay his sword at the Sultan's feet and to demand in return the heads of the Seraskier, the Syr-Kiatib and the Master of the Mint, his

[18] S. Canning to Palmerston, 26 Dec. 1831, in *F.O. Turkey*, 201; cf. Lane-Poole, I, 492 ff.

[19] Urquhart, the well-known champion of Turkey and extreme anti-Russian, editor of the *Portfolio*, had gone out with Lord Cochrane as a Philhellene, and taken part in Hastings' action in Salona Bay on 29 Sept. 1827; but his subsequent travels converted him to a fervent belief in Turkish regeneration. For his report (8 Feb. 1832) of this visit, see *F.O. Turkey*, 209.

father's enemies".[20] Stratford had no authority to promise material aid to the Sultan, but he made confident though guarded promises of support. He agreed to stop supplies to Egypt but at the same time told the English consul to keep on good terms with Mehemet, to whom as the established authority he must look for protection.

At last on July 21st, after a discussion lasting sixteen hours, the frontier negotiation was successfully ended. The evacuation was to be completed, and the compensation paid, by December 31st. The greater part of this sum was advanced by Russia in reduction of the Turkish indemnity, and afterwards repaid by Greece. There was to be eighteen months' grace for emigration both ways.[21] The Porte reserved some minor claims which were rejected on reference to London.[22] Perhaps neither party put much faith in the conventional ending: "les négociations sont closes de la manière a ne jamais se renouveler: enfin que la question grecque est irrévoquablement résolue". Nevertheless the settlement lasted for fifty years.

[20] S. Canning to Palmerston, 17 May, 22 July, in *F.O. Turkey*, 210, 211. Mandeville to Palmerston, 25 Aug., *ibid.* 212.

[21] The maps were not actually exchanged until 9 Dec. 1835, from which day the eighteen months were reckoned; so that actually there was nearly five years' grace.

[22] Viz. (*a*) limitation of Greek forces, (*b*) Greek neutrality in war, (*c*) extradition rights. See Protocols, 30 Aug., 12 Nov., in *F.O.* 97/234. For the report of the settlement, see *F.O. Turkey*, 219 (part in *S.P.* 22, 934).

CHAPTER XV

A NEW PHASE

To obtain the new Greek frontier Stratford had virtually pledged the British Government to support the Sultan against his vassal. He did his best to make good the assurances which he had given on his own responsibility, and sent letters to the English agents at Bagdad and Teheran, instructing them to uphold the Sultan's authority. Mahmud wanted to get these promises redeemed by more substantial help, and in October he sent an envoy to London to ask for political support, and even for naval assistance by a blockade of Alexandria. But he met with a non-committal answer, being merely told that Great Britain would consider the application.[1] Palmerston, it will be seen, was still wondering which horse to back. But the danger was too pressing for delay; on December 21st Ibrahim by the battle of Konieh opened the road through Asia Minor to the Bosphorus. The Sultan had turned first to England for help, refusing three times (July, September, October) the proffered mediation of France; for he already regarded France as the patron of Mehemet Ali and was offended by her attack on Algiers in which Mehemet had offered to take part. The reception given by England to this appeal made him lose all faith in the friendship so often professed by her foreign ministers. From Austria, which was not a naval power, he could expect no help. He thereupon fell back on French intervention (January 13th, 1833): Halil Pasha, sent to offer pardon, with the Pashaliks of Acre and Damascus, to Mehemet Ali, was supported by a letter from the French ambassador. But Russia now stepped in. She had already marked her disapproval of Mehemet's adventure by withdrawing her consul from Egypt (June 1832). In May Count

[1] Stratford's promises, in his report to Palmerston, 9 Aug. 1832, in *F.O. Turkey*, 211. The envoy was John Mavroyéni, Turkish *chargé d'affaires* at Vienna, followed by Namik Pasha. There is an account of this mission in *Les Mavroyéni*, by Th. Blancard, II (Paris, 1909). Palmerston's answer, to Mandeville, 5 Dec., in *F.O. Turkey*, 212 (received 1 Jan. 1833).

Kisselew, the Russian governor in the still occupied Danubian Principalities, had proposed to force his aid upon Turkey, and to extract a fortress on the Bosphorus in return; the Tsar had frowned on the plan but at the end of December consented to Kisselew's mobilisation of his army.[2] At the same time General Muraviev arrived in Constantinople on his way to Egypt, bearing threats of the Tsar's disapproval. Muraviev's instructions were, not officially to offer the military aid of Russia to the Sultan, but to agree as soon as he should ask for it. Without waiting for his consent, he hurried to Alexandria in order to anticipate Halil Pasha and French intervention; returning, he practically forced the Sultan, against the advice of the ministers, to accept an alliance even more hollow than that of the other Powers, and on February 2nd, 1833, obtained a request for Russian help. A naval squadron was waiting in readiness at Odessa; in spite of French anger and English warnings, the first contingent passed the Bosphorus on February 20th, while the Sultan was half inclined to cancel his request.

Meanwhile the British Government had been considering the Turkish application for armed support. The doubt in Palmerston's mind is reflected in his pencil comments on the margin of an urgent memorandum from Stratford, who had returned home in September and was now in Paris; he had been asked by Lord Grey to put his views on paper.[3] Against Stratford's argument about the danger that Mehemet Ali might replace the Sultan or deprive him of a large portion of his Empire, Palmerston notes, "Is not the unwieldy extent of the Turkish Empire one great check to the improvement of its industry and commerce, and possibly one great cause of its external weakness?" Stratford's assertion that the presence of a British squadron at Alexandria would suffice to ensure success is questioned; his belief that the very attempt would give Great Britain important influence operating for the progress of reform is answered thus: "We

[2] Schiemann, III, 211–14.

[3] Stratford Canning to Palmerston, 19 Dec. 1832 (dated from Paris on his way to Madrid), in *F.O. Turkey*, 211. Extracts are printed in *C.H.F.P.* II, 638, but the marginal notes are not described. I have printed this important despatch complete in Appendix V.

rescued Egypt once for Turkey...what was the beneficial result? Certainly no progress in civilisation or Reform...." Later—"Is authority built on the forcible suppression of minor authorities legitimate? and if not, in what would the Pasha's usurped authority differ from the Sultan's, if successful, but in degree?" If the Pasha's right to retain Syria or Egypt without the Sultan's consent could only be the right of force—"what other has the Sultan?" On the recommendation of a blockade of Syria and Egypt—"with a view to remote and precarious advantages to our commerce, are we to begin by prohibiting that which exists with Syria and Egypt?" On the view that France might reconcile herself to our single interference—"surely it would be very strange if she did"; or that Russia could hardly step forward to oppose its exercise—"perhaps not, but would she or could she be entirely neutral and passive on such an occasion?"

In the first days of January Palmerston refused Talleyrand's proposals for joint action against Mehemet Ali, fearing that the French would secretly favour him. He merely acknowledged an overture purporting to come from Mehemet Ali and promising to "open the canal of Suez to facilitate the communication between England and India".[4] Before the middle of February he had decided—too late this time—to support the Sultan, and had dismissed the arguments on the other side, plausible as they seemed. The assumption in favour of Mehemet was that a separate Egyptian Power, extending to Syria and Asia Minor, and even swallowing Constantinople too, would, in alliance with the Shah of Persia, be a firm barrier against Russian expansion. But it was equally likely that Mehemet might join with Russia in partitioning Persia, or he might create a strong Mediterranean Power blocking the way to India. Such a Mohammedan league might be as hostile to English rule in India as to Russia. Moreover, the advance of Mehemet seemed to be due less to his real strength than to the accustomed inactivity of the Turkish authorities in Syria. The other bait was the supposed advantage to commerce through Mehemet's civilised rule. But the boasted enlightenment of the Pasha was only a thin veneer. His manu-

[4] Col. Light to Palmerston, 6 Jan. 1833, in *F.O. Turkey*, 233.

factures, like the Sultan's modern soldiers, seemed to be a hobby more than a serious undertaking; the increased revenues won by his monopolies and by his strict control of the Nile waters were devoted solely to purposes of further conquest. As for his rule in Syria, the British consul there wrote: "His political system has the common defect of all Turkish rulers—it has no respect to public interests, sentiments and attachments". Again, the Turks put no obstacle in the way of commerce save that of inertia, whereas a rising Egyptian State might impose tariff barriers as stiff as those of Russia itself, absorbing the profits of our trade to Bagdad and the Persian Gulf.

But the strongest argument against giving countenance to a mushroom growth like that of Mehemet's power outside Egypt was the probability, almost the certainty, that it would dissolve soon after his death; his son Ibrahim was a brave but fatalistic soldier, not a wily statesman like his father. If Turkey were to collapse, better that it should be replaced by successive national growths than by the transitory conquests of ambitious Pashas. Incidentally, it was fortunate for the future of Balkan nationalities that England did nothing at this crisis towards establishing a dominion which, if it should last, would effectually stop their growth, or, if it should suddenly break up, might lead to a partition before they were ripe for the inheritance. But the last consideration did not weigh with Palmerston, who acted on a review of the immediate chances.[5]

The decision was made too late to be effective. Early in April the British admiral was ordered to threaten a blockade of

[5] For the substance of these arguments, see a *Memoir* (9 Jan. 1833) by Sir H. Ellis, a former minister to Persia (1814) and to China (1816) and at this time a member of the Board of Control. David Urquhart had some share in the discussion—see an account of his interview with the King, dated 12 Jan., and a paper on commerce with Turkey, 12 Feb. 1833. All in *F.O. Turkey*, 233. S. Canning's memorandum, 19 Dec. 1832, has been quoted; enclosed with it came the reports of Capt. Chesney on the prospects of steam-navigation on the Euphrates. On the state of Syria in 1832, Stratford had some valuable information in the despatches of Consul-General Farren. Some of these are in *S.C. Papers*, 25. Cf. Farren to Palmerston, 1832 (esp. 23 May), in *F.O. Turkey*, 215. By the end of the year, Stratford was himself in London and doubtless took part in the discussions, though no written record remains.

Alexandria if Mehemet should refuse terms, and to invite the co-operation of the French. As soon as peace should be signed, he was to go to the mouth of the Dardanelles and remain there until the departure of the Russian fleet: in no case was he to pass the Dardanelles without orders from home. In May, Mehemet accepted terms; in addition to the four Pashaliks of Syria proper (Saida, Tripoli, Acre, Damascus) for himself, he obtained for his son Ibrahim the important district of Adana, commanding the gateway of the Taurus Mountains. But still the Russian fleet did not depart, and the other Powers became extremely nervous. As in 1829, the fleets were again assembled at the mouth of the Dardanelles. The rumours of an impending treaty seemed to foreshadow a complete dependence of the Sultan upon Russia; but nothing could be done to prevent it. As the Reis-Effendi said: "If Russia takes hostile action against England and France, the Porte will be obliged by force of circumstances to make common cause with Russia". Talleyrand's proposal for a conference of four Powers was partly discredited by the hasty and unsuccessful action of Roussin, the new French ambassador at Constantinople; he vainly threatened both Russia and Mehemet in the name of the French Government, which was much embarrassed. The expected treaty between Russia and Turkey was signed on July 8th at Unkiar Skelessi, on the northern shore of the Bosphorus, at the house of Chosrew, once the bitterest enemy of Russian influence. Russia was to help the Sultan at need with ships and troops, for which he was to pay the cost. In return the Sultan promised, instead of giving material aid, to provide for the closing of the Dardanelles to foreign warships under all circumstances.[6]

Palmerston felt that he had been outwitted. He tried unsuccessfully to persuade the Porte not to ratify "this obnoxious treaty". Metternich, although surprised and annoyed at the treaty, had stood surety for the good faith of Russia in sending

[6] On Roussin, cf. Mandeville to Palmerston, 23 Feb., 26 Mar., 28 Apr. 1833, in *F.O. Turkey*, 221–2. Austrian comments in *Weisungen nach London*, 261, 9 Apr., and *Berichte*, 263, Apr., *passim*. Treaty of Unkiar Skelessi in *S.P.* 20, 1176. See above, p. 209, n. 17.

her fleet to the Bosphorus: he followed up the same policy in the understanding reached with the Tsar at Münchengrätz in September. Palmerston complained that Austria "now appears to have surrendered to Russia the exclusive protectorate of Turkey", and joined with France in a common protest (August 28th); both Powers, when they heard of the meeting at Münchengrätz, suspected an agreement to partition Turkey. They were mistaken, for the object was rather to preserve the existing state of things; but the possibility was provided for in a secret article, by which Austria and Russia agreed to consult each other if collapse became inevitable. Palmerston was so much impressed with the influence given to Russia by the Treaty of Unkiar Skelessi that he seems once more to have entertained the notion which he had discarded in January. "The influence of Great Britain and France has been and will be exerted to prevent Mehemet Ali from commencing any aggression"; but in return the Sultan must be exhorted not to provoke the Pasha: "If the alarms of the Sultan are really excited by Mehemet Ali, Great Britain can effectually control the Pasha....But if ever reduced to choosing between Mehemet Ali at Constantinople or the subjection of that capital to Russia, Great Britain *would prefer the former*". The English press, too, spoke for some weeks in very bellicose tones against Russia. But Palmerston failed to agree with Talleyrand for a counter-understanding between England and France.[7]

It is interesting to speculate whether this episode supplies a key to the dilemma of Canning in 1827. If Stratford Canning, who knew every side of the question, believed in 1832 that England could send naval support to the Sultan without much risk of war with Russia, might not George Canning have taken the same risk in 1827 and followed up Navarin by a squadron in the Sea of Marmora? In the general uncertainty after Canning's death, the proposal was actually made but rejected. But

[7] *Weisungen nach London*, 261, *passim*, esp. 23 Jan., 8 Mar., 9 June, 16 Aug. *Berichte*, 265, 16 Aug., and p. 266, 20 Nov. The despatches of 16 Aug. betray the puzzled Austrian diplomacy. Palmerston to Ponsonby, 6 Dec. 1833, in *F.O. Turkey*, 220. Cf. Molden, *Metternich's Orientpolitik*, pp. 93ff., and text of the agreement at Münchengrätz in the Appendix.

Stratford's proposal was for a demonstration at Alexandria only, and it is not clear that in 1832, still less in 1827, he would have recommended the passage of the Dardanelles. Twenty years later the British public was more ready to take the risk and face the consequences.

These events opened a new phase in Eastern affairs. The Greek question faded into the diplomatic obscurity which is often the best guarantee of a small nation's prosperity. If Greece did not take advantage of the opportunity, the blame lay more with the people or their rulers than with the protecting Powers. "The state of the Levant from 1833 was extremely favourable to the progress of Greece....The incapacity of the rulers of Greece and the rude social condition of the agricultural population, perpetuated by retaining the Ottoman system of taxing land, allowed this favourable opportunity for rapid improvement to escape."[8] Egypt now became the centre of interest: the year 1833 marked the final breach in that Anglo-Russian alliance which had been inaugurated by the Protocol of St Petersburg in 1826, and completed the definite conversion of the Whigs and Canningites to a pro-Turkish, because anti-Russian, policy. The Tsar's attitude towards Louis-Philippe, and his treatment of the Polish revolt, had already alienated most of the Whigs on points of principle which did not closely affect British interests. His gains at Unkiar Skelessi, coming close upon the dictated Peace of Adrianople, convinced also the followers of Canning, who took a more realist or more opportunist view of foreign politics. France too had become anti-Russian, but looked for an ally to Mehemet Ali rather than to the Sultan. France and England, therefore, in spite of their common fear of Russia, were kept apart; although Mehemet's power outside Egypt was finally overthrown in 1840, French resentment against Palmerston was not soon appeased. At the same time the Anglo-Russian diplomatic conflict in Persia became more acute, and led up to the unfortunate Afghan War.

Henceforth Palmerston was to share fully the traditional distrust and eventually to lead the hue and cry against Russia. In

[8] Finlay, II, 339.

1834 he was writing: "With Russia we are on a footing of cold civility. She is not ready to go to war for Turkey, and perhaps thinks it better to take the place by sap than by storm. We shall therefore have no war this year; and a year gained is a great deal in such matters...." "With Russia we are just as we were, snarling...bickering...." Soon he began to doubt the progressive decay of the Ottoman Empire—it was only that "Europe is becoming better acquainted with the manifest and manifold defects in the organisation of Turkey". "There is no reason whatever why it should not again become a respectable Power. Half the wrong conclusions at which mankind arrive are reached by the abuse of metaphors....All that we hear every day of the week about the decay of the Turkish Empire and its being a dead body or a sapless trunk and so forth is pure and unadulterated nonsense."[9] During the thirties a regular campaign was initiated in press and pamphlet; we are told that

> it was necessary in the first instance that the public mind should be aroused, before the Government could be either disposed or able to undertake measures involving responsibilities, and Mr McNeill accordingly, assisted by D. Urquhart who had just returned from Turkey, and by Baillie Fraser who had been travelling with a special mission in Persia, set to work to *write up* the Eastern Question.[10]

The solution of the dilemma by the encouragement of independent States in 'the Balkans' and the Middle East, obvious as it may seem to us now (though less complete a solution than it seemed to Gladstone), was hardly realised by Canning when he died. He made the first steps reluctantly, as an immediate escape from the Russian bogey, but there is no certain evidence to show that his policy looked to the complete independence of Greece, much less to a general extension of the principle. Bulgaria was unknown, Albania was merely a recruiting-ground for the Turkish armies, but Serbia and the Principalities had

[9] Bulwer, *Palmerston* (1870), II, 179 ff., 3 Mar., 21 Apr., 27 June 1834; *ibid.* II, 287, 22 Sept. 1838; II, 298, 1 Sept. 1839.

[10] Sir H. Rawlinson, *England and Russia in the East* (1875), pp. 52–3, quoted in the *Memoir* of Sir J. McNeill by his granddaughter (1910). For a fuller treatment of this question, see my article in the *Cambridge Historical Journal*, III, No. 1, esp. pp. 59 ff.

already won, with Russian help, an almost complete autonomy. English ministers noted with a grudging eye each gain of national privileges as a new field for the extension of Russian influence: it did not occur to them or to anyone else to go one step further and actively to promote independence. Indeed they could do very little without weakening the true foundation of independence, the sense not merely of a just *claim* to stand alone, but also of the *power* to do so. Extreme readiness to rely on the protecting Powers was one of the worst maladies of Greece. But the vigorous forces of national feeling were really the best defence against a great military Power. The independent States ground out between the upper millstone of Russian or Austrian domination and the nether millstone of Turkish tyranny may be infected by a swollen nationalism from which larger States of more placid growth are sometimes free.[11] But if such small States make for increased daily friction and more frequent petty quarrels, they may lessen the chances of a catastrophe on the grand scale. In another comparison, each spring of national feeling in the Balkans spread a widening pool around the centre of disturbance; the process was bound to go on until the whole surface was covered. Even then there was sure to be rough water at first where the currents met. But Balkan quarrels, so long as they could be isolated from Europe, did no great harm; each party must in time find its limits by exhaustion, if not by friendly arrangement. Europe cannot altogether justly accuse the Balkans of disturbing its repose: it was equally the aggressive political ambitions of the Eastern empires which allowed Balkan ripples to raise the waves over the whole lake. The powerful are too apt to find merely ridiculous, when produced on a small scale, the passions which they regard in themselves as the stirrings of a noble ambition. Considering the difference in civilisation between the rest of Europe and the Balkans a hundred years ago and their relative conditions now, it is arguable that Europe,

[11] The Greek Μεγάλη Ἰδέα soon made its appearance: in July 1833, diplomatists were fluttered by a rash visit of the new King of Greece to Smyrna—*F.O. Turkey*, 233. There were unpleasant results for the Greek notables who entertained him on landing—Th. Blancard, *Quelques détails additionnels à la monographie des Mavroyéni* (1921), pp. 48 ff.

which has inherited so much from the past, may have as much to be ashamed of as her well-abused neighbours of the Turkish fringe.

Yet it is equally shallow to lay all evils at the door of diplomacy, and to exhibit the strife among the Powers as mere petty and personal struggles unrelated to any real interests or ideals. Diplomatists act as sounding-boards—they catch up and blend a multitude of discordant notes issuing in every key and with varying force from all those individuals and groups, who, whether with influence or without it, whether sentimentally or materially, are interested in the result. That is true as much of 'secret diplomacy' as of diplomacy carried on in the columns of evening newspapers or in the publicity of a watering place on the Continent. Until this confused hum of voices is transformed in each country into a single predominant note, diplomatists cannot frame a course of action at all; and even then it remains to tune the yet more sharply discordant notes of the several countries concerned. The manœuvres of diplomacy can be made to seem contemptible enough; but they are often the alternative, not to 'friendly discussion', but to a direct clash of interests. It is a condition of the success of such delicate bargaining with words that the methods should be formal and precise; the business of 'finding a formula', the difference between a written and a verbal communication, and all the other niceties, have a real significance and importance which it is too easy to deride. It is obvious that if statesmen are to get to the root of differences without first irrevocably emphasising them, their methods must be careful and systematic rather than slipshod. If great issues can at best be focussed and handled only in the person of men who are as other men, in language borrowed from the expression of individual feelings, in the terms of personal relationships, that is not the fault of the spokesmen. As long as policy is negative and pacific, diplomats will probably retain the impersonal ideal; the man who breaks through the conventions and artificial grooves of diplomacy is seldom a prophet of peace, but a Bismarck or a Cavour who has an aggressive and definite policy in view. For the maintenance of a 'balance of power', conventional diplomacy is the only conceivable support. The doctrine is often supposed to be obsolete, by those who fear its consequences: but there is nothing to show that small-scale self-conscious nationalism, which is often only a less effective form of imperialism, can supersede or make superfluous some sort of balance of power in ordinary times.

When the Greek revolution began, racial and linguistic 'nationality' had not yet been exalted into a political principle. It was soon to enjoy its heyday of enthusiasm, and to do a great work of liberation. Forces unnaturally confined broke their barriers and released a new flood of energy. But the means are not the end: it is difficult for men bent on removing an obstacle which engages all their efforts, not to idealise their aim into a permanent object. So, when the forces of militant nationality have done their work, it is hard to turn them in time into another channel. Employed hitherto in breaking down barriers of alien rule within the community, they soon form, in contact with each other, a new network of barriers, political, economic, and linguistic, just as artificial as the old. Even tyrants with a sense of proportion may be more tolerable than patriots without it. A time comes when exaggerated nationalism must be looked upon as morbid obsession, to be treated, not by forcible confinement which merely aggravates the evil, but by leading the patient back to realities and by offering him wider and deeper interests.

APPENDIX I

SUMMARY OF LEADING EVENTS AND TREATIES

1770. Rising in the Morea, instigated by Catherine II, but soon suppressed.

1774, 21 July. *Treaty of Kutchuk-Kainardji*, Russia and Turkey (28 Articles).

Art. 18, 24. Russian frontier advanced to River Bug.

Art. 11. Straits and Black Sea ports open to Russian trade: Russia free to establish consuls anywhere in Turkey, with the same privileges as those enjoyed by France and England by their Capitulations.

Art. 5. Russia establishes an Embassy at Constantinople.

Art. 7, 14. Turkey promises to protect "the Christian religion and all its Churches", especially the Embassy Church at Constantinople.

Art. 16, 17. Stipulations for the better government of the Danubian Principalities and of the islands of the Archipelago.

Art. 1, 17, 24. Amnesty for all subjects of the Porte, and limited right of emigration.

1779, 10 March. *Convention*, Russia and Turkey (8 Articles), in explanation of the Treaty (1774).

Art. 8. Turkey promises to give equivalent indemnities to those inhabitants of the Morea whose lands and goods have been confiscated and appropriated to the use of mosques, etc.

1783, 21 June. *Commercial Treaty*, Russia and Turkey (81 Articles).

1792, 9 Jan. *Treaty of Jassy*, Russia and Turkey (13 Articles).

Art. 3. Russian frontier advanced to River Dniester.

Art. 2. Stipulations of 1774 Treaty confirmed.

1803. British Government takes over from the Levant Company the appointment of ambassadors, but not of consuls except in newly created consulates.

1805. Mehemet Ali becomes Pasha of Egypt.

1808. Accession of Sultan Mahmud II.

1809, 5 Jan. *Treaty of the Dardanelles*, Great Britain and Turkey (12 Articles).

Art. 11. Affirms the "ancient rule of the Ottoman Empire", closing the Straits at all times to foreign warships.

1812, 28 May. *Treaty of Bucarest*, Russia and Turkey (16 Articles).

Art. 4. Russian frontier advanced to River Pruth and River Danube (including Kilia, or Eastern, channel of Danube mouths).

Art. 8. Stipulations in favour of Serbia.

1814. Formation of *Hetaireia*, at Odessa.

1815, 5 Nov. *Treaty*, Austria, Great Britain, Prussia, Russia.

Ionian Islands guaranteed as a "Septinsular Republic", under the Protection of Great Britain.

1819, 24 Apr. *Recognition* by Turkey of the status of the Ionian Islands as defined in the Treaty of 5 Nov. 1815.

1821, Mar. Revolt attempted by A. Hypselantes in Moldavia, but disavowed by the Tsar.

1821, Apr. Revolt begun by local chieftains and clergy in the Morea.

1821, July. Russian ambassador leaves Constantinople.

1822, 27 Jan. *Proclamation of Independence* of the Greek Nation at Epidaurus.

1822, 29 Aug. *Declaration* addressed by the Greeks to the Congress at Verona.

1822, Aug. Capo d'Istria ceases to be the Tsar's adviser.

1822, 18 Sept. George Canning becomes Secretary of State for Foreign Affairs in England.

1823, Mar. British Government publicly accords to the Greeks the rights of belligerents (already observed by the Ionian Government).

1823, Oct. Meeting at Czernowitz between Tsar and Austrian Emperor. Russia resumes relations with Turkey by sending Minciaky as commercial representative.

1824, Jan. Russian *Mémoire*, proposing the creation of three autonomous provinces (in addition to the islands): published in May, in the *Constitutionnel*.

1824, Aug. Ribeaupierre appointed as Russian ambassador to the Porte, but delayed until Feb. 1827.

1824, 24 Aug. Letter of Greek Provisional Government to Canning, repudiating the *Mémoire*.

1824, 1 Dec. Reply of Canning, re-affirming strict neutrality.

1824, Dec. Minciaky made Russian *chargé d'affaires* at Constantinople.

1824, 16 Sept. Accession of Charles X in France.

1825, 24 Feb. Arrival of first Egyptian troops in the Morea.

1825, Feb.–June. British Government takes over the appointment of consuls from the Levant Company, which is dissolved.

1825, 30 June. *Act of Submission* of Greek Provisional Government, placing itself under the 'protection' of Great Britain.

1825, 30 Sept. British *Proclamations*, once more forbidding British subjects to take part in the contest or to export arms to either party.

1825, 20 Nov. Greek *Decree*, appointing the Duke of Nemours 'hereditary Sovereign'.

1825, ? Nov. Greek offer to submit to the protection of Russia.

1825, 12 Oct. *Instructions* to Stratford Canning, appointed ambassador to Constantinople.

1825, Oct.–Dec. Overtures, in England, towards an understanding between Russia and Great Britain.

1825, 1 Dec. Death of Tsar Alexander I, and accession, at Christmas, of Nicholas I.

1826, 17 Mar. Russian ultimatum to Turkey, demanding a Conference to settle points in dispute between them, other than the Greek question.

1826, 4 Apr. *Protocol*, Great Britain and Russia, for joint formulation, and joint or separate mediation, of a settlement between Turkey and the Greeks, on the basis of an autonomous and tributary Greek Principality: published in May, in *The Times*.

1826, 22 Apr. Fall of Missolonghi to the Turks.

1826, 7 Oct. *Convention of Akkermann*, Russia and Turkey (8 Articles).

Disputed points in Treaty of Bucarest (1812) settled in favour of Russia.

Two separate Acts, confirming and extending the privileges of Serbia and of the Danubian Principalities.

1827, Feb. Return to Constantinople of a Russian ambassador, absent since 1821.

1827, Apr. Greek 'National Assembly' elects, as President, John Capodistrias;

as Commander-in-Chief on land, General Sir Richard Church;
as Commander-in-Chief at sea, Admiral Lord Cochrane.

1827, June. Surrender of Athens (Acropolis) to the Turks; no insurgent forces left north of the Isthmus.

1827, 6 July. *Treaty of London*, France, Great Britain, Russia (7 Articles).

The three Powers will demand an armistice of both parties, and offer their mediation to the Porte on the basis of the arrangement proposed, which is to be guaranteed by any of the three Powers who can undertake it.

Additional and secret article. In case the Porte or the Greeks refuse mediation, the Powers will impose an armistice by means of their squadrons, without hostilities, and will "continue to pursue the work of pacification": the whole published, 12 July, in *The Times*.

1827, 8 Aug. Death of George Canning.

1827, 3 Sept. Greeks accept the armistice, but disregard it.

1827, 25 Sept. Ibrahim promises to remain inactive for twenty days at Navarin, but also disregards his undertaking.

1827, 20 Oct. Battle of Navarin. Turco-Egyptian fleet disabled or destroyed.

1827, 8–12 Dec. Ambassadors of the three Powers leave Constantinople.

1827, Nov.–Dec. Porte repudiates the Convention of Akkermann, and prepares local governors for war.

1828, 9 Jan. Duke of Wellington Prime Minister in England.

1828, 1 Feb. Arrival in Greece of Capodistrias as President.

1828, 26 Apr. Russian declaration of war on Turkey.

1828, June. Turkish declaration of war on Russia.

1828, 2 July. *Protocol*, three Powers, instructing their ambassadors from Constantinople to meet in the Aegean and to report on the details of a settlement for Greece.

1828, 19 July. *Protocol*, authorising France to send troops to the Morea.

1828, 6 Aug. *Convention of Alexandria*. Adm. Codrington secures Mehemet Ali's promise to evacuate the Morea.

1828, 13 Oct. Russian campaign ends with the capture of Varna and retirement of the Russians into winter quarters at Jassy.

1828, 16 Nov. *Protocol*, placing the Morea and Cyclades Islands under the protection of the three Powers.

1828, 12 Dec. *Report* of the Conference of Ambassadors at Poros, recommending a frontier from Arta to Volo or Zeitoun, and the inclusion of Candia and Samos.

1828, Sept.–1829, Mar. Advance of Sir R. Church in Western Greece, north of the Isthmus.

1829, Jan. Arrival of a French special envoy at Constantinople, and of a Russian special envoy in London.

1829, 22 Mar. *Protocol*, recommending the adoption of the Poros Report as a basis of negotiation, but excluding Candia and Samos: British objections to the Report, annexed to the Protocol.

1829, 18 June. Return of French and English ambassadors to Constantinople.

1829, 18 June. Fall of Silistria to the Russians.

1829, 21 July. Russian army across the Balkan mountains.

1829, 20 Aug. Russian army in Adrianople.

1829, 31 Aug. British fleet (16 ships) anchors beside Russian fleet (15 ships) in Besika Bay.

1829, 9 Sept. Porte agrees to accept any decisions of the Conference of three Powers under the Treaty of London.

1829, 14 Sept. *Peace of Adrianople*, Russia and Turkey (16 Articles and two separate Acts).

Arts. 2, 3. Russian frontier advanced to St George's, or Western, channel of Danube mouths.

Art. 7. Russian commerce given special privileges (hitherto only the same as the most favourable Capitulations of other Powers).

Art. 5 and Act I. Danubian Principalities, new system of administration under Russian guarantee and supervision.

Art. 6. Serbia, privileges granted to additional districts.

Art. 10. Greece, Turkish adherence to the Protocol of 22 Mar. 1829.

Act II. War Indemnity, etc.

1829, Dec. French troops, with the exception of 1000 men, evacuate the Morea.

1830, 3 Feb. *Protocols*, offering to Prince Leopold of Saxe-Coburg the sovereignty of Greece, with a frontier from the mouth of River Aspropotamos to Zeitoun, and without Samos or Candia.

1830, 20 Feb.–21 May. Acceptance, and resignation, by Prince Leopold.

1830, July. Revolution in France.

1830, Nov. Viscount Palmerston Secretary of State for Foreign Affairs in England.

British Resident in Greece instructed (28 Dec.) to delay the evacuation in Western Greece.

1830–1. Growth of disorder and opposition to the Government in Greece.

1831, 9 Oct. Assassination of the President, John Capodistrias, by George and Constantine Mavromichalis.

1831, Nov. Invasion of Syria by the Egyptian army.

1832, Apr. Flight of Agostino Capodistrias: anarchy in Greece.

1832, 7 May. *Convention*, France, Great Britain, Russia, and Bavaria.

Greece an independent kingdom under the sovereignty of Prince Otto of Bavaria, and under the guarantee of the three Powers, with a frontier from the Gulf of Arta to the Gulf of Volo.

1832, 27 May. Fall of Acre in Syria to the Egyptian army.

1832, 21 July. Porte agrees to the new frontier for Greece, Stratford Canning holding out hopes of support against Mehemet Ali.

1832, 21 Dec. Battle of Konieh, opening Asia Minor to the Egyptians.

1833, Feb. Russia sends, at the Sultan's request for protection, a squadron, with troops, inside the Bosphorus.

1833, May. Mehemet Ali signs peace with the Porte, obtaining the whole of Syria, and Adana.

1833, 8 July. *Treaty of Unkiar Skelessi*, Russia and Turkey (6 Articles).

Defensive Alliance, and promise of mutual assistance at need.

Secret Article. The Porte, in place of material assistance to Russia, promises not to admit foreign warships inside the Straits under any pretext whatever.

1833, Sept. Meeting of Tsar, Emperor of Austria, and King of Prussia at Münchengrätz.

Agreement to support the Ottoman Empire, or to consult before taking other action if forced to do so.

1833, 4 Aug. *Act* declaring the independence of the Orthodox Church in Greece from the Patriarch at Constantinople.

NOTE. The documents mentioned may be found in one or other or both of the following collections:

British and Foreign State Papers (Hertslet). See *Chronological Index* to vols. 1–20.

Martens, G. F., Murhard and others, *Recueil*, etc. See *Table Générale, 1494–1874* (1875).

APPENDIX II

TRADE STATISTICS

Table A

Great Britain—Imports from and exports to Russia, Turkey and the Ionian Islands in £1000 units ('Official' Values).

Year ending Jan. 5th	Russia		Turkey and Levant		Ionian Islands		*Parl. Papers*
	Imports from	Exports to	Imports from	Exports to	Imports from	Exports to	
1817	1316	1706	165	404	70	—	1826, XXII, 122 ff. (1817–1825)
1818	2194	2758	186	599	58	2	
1819	2851	2820	369	1061	87	13	
1820	2484	2036	251	767	49	6	
1821	2500	3668	417	962	93	14	
1822	1911	2097	371	583	85	7	
1823	2555	1219	386	972	84	13	
1824	2611	1841	447	1274	93	8	
1825	2606	2238	747	1397	132	15	
1826	3678	2063	1207	1151	113	11	1826–7, XVIII, 40
1827	2936	2221	818	1172	93	24	1828, XIX, 336
1828	4173	2654	598	1255	132	47	1829, XVII, 252
1829	3442	2753	732	525*	143	59	1830, XXVII, 213
1830	4180	3154	431	1476	109	39	1831–2, XXXIV, 205
1831	4024	3031	701	2885	100	94	1833, XXXIII, 379
1832	4585	2603	731	2204	187	85	1833, XXXIII, 419

These figures include exports of foreign manufactures. Of the exports to Russia, British manufactures were about seven-tenths, of those to Turkey about eight-ninths of the total, taking an average over the whole period.

* Russo-Turkish War; blockade began Oct. 1828.

Table B

Great Britain—Exports to Russia and Turkey in £1000 units ('Declared' Values).

Year	To Russia	To Turkey and Greece	*Parl. Papers*	Remarks
1827	1409	532		
1828	1319	186	1837–8, XLVII, 102 (totals only).	(*a*) Of our exports to Russia, cotton *twist and yarn* formed at first about 75 %, but these declined rapidly during the forties, a decline hardly counterbalanced by a large rise (after 1842) of exports of iron and steel and machinery, and (after 1844) of refined sugar. Woollens made up about 5 %, at first mainly manufactures, after 1842 mainly yarns.
1829	1436	569		
1830	1490	1149		
1831	1192	899		
1832	1587	925		
1833	1531	1045		
1834	1382	1245		
1835	1753	1360		
1836	1740	1821		(*b*) Of our exports to Turkey, *manufactured* cotton goods formed from 66% to 75%, cotton *twist and yarn* made up another 10 % to 20 %. Sugar, then iron and steel, were the largest items in the remainder. Exports to Syria and Palestine were first distinguished in 1836, and increased rapidly.
1837	2047	1179		
1838	1663	1976	1852, LI, 490 (analysed in detail). Cf. Porter's *Progress of the Nation* (1851 ed.) pp. 362–7. These figures include Turkey, Greece, Syria and Palestine, but not Egypt.	
1839	1776	1453		
1840	1603	1390		
1841	1607	1682		
1842	1886	1864		(*c*) These figures, unlike those of Table A, do not include re-exports of foreign manufactures. Even so, the discrepancy between the *official* values of Table A and the *declared* values of Table B (in the overlapping years 1827–32) is striking, the former being *on the average* about double the latter, but not corresponding at all closely year by year.
1843	1896	2332		
1844	2129	2897		
1845	2153	2879		
1846	1725	2406		
1847	1845	3226		
1848	1925	3401		
1849	1956	3220		
1850	1455	3114		

Table C

Number of British and foreign vessels engaged in trade between British ports, and Russian and Turkish ports.

Year	Russian ports				Turkish ports				Remarks
	Cleared from		Cleared to		Cleared from		Cleared to		
	British	Foreign	British	Foreign	British	Foreign	British	Foreign	
1817	1388	61	912	83	52	0	21	1	(*a*) These figures are from *Parl. Papers*, 1844, VIII, 225. The Russian Baltic trade employed disproportionately more vessels (compare Tables A and B), which brought bulky goods often in small vessels. Many of these returned to Russia in ballast, as is proved by scattered returns in *Parl. Papers*, showing tonnage exclusive of ships leaving in ballast (e.g. 1835, XLVIII, 537, for 1834 and 1835).
1818	1690	138	998	117	95	0	88	5	
1819	1509	104	772	91	93	0	61	7	
1820	1255	80	626	63	101	2	67	8	
1821	870	45	478	42	80	0	51	3	
1822	1208	66	584	44	75	0	55	5	
1823	1195	85	590	40	109	0	59	0	
1824	1293	146	799	84	168	1	151	7	
1825	1770	146	987	88	189	0	122	5	
1826	1178	88	787	55	137	0	107	5	
1827	1905	110	1230	94	138	1	88	4	
1828	1425	90	951	71	124	0	75	5	
1829	1829	85	1451	97	101	0	111	7	
1830	1661	90	1231	88	135	1	127	5	
1831	2065	132	1605	129	173	0	158	9	
1832	1419	117	1003	90	177	4	163	5	
1833	1382	152	1140	105	156	4	158	27	
1834	1519	228	1082	132	191	4	182	9	
1835	1279	257	992	196	242	4	214	15	
1836	1611	274	1244	273	237	3	220	18	
1837	1531	279	1223	227	216	2	211	11	
1838	1677 + 4	293	1304 + 1	207	224	3	341	12	(*b*) The additional figures (+) give the number of steamships, separately distinguished after 1837.
1839	2024 + 12	257	1484 + 11	283	282	5	278	49	
1840	1625 + 5	296	1073 + 6	213	239	8	250	18	
1841	1440 + 6	290	962 + 3	207	260	4	343	28	
1842	1303 + 6	215	889 + 5	186	306	24	371	38	
1843	1523 + 6	177	1096 + 3	179	325	11	376	64	
1818–42	1568		1018		173		162		Average, 25 years (1818 to 1842)

APPENDIX III

EXTRACTS RELATING TO NAVARIN AND TO CAPODISTRIAS

(1) *Lord Cochrane to Sir Richard Church*

Poros, 26 October 1827.

My dear Sir Richard

Reports have arrived from different quarters and by different persons situated on shore and at sea, of a battle in the Port of Navarin between the combined fleets & Turks. The action lasted from two hours before sunset until eight at night and between the commencement and twelve o'clock thirteen great explosions were counted. This affair (whatever the allies have suffered) must be ruin to the Egyptian and Turkish naval force.

Now therefore is the moment for the Greeks to act and for you to cover yourself with glory.

We are now proceeding to aid the insurgents in *different* quarters

yours ever sincerely

COCHRANE

P.S. If you become *rich* pray remember the poor for I have not a dollar to pay the men with, they are however at this moment inclined to trust, I think for a month.

B.M., Add. MSS. 36544, f. 183.

(2) *Circular letter of Sir Richard Church*

Head Quarters, Diakophto, 16/28 Oct. 1827.

The tremendous roar of the artillery of hundreds of ships of war, and the continual lightning of consuming fire, blazing awfully to announce the repeated peals bursting like thunder from thousands of heavy cannon will have already announced to many the glorious event of the destruction of the Turko-Egyptian fleet in the harbour of Navarino by the allied fleet of England, France and Russia under the supreme direction of His Ex[y] Admiral Sir E. Codrington, and his noble supporters Admirals De Rigny and De Heyden—To those who from distance from the shores of Navarin could not have had the extreme delight of hearing the thunder of the Battle I have now the pleasure to communicate this signal interposition of divine Providence by the chastizing hands of the three Christian powers in favour of Greece in favour of the Hellenic race. I need say no more I think to tell you to redouble your efforts in the service of your Country—Ibrahim Pasha who makes war even on your fruit trees and who avoids the serious and bloody combat with men, to make slaves of your helpless children of both sexes for brutal purposes—whose most sacred and most secret asylums are assail'd by his ferocious bands whilst he keeps aloof from manly warfare—this Pasha this ferocious Pasha now contemplates with dismay the remains and wrecks of that late mighty Turko-Egyptian fleet which had brought so many thousand Turks and Arabs to your shores and which had so amply provided them with all their wants—It is with a truly joyful heart that I communicate to you this great event, and desire you to make it known—to all the troops and inhabitants in your vicinity.—I salute you.

RICHARD CHURCH, *Generalissimo.*

To the Generals
and Officers commanding troops.

Copies in Greek and English in *B.M.*, *Add. MSS.* 36554, ff. 94–6.

(3) *The Character of Capodistrias*

Count Capodistrias seems to be a well-informed man; he has studied men and affairs; but he is rather a philosopher than a statesman, with particularly liberal and constitutional ideas. He sympathises with the sentiments of the age without going so far as to agree with its errors; he considers that one should not attempt to stop a strong tendency, but should restrict oneself to curbing it and obviating as much as possible the evils that may be produced by its action. He is a man at once systematic and of a speculative turn of mind, possessing great eloquence, only saying exactly what he wants to, and always anxious to produce an impression. He never utters a word too much, but speaks deliberately in order to show to the best advantage; his arguments are so subtle as to lend themselves nearly always to a double meaning, and although one cannot always approve of them, on the other hand one cannot wholly condemn them. In order to understand him one would have to get to the bottom of his ideas, and this he does not let you do, always avoiding any discussion that would oblige him to explain and develop his thoughts. When he went away he left everyone delighted with his manners, his wit and his behaviour.

Diary of Philip von Neumann (Austrian Chargé d'Affaires in London), Sept. 1st, 1819.

C'est encore avec Pozzo que j'ai fait ce voyage, et quand tu sauras que c'est à lui que je dois d'avoir roulé dans une bonne voiture à quatre places, tu lui pardonneras, j'espère, les torts que tu lui supposes. Quant à moi je t'avoue franchement que je ne connais personne qui lui soit supérieur. C'est aujourd'hui le seul homme en Europe auquel je reconnaisse les qualités qui constituent le véritable homme d'Etat. Je conviens avec toi que Capo d'Istria a l'âme plus pure, les sentiments plus nobles, plus désintéressés, avec moins de passions et de vanité, mais il est loin d'avoir les moyens, le bon sens et les connaissances de Pozzo, et surtout *cet esprit pratique* indispensable pour bien conduire les affaires de ce bas monde. Capo d'Istria a beaucoup d'esprit, mais il a souvent l'esprit faux, et malgré une grande sagacité, son jugement est quelquefois en défaut; il a de la perspicacité et de la finesse, mais pas toujours de la logique; il manque surtout de l'expérience des hommes et des choses. Il a l'air de travailler pour un monde composé d'êtres aussi parfaits que lui. Si le sort l'avait jeté dans les affaires de la France, il aurait été doctrinaire avec les meilleures intentions du monde. Ainsi rien ne l'a tant séduit que le livre de Guizot, qui est rempli de sophismes et de fausses assertions. Telle est, chère amie, ma profession de foi sur l'un et l'autre de ces personnages; je voudrais avoir Pozzo pour ministre et Capo d'Istria pour ami.

Nesselrode to his wife, from Laybach,
9 Jan. 1821—*Lettres et Papiers*, VI, 114–5.

APPENDIX IV

GREEK BALLADS

(*a*) *Karaïskaki*

Three little birds sit perched aloft, above Piraeus town,
On high they sing a mournful dirge, whose burden thus floats down:
"Tuesday, Wednesday, hapless days, but Thursday bitter gall:
Then Friday came, ah! would that day had never dawned at all.
The island men gave counsel rash to try the chance of war;
Karaïskaki was full of wrath, foreboding doom afar.
But he shouted for his serving man and cried with all his might:
'Saddle my horse, man, fetch my sword, make ready for the fight!'
He rides into the battle there, but close upon the Turks
Falls stricken by a deadly shaft, wherein black poison lurks.
The host stands fearful in amaze, the palikari quail,
But he bids the ranks unbroken stand, implores them not to fail:
'My children, do not melt away, but rally to your place,
While I go unto Koulouri[1] to heal my wounds apace;
For here I'm now but half a man, yet whole I'll soon return'.
And the warriors, hearkening to his voice, went on to battle stern.
Kiutayeh[2] there attacked them and drove his mob to fight,
With eight and twenty companies he slew them and put to flight.
He took a thousand heads of them,[3] three hundred captive made,
So there the palikari's flower is to rest for ever laid".

From the Greek in Passow's *Popularia carmina Graeciae recentioris*, CCLXVI.

(*b*) *Tzamis and the Constitution*

"What murmur's this o'er plain and hill, Rumelia's bitter cry?"
The answer, countryman of Greece, none better knows than I.
I've fought the Sultan twelve long years, shed blood o'er plain and hill;
And, now my heritage is won, the monarchs wish me ill.
They've sent me Capodistrias to lord it o'er the land,
A proud and scornful man is he, and mocks our warlike band.

[1] Salamis.

[2] The Turkish general.

[3] Literally, not metaphorically; the ears were sent in bags to Constantinople; the 300 prisoners were put to death some days later in revenge for the affair at St Spiridion.

He bids the chieftains all disarm, but they'll not bow the knee;
A *Constitution* they demand, *Assembly* there must be.[1]
In wrath he orders General Ranck, and Kitsos[2] whom he's gained,
To bring him Karatassos' son, Tzamis, alive enchained;
Kallergi[3] leads the horsemen forth—vile Cretan, full of lies;
But Tzamis, while he yet draws breath, '*The Constitution*' cries.

E. Legrand, *Recueil de chansons populaires grecques*, LXXX.
(There translated into French prose.)

[1] Σύνταγμα, Συνέλευσι.

[2] Kitsos Tsavellas, who took possession of the fort of Patras and ruled the town; he is described, under the name Giavellas, in *Sketches in Greece and Turkey* (anon. 1833). *B.M.* 1047. k. 6.

[3] Commander of the regular cavalry under Capodistrias.

APPENDIX V

MEMORANDUM ON THE TURCO-EGYPTIAN QUESTION BY SIR STRATFORD CANNING

Enclosed in S. Canning's letter from Paris, 19 Dec. 1832. This covering letter, which is endorsed "Returned by the King, Jan. [?] 1833", explains that the Memorandum was written in some haste, at the request of Lord Grey. *F.O. Turkey*, 211. [With pencil comments by Palmerston—indicated in the text by italics, and enclosed in square brackets.]

The Turkish Empire has reached, in its decline, that critical point, at which it must either revive and commence a fresh era of Prosperity, or fall into a state of complete dissolution. To Great Britain the fate of this Empire can never be indifferent. It would affect the interests of her Trade and East-Indian Possessions, even if it were unconnected with the maintenance of her relative Power in Europe. Nearer and more pressing Duties may forbid His Majesty's Government to take an active part in the Contest which now agitates Turkey; but the issue of a struggle so likely to prove decisive of the Sultan's independence, can hardly be overlooked and left to chance on any sound Principle of English Policy.

Often as the Sultan and his Predecessors have had occasion to maintain their Authority by force of Arms, they have always done so with ultimate Success, except in the recent instance of the Greeks. But the Egyptian War, though originating in the same vicious system of Government, which has caused so many Convulsions in Turkey, is far more dangerous to the Porte than any preceding Rebellion, whether it be considered with reference to the Character and Resources of Mehemet Ali, or to the difficulties of the Sultan's Position. The Pasha, however, if he succeed in the end, will not be able to carry his point without a severe and protracted Contest. Already overstrained by his exertions, he can only sustain them by imposing Additional Burthens on Egypt and Syria, increasing thereby the hazard and odium inseparable from the prosecution of his enterprise. His Sovereign, who has publicly branded him as a Rebel and Outlaw, is urged by the strongest motives to reject such terms of compromise as, on any probable supposition, it would agree with the views or safety of the Pasha to offer of his own accord. If Mehemet Ali be superior in point of capacity, if he can dispose more completely of the resources of his Country, and exhibit a higher degree of discipline in his Fleet and Army, the Sultan, on the other hand, has those advantages, which belong to an acknowledged Right, and a greater extent of Territory. He cannot be blind to the consequences of allowing his Vassal to form a separate Sovereignty within the Limits of his Empire. The Erection of Syria and Egypt into an independent State would in fact cut off the communication between Constantinople and Mecca, and while it weakened Mahmoud's Title to the Caliphat, would place the most important Parts of Arabia and Mesopotamia under the control of his Enemy.

The extraordinary Progress made by Ibrahim Pasha during the last Campaign has given rise to an idea, that the Capital itself is not beyond his reach. In Turkey no kind or description of Revolution is impossible. But the Egyptian Army has paused in its Career. The Sultan has had time to repair, in some measure, his losses; and the Grand Vizir at the head of a considerable Force, composed in part of new Levies, and partly of the Albanian Troops, which he commanded with so much credit in Bosnia, will afford a rallying point for the remains of the Army defeated under Hussein Pasha, and, if not strong enough to attack the Egyptian cantonments, will at least be able to make a stand in the fastnesses of Mount Taurus. But let us suppose an extreme case. The Vizir, no doubt, may experience the fate of his Predecessor; his Army may be dispersed; the Country may rise in favour of the Egyptians; and Ibrahim Pasha, encouraged by these circumstances, may possibly follow up his Victory even to the Shores of the Bosphorus, and dictate the most humiliating Terms to the Sultan.

In this case one of two results would be unavoidable. The Sultan must either abandon his Throne altogether, or consent to such a reduction of his Empire, as would leave Mehemet Ali in permanent Possession of Egypt and Syria with all the Country behind those Provinces as far as the Persian Frontier. Supposing the triumphant Viceroy to occupy and maintain himself on the vacant Throne of Constantinople, it is evident that he would be placed towards the Powers of Europe in the same position as the Sultan, with the additional weakness belonging to an usurped Title, and the necessity of flattering the religious prejudices of the Turks. The Interests of England and of Christendom would gain little by such a change. Whatever price the Chief of a new Dynasty would be willing to pay for recognition, could equally be obtained from the reigning Sultan in return for support and cooperation. Supposing the contest to terminate in the formation of a separate Government under the Sceptre of Mehemet Ali or of Ibrahim Pasha, the Sultan, deprived of so large a Portion of his Empire, and degraded in the opinion of his Subjects, would find it more difficult than ever either to make head against the encroachments of Russia, or to carry on that system of improvement, which is become essential to the maintenance of his Independence. [Marginal note by Palmerston—*Is not the unwieldy extent of the Turkish Empire one great check to the improvement of its industry & resources & possibly one great cause of its external weakness?*]

If the contending Parties were left to themselves, it is but too probable that a long and arduous War would drain their respective resources, and, by adding another cause of desolation to those which have long worn down the Turkish Empire, render it an easy prey to the first Invader. Nor is it in this respect alone that a protracted Contest in the Mediterranean Provinces of Turkey would be detrimental to European Interests. The necessities of both Parties would oblige them to employ every kind of Extortion and violence injurious to life and property, and it is difficult to conceive how Commerce more than civilization could expand, or even exist, under such a pressure. [*Is it quite clear that war on an extensive scale in an Empire which at all times & during what is called peace is the theatre of perpetual turbulence & petty disturbance, is really so injurious to its commerce & improvement as this paragraph supposes?*]

So many indeed and great are the Evils which this Contest is likely to generate in its Progress, that it becomes a duty to enquire by what means Great Britain, either alone or in concert with any of her Allies, may best contribute to hasten its Termination. [*This assumes more than is proved.*] No pretext for interference is wanting. The Sultan and the Pasha have both appealed to the friendly and equitable disposition of the British Cabinet, but with this difference, that the former applies for our assistance, and the latter for our mediation. It is not surprising that the Sultan, whose Honour and Independence are at Stake, should look for succour to that Power, which has once already been the instrument of restoring Egypt to the Porte; nor is it less natural, that Mehemet Ali should reckon, however erroneously, upon Great Britain for the means of securing to him that independence, of which the Greek Insurrection has probably given him the idea and the occasion.

Unfortunately this very consideration indisposes the Sultan to every kind of foreign interference unaccompanied with a moral or physical cooperation in his favour. He must necessarily feel that his plain unquestionable Interest is to put down the Pasha of Egypt, and to reestablish his own Authority in that Province and Syria. What he wants is the effectual aid of Great Britain for the accomplishment of this purpose, and there is little doubt, that, if His Majesty's Government could find in the present circumstances of the Turkish Empire adequate motives for acceding to this request, the presence of a British Squadron would suffice to ensure success. [*Is even this quite certain?*]

The principal difficulty with which the Sultan has to contend in directing his operations against Mehemet Ali, arises out of the distant and insulated position of Egypt, the ease with which Syria can be defended against an Army invading it from the North, and the disadvantage of having a Fleet, which though superior in numerical Force to that of Egypt, is by no means so well manned and manœuvred.

With the assistance of a British Squadron there is great reason to believe, that the Sultan would easily surmount these obstacles. Instead of attacking the Egyptian Forces in Syria, he might send an Expedition by Sea against Egypt itself. To the East of Damietta the Coast affords Facilities for landing Troops, and an invasion properly directed on that side would not only compel Ibrahim Pasha to retreat, but would also menace Cairo, and bring into the field all those, who, secretly attached to the Sultan's cause, are nevertheless kept down at present by the want of support and the fear of Punishment. Whatever just or insuperable objections may be raised on the score of expence, or on any other account, to the participation of Great Britain in this measure, the probable result of it would be beneficial in no small degree to her Interests. The very attempt indeed would give her an important Influence in the Counsels of the Divan. That influence would operate most powerfully in promoting the Progress of reform and civilization throughout Turkey [*We rescued Egypt once for Turkey—We acquired or supposed that we acquired influence in the Divan. What was the beneficial result? certainly no progress in civilization or Reform nor any such improvement of Turkish resources as is here contemplated*]; and the spirit of improvement, thus encouraged and directed, could hardly fail to revive the overlaid resources of a Country so rich in natural advantages. The Treaty of Alliance which would naturally be formed to regulate the operations of the combined Forces, and to provide for the reception and refreshment of the British Squadron, might also contain Stipulations in favour of any specific concession desired by His Majesty's Government, as well as an engagement to indemnify our Merchants at Alexandria for any losses arising out of the participation of Great Britain in the Contest. The Sultan's Pardon and a suitable Provision for Mehemet Ali and his Son Ibrahim, in the event of their overthrow, might be secured by means of the same Instrument.

It is obvious, that, as far as Great Britain is concerned, the only ground [*this is most just and true*] on which this Plan could be recommended, is the necessity of interfering to rescue the Turkish Empire from a War, which threatens to lay it at the feet of a Power already too great for the general Interests and Liberties of Europe. It is impossible at the same time to contemplate such a necessity without an encreased Feeling of regret that a Contest fraught with such consequences should ever have commenced; and hence arises an anxious desire to discover some means of restoring matters, as nearly as may be practicable, to the state in which they stood before the Pasha's attempt upon Acre.

If it be true, as the Sultan alleges, that Mehemet Ali has embarked in an enterprize of mere Ambition; if he has taken advantage of his Sovereign's embarrassments with the sole view of establishing an independent Sovereignty for himself and his Family, there is evidently no middle course; he must either succeed altogether or fail altogether.

[*Do not see that this conclusion follows from the premises.*] The question in that case is whether the object of enabling the Sultan to hasten the conclusion of the War by an attack upon Egypt, be sufficient to overbalance the objections which His Majesty's Government may entertain in general to extending their interference in foreign quarrels. Of their right to interfere upon an invitation from the Sultan there can be no doubt; and it is probable that the mode of interference suggested alone would prove effectual.

But to judge impartially of the Viceroy's motives we must call to mind the situation in which he was placed before his Expedition into Syria. The main object of the Sultan's internal Policy throughout his Reign has been the suppression of all minor Authorities [*Is the authority built on the forcible suppression of minor authorities legitimate? & if not, in what would the Pasha's usurped authority differ from the Sultan's if successful but in degree? Both would be usurpation*] which had acquired in any degree an abusive power of checking his own. Having destroyed the Janissaries, who formed the great obstacle to his designs, and having reconciled himself to the loss of Greece, that perilous bone of contention between him and Christendom, his views were turned to the establishment of a more regular system of administration in the Provinces of his Empire, and to the cultivation of a better understanding with the Powers of Europe, and principally with Great Britain. Such being the case it is far from improbable that Mehemet Ali may have looked with apprehension to the moment, when measures arising out of this policy would be applied to Egypt, which he had advanced, during an administration of twenty years, from a state of confusion and comparative poverty, to a degree of improvement, in point of order and production, which filled his Coffers, and placed him at the head of a considerable military and naval force. He may have thought that the Sultan's designs, coinciding with his necessities, would shortly lead to the spoliation of these fruits of his eminent capacity for Government, and therefore that it would be better to avail himself of the latter, in order to increase his means of resisting the execution of the former at his expence. Upon this supposition prudence and not ambition would be the motive of his conduct; security, rather than aggrandizement, his object. In a question of so much difficulty and complication, it may, therefore, be worth while to ascertain how far a reasonable security, consistent with what is due to the rights and character of the Sultan, might by possibility be obtained from him by means of British interference.

To go at once to the point, it is clear that the Pasha cannot be left in possession of Syria, on any imaginable terms whatever, without a considerable loss of credit, if not of actual strength, to the Sultan's Government. His right to retain possession either of Syria or of Egypt without the Sultan's consent can only be the right of force. [*What other has the Sultan?*] The obvious inference is that no arrangement intended to give security to the Pasha can be fairly proposed to the Porte, unless it be attended with the recall of the Egyptian forces from Syria. Nor is it likely that any proposal would prove effectual, which should not be accompanied with a distinct understanding as to the amount of revenue and the contingent of troops and ships that the Pasha would be ready henceforward to hold at the Sultan's disposal, in consideration of his continuing to hold the Viceroyalty of Egypt for life, and co-operating with the Sultan for the advancement of those plans of reform, upon the execution of which the best and only hope of maintaining the independence of the Turkish Empire, and improving the condition of its inhabitants, may be truly said to depend. An arrangement comprizing these points, and concluded under the sanction, though not necessarily with the guarantee, of Great Britain, might be expected to allay the Pasha's apprehensions, supposing his present conduct to have originated rather in them than in any ambitious impulse. But in order to reconcile the Sultan's mind to a transaction which, at best, would be far from palatable to a Prince of his temper and policy, something more than the recollection of his disasters in the late campaign would be necessary. He would no doubt expect of Great Britain to declare Herself openly in favour of his cause, and to follow up that declaration with measures tending to uphold his authority in the eyes of his subjects, and to facilitate his operations against the Egyptian forces. The most obvious measures of this description are a prohibition to His Majesty's Subjects to convey provisions or warlike stores to Egypt and Syria, [*i.e. with a view to remote and precarious advantages to our commerce to begin by cramping & prohibiting that which exists with Egypt & Syria*] the establishment of Cruizers on the Coast to prevent the importation of those Articles, the recall of all British Subjects serving under the Pasha, an arrangement for introducing Engineers and Naval Officers into the Sultan's service, and a refusal to acknowledge the Egyptian Flag. To these might be added such diplomatick proceedings at the Courts of Persia and Greece, and at Bagdad, and in parts of Syria which are not actually occupied by Ibrahim Pasha, as would counteract the intrigues of Mehemet Ali, and contribute to the promotion of the Sultan's interests in those Quarters.

Great Britain, by adopting these measures, or measures like these, might perhaps be able to gain in a sufficient degree the confidence of the Sultan; but much would still remain to be done in order to bring the Viceroy of Egypt into an arrangement on the above-mentioned terms. It would be necessary, in the first place, to extinguish his hope of our ever consenting to the accomplishment of his schemes of independence, in the second, to provide in some degree for Ibrahim Pasha's interests, and, in the third, to soften his mortification at the loss of Syria by making some change in the Authorities of that Country more acceptable to him than the reinstatement of those whom he has forcibly removed. On the second and third of these points, it would of course be advisable to consult the views and feelings of the Viceroy himself, but as far as a conjecture may be hazarded, it is not impossible that an immediate transfer of the Government of Candia to Ibrahim Pasha, or a promise of the reversion of that of Egypt to him during his lifetime on the same conditions under which it is proposed that Mehemet Ali should hold it in future, would be satisfactory on that point; and that as to Syria, the Sultan might be induced to consign the Pashalick of Acre to one of Mehemet Ali's Grandsons, provided no Egyptian Troops were allowed to remain there, and that the Fortress of Acre were garrisoned by a detachment of the Sultan's Guard, and commanded by a Governor enjoying his confidence.

The effect of this plan, if it were carried into execution, would be to restore the matters in question as nearly as possible to their former state. It is grounded on the threefold persuasion that nothing but absolute necessity would induce the Sultan to consent to the union of the two Provinces of Egypt and Syria under Mehemet Ali; that his efforts to avert that necessity would exhaust his resources, and render the independence of his Empire still more precarious than now; and, finally, that His Majesty's Government might either find insuperable objections to co-operating with the Sultan by means of an auxiliary Squadron, or, at all events, that they would prefer withholding that kind of assistance until the experiment of milder measures had been made without success. The very apprehension of their recurring eventually to such an extremity would doubtless contribute to produce in the Viceroy's mind a disposition favourable to the acceptance of their proposals.

How far it may be practicable to render the proposed Alliance respecting Egypt, on either of the preceding suppositions, available to the acquisition of any exclusive advantage for Great Britain, is by no means so clear as the benefit which would in all probability accrue from it to the general interests of Europe and of Turkey itself. It is not to be doubted that our support, and more particularly our assistance under such circumstances, would secure the confidence and gratitude of the Sultan, and that He would be ready to make any reasonable sacrifice in return for such important aids. But the Porte is so bound by her Treaties with the principal European Powers, that no commercial privilege granted to one could long be withheld from the others, and it would be difficult to point out any special object of interest not coming under that head, unless it were the grant of certain facilities for navigating the River Euphrates by Steam, with a view to the promotion of a more direct intercourse with India, the feasibility of which very important project, though probable in the highest degree, has not yet been submitted to actual experiment, or the privilege of obtaining Ship-timber from the extensive forests of Turkey, which could only be of value to Great Britain in the event of Her being engaged in a naval war in some degree similar to the last. But it stands to reason that the same motives which induce the Sultan to court an Alliance with Great Britain would render the existence of that Alliance favourable to the promotion of our interests in Turkey. Nor can it be necessary to repeat that if it be a British and an European object to uphold the Turkish Empire as a barrier against encroachments from the North, and if the Sultan's independence be endangered by the chances of a contest indefinitely prolonged against Egypt, and the consequent interruption of measures essential to its maintenance, there are sufficient motives for acceding, under proper restrictions, to the Sultan's overture without the additional inducement of a special or exclusive British interest.

Another part of the subject remains to be examined, and it is one which embraces such various and extensive considerations as scarcely to find place in a memoir grounded on the presumed facility of access to local information. The question of British interference in the Egyptian contest is, however, indissolubly connected with the policy of the Courts respecting Turkey. Nor is it possible to arrive at a satisfactory conclusion on the subject, without referring in some measure to the opposition or concurrence which Great Britain would have to expect from them in the event of her determining to support the Sultan's cause, or to offer her mediation between him and the Pasha of Egypt. But it is by no means necessary to go over the whole ground of inquiry on this occasion. What can be stated with some degree of confidence, or prospect of utility, it is not difficult to bring within a narrow compass.

There is no doubt that the Sultan would in any emergency look with preference to the counsels or assistance of Great Britain. No Christian State ranks so high in his estimation either for power or for good faith. If England were to take up the affair of Egypt in concert with France, he would not perhaps regret their joint interference accompanied with the support of his cause, but in all probability he would only consent to it from deference to His Majesty's Government. Many acts of France during the last forty years, concluding with the occupation of Algiers, have rendered the Porte extremely mistrustful of that Power. The concurrence of France in the supposed case could therefore be desirable to Great Britain, only as it might tend to allay jealousy, or enable her to operate more effectually on the Pasha of Egypt. The motives which at present prevail with the French Ministers to cultivate the good-will and confidence of England, might possibly suffice to reconcile them to her single interference in the Affairs of Turkey: [*Surely it would be very strange if it did—Should we be easily reconciled to the 'single' interference of France? Yet France is both by position and by antient connection more directly interested in Turkish affairs than ourselves*] but the counteraction, however disguised, of a Power like France could hardly fail to increase the difficulties already existing, and it is well known that the French Cabinet has long regarded the Levant, and Syria and Egypt in particular, with more than common interest.

Of the two remaining Powers, whose disposition with respect to Turkey is of any immediate consequence, Austria would no doubt behold with satisfaction the influence and energy of Great Britain employed in support of the Sultan's authority and the preservation of his empire from dismemberment. It is equally clear that a similar interference for such purposes could never be agreeable to Russia, although the feelings, which it would be likely to excite in that quarter, might soften in proportion as British influence was pointed to the overthrow of rebellion; and the Court of St Petersburgh, though no less adverse to our interference than to the Sultan's application for it, could hardly with a due regard to its own principles and professions of peace, step forward to *oppose* its exercise [*perhaps not, but would she or could she be entirely neutral & passive on such an occasion—America is not glanced at but she has commerce in those parts & by interfering we sanction her right of interfering too*].

To return to the main question, there is no denying that whether it be contemplated with reference to a single or to a joint interference, the difficulties are great, the hazards considerable. In one respect, however, the prospect is clear. Let Mehemet Ali succeed in constituting an independent State, and a great and irretrievable step is made towards the dismemberment of the Turkish Empire. That Empire may fall to pieces at all events; and he must be a bold man who would undertake to answer for its being saved by any effort of human policy. But His Majesty's Government may rest assured that to leave it to itself is to leave it to its Enemies.

APPENDIX VI

(*a*) *Chief Ministers of the Powers*, 1821–1833

		Prime Minister	*Foreign Secretary*	
England		Earl of Liverpool, retired 1827, Feb.	Viscount Castlereagh, d. 1822, Aug.	
			George Canning	1822, Sept.
	1827, Apr.	George Canning (d. Aug.)	Earl of Dudley	1827, Apr.
	Aug.	Lord Goderich	Earl of Dudley	
	1828, Jan.	Duke of Wellington	Earl of Dudley	
			Earl of Aberdeen	1828, May
	1830, Nov.	Lord Grey	Viscount Palmerston	1830, Nov.
		Head of Ministry	*Foreign Affairs*	
France	1821, Dec.	Duc de Richelieu	Duc Pasquier	
		Comte de Villèle	Vicomte M. de Montmorency	1821, Dec.
			Vicomte de Chateaubriand (Verona)	1822, Sept.
			(Minister)	Dec.
			Baron Damas	1824, Aug.
	1828, Jan.	Vicomte de Martignac	Comte de la Ferronays (during his illness, M. de Rayneval)	1828, Jan.
			Comte Portalis	1829, Jan.
	1829, Aug.	Prince de Polignac	Prince de Polignac	
	1830, Aug.	M. Lafitte	Comte Molé	1830, Aug.
			Comte Sebastiani	1830, Nov.
	1831, Mar.	M. Casimir Périer	Duc de Broglie	1831, Sept.
Austria		Prince Metternich, *Chancellor* since 1809 (Chevalier de Gentz, d. 1832)		
Prussia		Prince von Hardenberg, d. 1822, Oct.		
		Count von Bernstorff, retired 1832		
	1832	M. Ancillon (since 1815 head of political division in Foreign Office)		
Russia		Count Nesselrode, *Chancellor*		
		Count John Capo d'Istria, retired 1822, Aug.		

APPENDIX

(*b*) *Ambassadors and Special Envoys † of the*

	London	Paris	Vienna
England		Sir C. Stuart 1825 Visc. Granville 1828, July Lord Stuart de Rothesay (formerly Sir C. Stuart) 1831, Jan. Visc. Granville	Hon. R. Gordon 1823 Sir H. Wellesley (1828 became Lord Cowley) 1832 Sir F. Lamb
France	Duc Decazes 1822, Jan. Vic. de Chateaubriand 1823–1829 Prince de Polignac 1829, Aug. A. de Montmorency, Duc de Laval 1830, Sept. Prince Talleyrand		1815 M. de Caraman 1828 A. de Montmorency, Duc de Laval 1830 Comte de Rayneval 1833, Jan. Comte de S. Aulaire
Austria	1815–1842 Prince Paul Esterhazy and (to 1826) Baron Philip de Neumann (*chargé*)	1826–1849 Count A. Apponyi	
Prussia	1821 Baron H. v. Werther 1824 Count M. v. Maltzahn 1827–1841 Prince H. von Bülow	1825 Baron H. v. Werther	Prince Hatzfeldt 1827 Count M. v. Maltzahn
Russia	1812–1834 Count (from 1826 Prince) C. de Lieven (and Princess de Lieven) 1829–1830 Count Matuscewitz†	1815–1839 Count C. Pozzo di Borgo	Count Golowkin 1822 Count Tatistchev†

VI

Powers at Foreign Capitals, 1821–1833

Berlin	St Petersburg	Constantinople	Greece
Sir G. Rose 1823 E. of Clanwilliam 1827 G. H. Seymour 1828 Sir Brook Taylor 1830 G. W. Chad 1832 Lord Minto	Sir C. Bagot 1825, Jan.–June Stratford Canning 1825, Nov.–1826, June Visc. Strangford 1826, Mar.–Apr. D. of Wellington† 1826, June–1828, June E. C. Disbrowe (*chargé*) 1828, Aug. Lord Heytesbury	Visc. Strangford 1825 W. Turner (*chargé*) 1826, Feb.–1827, Dec. Stratford Canning 1829, June–1831, Aug. Sir R. Gordon 1831, Nov.–1832, Aug. Sir Stratford Canning (D. Urquhart, *secretary*) 1832 H. Mandeville (*chargé*) 1833, May Lord Ponsonby	1826, Jan. (Hydra) 1828, Oct.–Dec. (Poros) Stratford Canning (accredited to the Porte) 1828, Dec. E. Dawkins (*Resident*)
1821, Dec. M. de Rayneval 1825 Comte de Saint-Priest 1827 Vic. d'Agoult 1830, Oct. Comte de Rumigny 1831–1833 Maréchal Maison	1818 Comte de la Ferronays 1828 Marquis de Mortemart 1832 Maréchal Mortier 1833 Maréchal Maison	1824 Marq. Latour-Maubourg 1824, June–1827, Dec. 1829, June–1831, June Lieut.-Gen. Comte Guilleminot 1829, Jan.–1830 M. J. P. Jaubert 1831 M. de Varenne (*chargé*) 1833, Feb.–1834 Adm. Baron Roussin	1828, Oct.–Dec. Lieut-Gen. Comte Guilleminot (at Poros) (accredited to the Porte) 1828, June–Dec. Baron Juchereau de Saint Denys 1829, June Baron Rouen (*Resident*)
1810 Count Stefan Zichy 1827–1834 Baron J. v. Werner	1815–1826 Count Ludwig Lebzeltern 1824, and 1826, Feb. Comte de Clam† 1827–1829 Count Stefan Zichy 1828–1829 Prince Philip of Hesse-Homburg† 1829, Jan.–1839 Count K. Ficquelmont	1818 Count R. Lützow 1823 Baron F. Ottenfels-Schwind 1832–1850 Count B. Stürmer	1831 Consul Gropius 1834–1848 Baron A. Prokesch v. Osten
	M. Schöler M. v. Küster (*chargé*)	1820 M. A. v. Miltitz 1828 Baron v. Canitz 1829, Aug. Gen. Baron Müffling†	
Count D. Alopeus		to 1821 Count P. A. Stroganov 1824, Aug.–1826 M. de Minciaky (*chargé*) 1827, Feb.–Dec. M. de Ribeaupierre (nominated 1824, Aug.) 1830 M. de Butenev 1832, Dec. Gen. Muraviev 1833, May Count Alexis Orlov	1828, Oct.–Dec. M. de Ribeaupierre (at Poros) 1828, Sept. M. Bulgari 1830 Baron Rückmann (*Resident*)

APPENDIX VI(*c*)

	Mediterranean Squadrons.	*Miscellaneous.*	*Missions to Egypt.*
England	Adm. Sir E. Codrington, 1827–8 Adm. Sir Pulteney Malcolm, 1828, Oct.	Capt. G. W. Hamilton (Greek waters)	Col. Cradock, 1827, Aug.; 1828, Mar. Col. P. Campbell, 1833 Consuls H. Salt and (1828) J. Barker
France	Adm. H. de Rigny	(Expedition to the Morea) Gen. Maison, 1828, Sept. Gen. Schneider, 1829	(Gen. Boyer in command of the Egyptian army, 1825–6)
Russia	Adm. Heyden, 1827, Oct. Adm. Ricord, 1831	M. Katakazy (diplomatic attaché to the naval squadron)	Gen. Muraviev, 1833, Jan.
Austria	Adm. Paulucci Adm. Dandolo	Major Prokesch (diplomatic attaché to the naval squadron, 1827–1830)	Major Prokesch, 1826, Sept.–1827, June; and 1833, Apr. (from 1830 Baron P. v. Osten)

BIBLIOGRAPHY

I have been guided mainly by the bibliography in the *Cambridge Modern History*, vol. x, cc. 6 and 17, supplemented by that of the *Cambridge History of British Foreign Policy*, vol. II, c. 2. There is a very full list of contemporary publications in G. Bengesco's *Essai d'une notice bibliographique sur la question d'Orient: Orient Européen*, 1821–1897 (Brussels, 1897). The titles show how the flow of pamphlets begins with historical essays and appeals for sympathy and money for Greece, and passes from 1827 onwards to partitions of Turkey, anti-Russian outbursts, attack and defence of Capodistrias, the future expansion of Greece, etc. See too *English Bibliography of the Near Eastern Question* by V. M. Jovanović (Belgrade, 1908), and the *Sale-Catalogue* of the library of A. Z. Mamouka (Athens, 1886).

NOTE. Books published in London unless otherwise stated. Abbreviations used in the footnotes are shown here in heavy type. I have referred throughout in the footnotes to printed sources in preference to MSS.; and, among printed documents, to the most accessible in each case, so far as possible, or to the most complete: e.g. letters from Metternich to Gentz are referred, not to Metternich's *Mémoires*, but to the complete collection of *Briefe von und an Gentz*, vol. III (ed. Wittichen). Documents printed in strict chronological order are as a rule referred to by date only: e.g. Princess Lieven's *Letters* to her brother, and her *Correspondence* with Lord Grey.

I. MANUSCRIPTS

PUBLIC RECORD OFFICE (P.R.O.)

Foreign Office. **F.O. Russia** (65) and **F.O. Turkey** (78). Out-letters only, 1821–5. Out- and In-letters, Oct. 1825–Dec. 1833. Occasional "Domestic" and "Consular" volumes. **F.O. France** (27), **F.O. Austria** (7), **F.O. Prussia** (64)—occasional volumes. **F.O. Greece** (32), 1828–33. The reports of Edward Dawkins give copious information, with a strong bias against Capodistrias.

Colonial Office. **C.O. Ionian Is.** *Greek Revolution*, 1822–30. These volumes contain a large number of intercepted letters: the quarantine was used throughout the East for opening letters in the post. No. 1260, *Review of the Conduct of the English Government in the Protection of the Ionian Islands* (undated), is an official explanation of the constitution and an able defence of its limitations.

Stratford Canning Papers (**S. C. Papers**) (F.O. 352), 1826–33. For extracts also printed in Lane-Poole's *Life of Lord Stratford de Redcliffe*, reference has been made to the book and not to the papers.

Howard de Walden Papers (H. de Walden Papers) (F.O. 360), Nos. 2–5. Austrian and Russian intercepted letters, 1826–8. Lord Howard de Walden was the eldest son of Canning's friend, Charles Ellis. After a short career in the army, he was made in 1824 Under-Secretary of State for Foreign Affairs at the age of twenty-five.

Admiralty (Ad.). Occasional volumes, especially Ad. II, 1694 (secret instructions).

British Museum (B.M.)

Add. MSS. 37294 (Wellesley Papers). Greek letters, 1825.

Add. MSS. 38294 (Liverpool Papers). Canning in Paris, 1826, f. 136.

Add. MSS. 36544–7, 36554, 36563–5 (Church Papers). Correspondence, Narrative, 1827–9, News-cuttings, etc.

Add. MSS. 36461–4 (Broughton Papers). Greek Committee, Lord Cochrane, etc.

Vienna, Archives

Weisungen nach London (Weisungen), Berichte aus London (Berichte), 1828–33. Extracts from the same correspondence (between Metternich and Esterhazy) for 1826–7 were kindly lent to me by Prof. H. W. V. Temperley—reference in footnotes to Austrian Extracts.

Munich, Archives

Hausarchiv and Staatsarchiv, relating to the Bavarian candidature for the throne of Greece. I am indebted for help in this search to Archivrat Dr J. Weiss, of the Hausarchiv.

Lent by Mr F. F. Urquhart

MS. Diary of Col. C. G. Urquhart (brother of D. Urquhart), 1827–8. He was killed in attacking the pirates of Grabusa, March 1828.

II. PRINTED BOOKS

(*a*) Documents, collected

British and Foreign State Papers (Hertslet). Reference in footnotes to S.P.

Hansard, *Parliamentary Debates*, 3rd series, 1820–32.

Martens, F. de. *Recueil de Traités et Conventions conclus par la Russie*. St Petersburg, 1874– . With a continuous narrative taken from Russian despatches. Vol. IV, Austria; vol. XI, England; vol. XV, France. The narrative is not very trustworthy.

Martens, G., and Murhard. *Recueil*, *Suppléments*, *Nouveau Recueil*, *Nouveaux Suppléments*. Göttingen. As this collection is provided with a complete chronological index (*Table générale*, 1494–1874, Göttingen, 1875), I have not used it for reference as a rule. The *Nouveaux Suppléments* contain many documents from the *Portfolio*, but not all.

Parliamentary Papers (Parl. Papers), especially 1830, XXXII, including Protocols of London Conference, 12 July 1827 to 14 May 1830; 1831–2, XLVIII, including Protocols, 22 May 1830 to 25 July 1832.

Portfolio, 6 vols., 1836–7; and *New Portfolio*, 4 vols., 1842–3. Ed. by David Urquhart. A strongly anti-Russian periodical consisting, in part, of Russian despatches found at Warsaw during the Polish Revolution of 1830. Their authenticity was never denied: a few of them are to be found in the English F.O. records. Copious commentary by the editor.

Prokesch v. Osten, Baron A. F. *Geschichte des Abfalls der Griechen vom Türkischen Reiche*. 6 vols. Vienna, 1867. Vols. III–VI contain the most important Austrian documents, some Russian and a few English. Reference in footnotes to P.O.

Recueil de documents relatifs à la Russie. Paris, 1854. (Recueil, 1854.) Miscellaneous documents, selected to rouse feeling against Russia.

Wellington, Duke of. *Despatches, Correspondence and Memoranda, in continuation of the former series* (1819–32) (Wellington's Despatches). 8 vols. 1867.

(*b*) GENERAL

Aberdeen, Earl of. *Life*. By Lord Stanmore. 3rd edn. 1905.

—— *Life*. By Lady F. Balfour. 2 vols. 1923.

About, Edmond. *La Grèce Contemporaine*. Paris, 1854. *Le Roi des Montagnes*. Paris, 1867. Amusing and satirical sketches of Greek life, the first in the form of traveller's essays, the second a novel of brigandage.

Adams, J. Q. *Memoirs of J. Q. Adams, comprising portions of his diary*, 1795–1848. Vols. V and VI. Ed. C. F. Adams. 12 vols. Philadelphia, 1874–7. Abridged edn., ed. Nevins, 1928.

Beaujour, L. A. *Tableau du Commerce de la Grèce* (1787–97). Eng. trans. 1800.

Bikélas, D. *Loukis Laras: Reminiscences of a Chiote merchant during the War of Independence* [J. Gennadius]. 1881. *La Grèce Byzantine et Moderne*. Paris, 1893. Some chapters appeared, translated by Lord Bute, in *Seven Essays on Christian Greece*. 1890.

Blaquière, E. *The Greek Revolution, its origin and progress*. 1824. *Narration of a second visit to Greece*. 1825. *Greece and her Claims*. 1826. The author was a prominent member of the Greek Committee in London, and carried the first instalment of the loan to Greece.

Bowring, Sir J. *Autobiographical Recollections*. 1877. A promoter of the Greek Committee, and the disciple and executor of Bentham.

Broughton, Lord (J. C. Hobhouse). *Recollections of a Long Life*. Vol. II, 1822–9. 6 vols. 1909–12.

Byrne, M. *Memoirs of Miles Byrne*. Ed. S. Gwynn. Dublin, 1907. A commander in the French army of occupation in the Morea.

Byron, Lord. *Life*. By T. Moore. 1832. *Letters and Journals*. *Correspondence*, vol. II. Ed. J. Murray. 1922.

Cambridge History of Foreign Policy (C.H.F.P.). Vol. II. 1923.

Cambridge Modern History (C.M.H.). Vol. X. 1910.

Canning, George. *Life* (1822–1827). By A. G. Stapleton. 3 vols. 1831.

—— *Canning and his Times* (C. and his Times). By A. G. Stapleton. 1859.

—— *Some Official Correspondence of G. Canning* (Some Official Correspondence). Ed. E. J. Stapleton. 2 vols. 1887.

—— *Canning and his Friends* (C. and his Friends). By J. Bagot. 2 vols. 1909.

Canning, George. *Life*. By H. W. V. Temperley. 1905.

—— *The Foreign Policy of Canning*. By H. W. V. Temperley. 1926.

Canning, Stratford. *The Eastern Question*. 1878.

—— *Life of Lord Stratford de Redcliffe*. By S. Lane-Poole. 2 vols. 1888. Based on the S. Canning Papers, now in the Public Record Office.

Capefigue, J. *Les Diplomates Européens*. 2 vols. Paris, 1845. A series of biographical and character sketches.

Capodistrias, J. *Mémoire* (1798–1822), written by Capodistrias for the Tsar in Dec. 1826, in *Sbornik*, III, 163–292. Minimises his own interest in the preparation of the revolt.

—— *Lettres et Documents*. [Ed. J. G. Eynard.] Paris, 1831.

—— *Correspondance*. 4 vols. Geneva, 1839. Selected in defence of his memory, but fairly representative.

—— *Renseignements sur la Grèce et sur l'administration du Comte Capodistrias, par un Grec*....Paris, 1833. A defence.

—— *Mémoires*. By A. Papadapoulovrétos. 2 vols. Paris, 1837. A panegyric.

—— *Deux Études*. By J. A. de Gobineau. Paris, 1905. One is from *Revue des deux Mondes*, Apr. 1841, and is criticised in *Capodistrias—Zur Vorbereitung für die künftige Geschichte*....Anon. Aarau, 1842.

—— *La Grèce et les Capodistrias*. See under Pellion.

—— *Graf Capodistrias*. By K. Mendelssohn-Bartholdy. Berlin, 1864. Severely critical, by a doctrinaire liberal.

—— ''Ι. Καποδίστριας.' By 'Α. Μ. 'Ιδρώμενος. Athens, 1900. A critical defence, but not many sources used.

—— 'ὁ Καποδίστριας ὡς Θεμελιώτης τῆς δημοτίκης ἐκπαιδεύσεως.' By Λ. Βελελι. Athens, 1908. A prize essay on the schools of Greece before and after the Revolution.

—— *Capodistrias avant la Révolution grecque*. By T. Lascaris. Lausanne, 1918.

—— *Essai sur la vie du Comte Capodistrias* (Aug. 1822–Jan. 1828). By L. Oeconomos. Paris, 1926. Traces his activity in retirement.

Castlereagh, Viscount. *The Foreign Policy of Castlereagh*. (Castlereagh.) By C. K. Webster. 1925.

Chesney, Col. F. R. *The Russo-Turkish Campaigns*, 1828–1829. 1854.

—— *Narrative of the Expedition for the Survey of the Euphrates and Tigris*, 1835–1837. 1868.

—— *Life*. Ed. S. Lane-Poole. 2nd edn. 1893. Chesney's preliminary reports on the Euphrates influenced Stratford Canning in Dec. 1832. See Appendix V.

Church, Sir R. *Observations on the Greek Frontier*. 1830. Pamphlet.

—— *Life*. By S. Lane-Poole. (From *E.H.R.* v, 7, 293, 497.) 1890.

—— *Chapters in an adventurous Life*. By E. M. Church. 1895.

—— *Some English Philhellenes* (VII). By Z. D. Ferriman. 1919.

Cochrane, Lord. *Life*. By his son. 2 vols. 1869. *Life*. By J. W. Fortescue. (English Men of Action.) 1889. *Correspondance entre deux Philhellènes* [Lord Cochrane and L. A. Gosse]. Ed. E. Rothpletz. Paris, 1919.

Cochrane, G. *Wanderings in Greece*. 1837. A relative, who accompanied the Admiral to Greece.

Cradock, Col. *Cradock's Missions to Egypt*, 1827–1828. A. Stern in *E.H.R.* XV, 277.

Dragoumes, N. *Souvenirs historiques*. Trans. J. Blancard. Paris, 1891.

Ellenborough, Lord. *A Political Diary*, 1828–1830 (Diary). Ed. Lord Colchester. 2 vols. 1881. Valuable evidence for the Duke of Wellington's administration.

Emerson, J. (Sir J. E. Tennent). *Picture of Greece in* 1825. 2 vols. 1826. *Letters from the Aegean*. 2 vols. 1829. A not very critical Philhellene.

English Historical Review (E.H.R.).

Eton, W. *A Survey of the Turkish Empire*. 4th edn. 1809. Contains a good deal of statistical matter.

Études diplomatiques sur la Question d'Orient, 1826–1827. Stuttgart, 1870. Argues that Protocol and Treaty were a victory for Russia over Canning.

Eynard, J. G. *Der Genfer J. G. Eynard als Philhellene*, 1821–1829. By E. Rothpletz. Zurich, 1900.

Fabvier. *Le Général Fabvier en Grèce*. By A. Debidour. Paris, 1904. Numerous references to French archives.

Fallmerayer, J. P. *Geschichte der Halbinsel Morea während des Mittelalters*. 2 Theile. Stuttgart, 1830, 1836. *Schriften und Tagebücher*, selected by H. Feigl and E. Molden. München, 1913. The introduction, pp. xxviii–xxx, gives references to later criticism of Fallmerayer's theory.

Festing, G. *J. H. Frere and his Friends*. 1899.

Finlay, G. *History of the Greek Revolution*. 2 vols. 1867. (= *History of Greece*, VI–VII.)

Gentz, F. von. *Dépêches inédites aux hospodars de Moldavie et de Valachie*, 1813–1828 (Dépêches inédites). 3 vols. Paris, 1876. Gentz was paid for supplying information in this correspondence, which ceased abruptly on its discovery by the Tsar in 1828.

—— *Zur Geschichte der Orientalischen Frage*, 1823–1829 (Zur Geschichte). Vienna, 1877. A volume of letters to and from Gentz.

—— *Briefe von und an F. v. Gentz* (Briefe). Ed. C. Wittichen. Berlin, 1909. Private correspondence with Metternich, 1819–1832, in vol. III².

Gordon, T. *History of the Greek Revolution*. 2 vols. 1833.

—— *Some English Philhellenes* (III). By Z. D. Ferriman. 1918.

Goriainow, S. *Le Bosphore et les Dardanelles* (1774–1878). Paris, 1910. A valuable work based on Russian archives.

Goudas, A. N. 'Βίοι Παράλληλοι' (of heroes of the revolt). 8 vols. 1870.

Green, P. J. *Sketches of the War in Greece*. 1827. Green was consul at Patras in 1821, but retired to Zante during the revolt.

Grey, Earl. *Lord Grey of the Reform Bill*. By G. M. Trevelyan. 1920.

Guilford, Lord. *Some English Philhellenes* (VI). By Z. D. Ferriman 1919.

Hammer, J. v. *Des Osmanischen Reiches Staatsverfassung und Staatsverwaltung*. 2 vols. Vienna, 1815.

—— *Geschichte des Osmanischen Reiches*. In vol. IX, *Verzeichnis...der Ämter*.... Pest, 1833.

Hastings, F. A. Biographical notice by G. Finlay in *Blackwood's*, Oct. 1845.

—— *Some English Philhellenes* (I). By Z. D. Ferriman. 1917.

Howe, S. G. *Letters and Journals*. 1907. The writer (an American doctor) was engaged on relief work: many sidelights on the Greek leaders.

Isambert, G. *L'Indépendance grecque et l'Europe*. Paris, 1900. Based on French archives.

Jourdain, Capt. *Mémoires historiques*. 2 vols. Paris, 1828. An ardent Philhellene.

Jurien de la Gravière. *Station du Levant*. Paris, 1876. Of the French Mediterranean squadron at this period, afterwards Admiral.

Kolokotrones, T. *Kolokotrones, Klepht and Warrior*. Autobiography, trans. with introduction and notes by Mrs Edmonds. 1892.

Kuriakos, A. D. *Geschichte der Orientalischen Kirchen*, 1453–1898. (Trans. from Greek.) Leipzig, 1902.

Lebzeltern, L. v. *Les Rapports diplomatiques de Lebzeltern, ministre d'Autriche à la Cour de Russie*, 1816–1828 (Les Rapports de Lebzeltern). Ed. Grand-duc Nicholas Mikhailovitch. St Petersburg, 1913. This volume contains also a selection of letters and despatches from Metternich.

Leopold I von Belgien. By E. C. Corti. Vienna, 1922. French (enlarged) edn., *Léopold Ier, Oracle politique de l'Europe*. Brussels, 1927.

Levant Company. *Proceedings of the Levant Company respecting the surrender of its charters*. 1825. See, also, under Walsh, R.

Lieven, Princess. *Correspondence with Lord Grey* (Correspondence). Ed. G. le Strange. 3 vols. 1890.

—— *Letters* to her brother. Ed. L. G. Robinson. 1902.

—— *Diary*. Ed. H. W. V. Temperley. 1925.

Liverpool, Second Earl of. *Life*. By C. D. Yonge. 3 vols. 1868.

[Lowe, Sir H.] *Observations upon the affairs of Russia, Greece and Turkey*. (Anon.) 1829.

Ludwig I von Bayern. By K. Heigel. München, 1872.

Lytton, Sir H. B. *An Autumn in Greece*. 1826. A visit in connection with the loan.

Maitland, Sir T. *Life*. By W. F. Lord. 1897.

Mendelssohn-Bartholdy, K. *Geschichte Griechenlands*. 2 vols. Leipzig, 1873–4. See, also, under Capodistrias.

Metaxas, C. *Souvenirs de la Guerre*. Trans. J. Blancard. Paris, 1887.

Metternich, Prince. *Mémoires*. 8 vols. Paris, 1880–4. References to the documents as numbered.

Miaoules, A. A. Ἱστορία...τῶν...ναυμαχιῶν.... (By a son of the admiral.) Nauplia, 1833. Ἱστορία τῆς νησοῦ Ὕδρας.... Athens, 1874.

Michaud, J. *Correspondance d'Orient*, 1830–1831. 4 vols. in 2. Paris, 1833. Learned and shrewd commentary by the historian of the crusades.

Miller, W. *The Ottoman Empire and its successors*, 1801–1927. 1927. *History of the Greek People*, 1821–1921. 1922. Articles on Greece before nineteenth century in *E.H.R.* XIX, 646 and XXXV, 343.

Molden, E. *Metternich's Orientpolitik*, 1829–1833. Vienna, 1913.

Moltke, H. C. B. v. *Der Russisch-Türkischer Feldzug*, 1828–1829. Berlin, 1845. Eng. trans. *The Russians in Bulgaria*, 1828–1829. 1854.

Mouradja d'Ohsson, I. *Tableau général de l'Empire Othoman*. 4 vols. in 5. Paris, 1788–91. Deals mainly with Ottoman legal and religious institutions.

Müffling, F. C. F. v. *Aus Meinem Leben*. Berlin (1851). 2nd edn. 1855. Four episodes from his life, left for posthumous publication by his son. The fourth was translated (1855) by D. Jardine, *Narrative of my Missions to Constantinople and St Petersburg*, 1829–1830.

Napier, Sir C. J. *The Colonies* (Ionian Is.). 1833. A defence of his administration and attack upon Sir F. Adam, High Commissioner.

—— *Life*. By his son. 2 vols. 1857.

—— *Some English Philhellenes* (II). By Z. D. Ferriman. 1917.

Nesselrode, Comte C. de. *Lettres et Papiers*, 1760–1850. Ed. Comte A. de Nesselrode. 11 vols. Paris, 1904– . In vol. II, fragment of autobiography to 1815; vols. VI–VII cover this period, mostly letters to his wife, and some to Lieven.

Nicholas I, Tsar. Letters to and from Grand Duke Constantine, 20 Feb. 1826–June 1831 (in French), in *Sbornik* CXXXI–CXXXII.

Nonnenburg-Chun, M. *Der französische Philhellenismus.* (*Romanische Studien*, Heft 10.) Berlin, 1909.

Ottenfels, Franz Freiherr v. (*Beiträge zur Politik Metternichs im griechischen Freiheitskampfe.*) By J. Krauter. Salzburg, 1914. Based on the Internuncio's unpublished memoirs, and on letters from Gentz and Metternich, 1822–32.

Palmerston, Viscount. *Life.* By Lord Bulwer. 3 vols. 1870.

Paparrigopoulo, C. *La Civilisation Hellénique.* Paris, 1878.

Parish, H. H. *Diplomatic History of the Monarchy of Greece from* 1830. (From *Portfolio*, III.) 1838. Parish had been Secretary of Legation to Dawkins in Greece, and became a disciple of Urquhart with regard to Russia.

Pellion, Général. *La Grèce et les Capodistrias pendant l'occupation française de* 1828 *à* 1834. Paris, 1855. Pellion was an officer in the French army of occupation: strongly anti-Russian in tone.

Phillips, W. Alison. *The War of Greek Independence*, 1821–1833. 1897.

—— *C.M.H.* vol. X, cc. 6 and 17, with valuable bibliography.

Politis, A. G. *L'Hellénisme et l'Égypte moderne.* Tome I (1798–1927). Paris, 1929. Illustrates the strong Greek element in trade and administration under Mehemet Ali.

Pouqueville, F. C. *Histoire de la régénération de la Grèce.* 4 vols. Paris, 1824. French consul at Patras, and a Philhellene: not very reliable.

Prokesch v. Osten, Baron A. F. *Kleine Schriften.* 7 vols. Stuttgart, 1844.

—— *Geschichte des Abfalls der Griechen vom Türkischen Reiche.* 6 vols. Vienna, 1867. The history (vols. I–II) was written 1834–48 at Athens, where the author was Austrian minister; it was printed in 1853 at the expense of the Imperial Academy, but publication was delayed by the censor for fifteen years. It is a laborious, but not uncritical, defence of Metternich's policy, based (from 1824) on personal knowledge of the conditions on the spot. For vols. III–VI (documents), see section II (*a*), above.

—— *Mehemet Ali.* (*Aus meinem Tagebuche*, 1826–1841.) Vienna, 1877.

—— *Aus dem Nachlasse.* (Correspondence with Gentz, 1826–32, and with Metternich, 1832–55.) Ed. by his son. 2 vols. Vienna, 1881.

—— *Aus den Tagebüchern.* (Mar. 1830–Sept. 1834.) Ed. by his son. Vienna, 1909.

Rawlinson, Sir H. *England and Russia in the East.* 1878.

Ringhoffer, K. *Ein Dezennium Preussischer Orientpolitik,* 1821–1830. Berlin, 1897. A not very successful attempt to vindicate the independence of Prussian policy between Austrian and Russian pressure.

Sbornik = *Imperatorskoe Istoricheskoe Obchestvo* (Russian Imperial Historical Society). See under Capodistrias and Nicholas I.

Schiemann, T. *Geschichte Russlands.* Berlin, vol. I, 1904; vol. II, 1908; vol. III, 1913; vol. IV, 1919. Based throughout on Russian archives and printed sources, and especially valuable to those unfamiliar with Russian.

Sketches in Greece and Turkey. Anon. 1833. Lively characters of Greek leaders. B.M. 1047, k. 6.

Sorel, A. *Essais d'histoire.* Pp. 95–112. *L'Alliance russe et la Restauration.* Paris, 1894.

Stanhope, Col. *Greece*, 1823–1824. 1825. The 'typographical' Stanhope.

Stockmar, Baron. *Memoirs*. 2 vols. 1872. Throws light on Leopold's candidature.

Strangford, Viscount. *Selected Writings*. Ed. by his widow. 2 vols. 1869. In vol. i, 'Chaos' (a clever essay on Slav nationalism), and 'Occasional Notes' on Turkey and Greece.

Strong, F. *Greece as a Kingdom* (Bavarian statistics). 1842.

Thiersch, F. *De l'état actuel de la Grèce*. Leipzig, 1833. Very unreliable, a partisan of Kolettes.

—— *Leben Thiersch's*. By H. Löwe. Vol. i. München, 1925.

Trelawny, E. J. *Letters*. Ed. H. B. Forman. Oxford, 1910. Trelawny married the sister of a *klepht* known as 'Odysseus'.

Trikoupes, Sp. Ἱστορία τῆς Ἑλληνικῆς Ἐπαναστάσεως. 4 vols. London, 1853–7. 3rd edn., Athens, 1888. The standard Greek history of the revolt; on the whole very fair-minded.

Urquhart, David. *Turkey and its Resources*. 1833. Commercial and statistical argument.

—— *The Spirit of the East*. 2 vols. 1838. Partly a record of travel in the East.

—— *Life*. By Gertrude Robinson. Oxford, 1920.

Viel-Castel, L. de. *Histoire de la Restauration*. Vols. xvi–xvii. 20 vols. Paris, 1860. Copious extracts from speeches made in the Chamber, etc.

Voyage de D. et N. Stephanopoli en Grèce, 1797–1798. 2 vols. Paris, an viii (1799). See above, p. 10, n. 13.

Waddington, G. *Visit to Greece*, 1823–1824. 1825. *The Greek Church*. 1829. 2nd edn., 1854. The writer was a Fellow of Trinity College, Cambridge.

Waliszewski, K. *Le Règne d'Alexandre I*, 1818–1825 (vol. iii). Paris, 1925.

Walpole, R. *Travels in Turkey*. 1817.

Walsh, R. *Account of the Levant Company*. 1825. Dedicated, on its dissolution, to Lord Grenville, its President for twenty-five years.

(c) Contemporary Periodicals

Annual Register. *Annuaire Historique* (C. Lesur). *Blackwood's*, 1826 (xx, 542)—origins and beginning of the revolt. *Foreign Quarterly Review*, Nov. 1829 (v, 271)—attacks Wellington's policy, defends Navarin and Capodistrias. *Foreign Review*, 1828 (vol. ii)—Russia, India and Persia. *North American Review*, Oct. 1823 (xvii, 398)—appeal for help; why should not America recognise Greece? 1832 (xxxiv, 1)—Greek education. *Quarterly Review*, Jan. 1823 (xxviii, 474)—a benevolent philosophic article. Apr. 1823 (xxix, 86)—Ionian Islands; reply to the charges of Hume and the Radicals. Apr. 1828 (xxxvii, 386)—blockades of Dardanelles. July 1828 (xxxviii, 190)—argues for Greek independence as a barrier-state. Jan. 1829 (xxxix, 1)—anti-Russian. Nov. 1829 (xli, 470)—Turkish reforms. Mar. 1830 (xlii, 520)—against surrendering Ionian Islands to Greece. Oct. 1830 (xliii, 590)—by Dean Phillpotts, a defence of Wellington's policy, hostile to Philhellenes. *Spirit of the Public Journals*, 1823–5—poems and epigrams. *Westminster Review*, 1823 (i, 453)—Great Britain and Russia; Greece the best barrier. 1824 (ii, 149, 225)—Philhellenes, Byron. 1830 (xii, 522)—a protest against Leopold's candidature, 'from Cephalonia'.

(*d*) Biographical Dictionaries

Michaud's *Biographie Universelle*. Paris, 1843–63. *Dictionary of National Biography*. *Allgemeine Deutsche Biographie*. Leipzig, 1875– Wurzbach's *Biographisches Lexikon des Kaisertums Oesterreich* (1750 onwards). Vienna, 1856–91.

(*e*) Note on the London Greek Committee

(i) *Loan*

Blaquière, Byron, Lytton, Stanhope—see under (*b*).

Cobbett's *Weekly Register*, Nov.–Dec. 1826, 'The Greek Pie'. *Greek Loans, 1824–1825; Opinions of the Day*. London, 1878. A collection of articles from *The Times*, Sept.–Dec. 1826, accusing the Greek Committee of incompetence and dishonesty, but acquitting Luriottes, one of the Greek deputies. [Ed. J. Gennadius.] *Greek Loans*, 1824–1825. Their conversion and settlement and the Dutch protest. [By J. Gennadius.] 1880. *Quarterly Review*, Jan. 1827 (xxxv, 221)—another exposure. *Westminster Review*, 1826 (VI, 113)—a defence of the Committee, but not of the Greek deputies. *The Ghost of Miltiades*. By Tom Moore. First appeared in *The Times*, 8 Nov. 1826. *The Greek Bubble*. 1826. A satirical poem. *Letter to holders of Greek Bonds*. By 'Philogordo'. 1830. *Letters* from F.O. to representatives of the bond-holders, refusing to stipulate for their claims, but promising to urge them upon the Greek Government. 1830–4. S.P. 28, 967. Jenks, L. H., *Migration of Capital*, pp. 50–1. New York, 1927.

(ii) *Steamboats*

American Quarterly, 1827 (I, 254)—a full account, based on all the evidence, of the Steamboats: a severe censure on the Arbitrators and on one at least of the two contracting firms. *North American Review*, July 1827 (xxv, 33)—a shorter article to the same effect.

The evidence is in six printed pamphlets, bound together in B.M. 1312, d. 4, all New York, 1826. (1) Platt, J. (and others). *Report of the Evidence by the Arbitrators*. (August.) (2) Sedgwick, H. D. *Vindication of Conduct and Character of*—reply to (1). (21 Sept.) Sedgwick was the counsel representing the Committee before the Arbitrators. (3) Contostavlos, A. *Narrative of Material facts*. (24 Oct.) (4) Bayard, W. *Exposition of Conduct of the Two Houses*—reply to (3). (Nov.) (5) Sedgwick, H. D. *Refutation of reasons assigned by Arbitrators*. (2 Nov.) (6) Sedgwick, R., and Duer, J. *An Examination of the Controversy*. (Dec.)

(*f*) Greek Ballads

Fauriel, C. *Chants populaires de la Grèce moderne*. Paris, 1824.

Legrand, E. *Recueil de chansons populaires grecques*. (French prose translation.) Paris, 1874.

Passow, A. *Popularia Carmina Graeciae recentioris*. (In the original dialect.) Leipzig, 1860.

Sheridan, C. B. *Songs of Greece*. (Translated.) 1826.

INDEX

OF PERSONS, PLACES AND SELECTED TOPICS

Diplomatic representatives merely mentioned in the footnotes may be identified in Appendix VI, books and authors in the bibliography; they will not be found in this index.

For EU product safety concerns, contact us at Calle de José Abascal, 56–1°, 28003 Madrid, Spain or eugpsr@cambridge.org.

www.ingramcontent.com/pod-product-compliance
Ingram Content Group UK Ltd.
Pitfield, Milton Keynes, MK11 3LW, UK
UKHW010345140625
459647UK00010B/840

* 9 7 8 1 1 0 7 6 2 6 5 1 5 *